The Alabama Folk Lyric:

A Study in Origins and Media of Dissemination

The Alabama Folk Lyric:
A Study in Origins
and Media of Dissemination

Collected and Edited
With An
Introduction and Notes

By

Ray B. Browne

Bowling Green University Popular Press
Bowling Green, Ohio 43403
1979

Library of Congress Catalog Card No.: 78-61076

Copyright © 1979 by the Bowling Green University Popular Press. Ray B. Browne, Director; Pat Browne, Editor.

ISBN: 0-87972-129-4 Clothbound.

Printed in the United States of America.

Cover design by Gregg Swope.

Dedicated to the Memory of
My Parents
Garfield Browne
and
Nola Browne
and My Sister
Joan Burns

Contents

Contents

Contents

Contents

The Sad Tale of a Star-Crossed Manuscript

The history of this manuscript from composition to publication may be of interest to some readers and will serve as an explanation of the long time between completion and publication.

The manuscript was submitted as my dissertation in the English Department at U.C.L.A. in 1956. After that time I spent four years in the Library of Congress and other libraries checking out and amplifying references to songsters, song books and other such publications. While reworking this manuscript I finished and submitted to the University of Alabama press the manuscript for my *"Night with the Hants" And Other Alabama Folk Experiences,* which was accepted for publication. Some years later, however, the editor of the Press decided that it would be politically dangerous to publish that book because of the content. It was decided that the "Hants" manuscript would be returned to me and I would submit the Alabama folksongs manuscript, which I had just finished, as a replacement. The exchange was made, and subsequently the second manuscript was accepted for publication.

Publication at the University of Alabama Press, as at many other university presses, was not the most expeditious. After the manuscript had been in his hands for two years, the Editor told me that he had finally found someone in Europe who could set the musical notations and that publication would proceed. However, after another two years I inquired about the progress of publication and received no answer despite repeated letters; even telephone inquiries could get no definite statement. Finally, in exasperation while I was at the University of Alabama one day in 1974 I had a friend check out in person the manuscript's fate at the Press. He was informed that the manuscript had been burned in the "Great Fire" at the University Press in 1970.

Unfortunately I had sent to the Press my only copy of the revised manuscript. Thomas Carlyle when told that his manuscript for *The History of The French Revolution* had been burned by Mrs. John Stuart Mill went home, at least so the legend goes, and that night began rewriting it. But I had many other interests taking up my time. So I could not immediately turn to reworking the material yet again. But through the years my belief and interest in the manuscript remained high. In the winter of 1977-78, I did find time to revise the manuscript. The Editor of the University of Alabama Press in reply to my carefully phrased letter of inquiry about interest in publishing the manuscript told me that he would be glad to look at it again but that if it were reaccepted it might take up to two years to bring the book out. I have always felt the importance of the manuscript and would like to break it out of the star-crossed lover syndrome, and, as Archer Taylor and Jere Whiting confessed in the Preface to their book *Proverbs and Proverbial Expressions in American Literature* under similar circumstances, I would like to see it published in my lifetime. I decided therefore that the Popular Press was the proper medium to get the book to the public.

In preparing the manuscript for publication I rewrote the Introduction and the headnotes to the individual songs insofar as needed. In the headnotes I especially reworked the material on the songsters. I intentionally, however, refrained from enlarging and bringing up to date references to other collections of folk songs that my pieces might be found in and from changing the present tense of the verbs in the references to the singers from present to past, though it might seem to some that the present tense of 1952 sounds strained in 1978. I did not update the references because such bits of information would not be of great value and because my purpose in this volume is really something else — to demonstrate what songs were sung by the folk of Alabama in the early 1950s and the origins and the media from they which did get or might have got this song literature.

Through the years I have felt that it would be interesting and informative to return to my original informants — where they are still alive — or their descendants, as Cecil Sharp did in the Appalachians years ago, to see what they or their children, and the communities in which they live, are singing now. Are these people, who obviously were influenced by "non-folk" songs still singing the old pieces, have they switched to more songs from the electric media and printed sources, do their actions tell significant facts about "folk" and "non-folk" songs"? I know now, however, that I shall never do the collecting necessary to develop these points. I can only hope that some other scholar will take the work begun here and develop it more. The results could have profound effects on the study of folk culture and of American culture in general.

Acknowledgments

My indebtedness far exceeds the space I have to acknowledge it. To the many singers who gave of their time and energy I should like to express my deep gratitude, and the hope that they enjoyed singing the old songs as much as I enjoyed listening to them. Three singers, especially, I should like to thank: Miss Drucilla Hall, who sang sixty-seven songs in one day and 302 altogether; my mother, Mrs. Nola Browne, who sang more than three hundred songs, although some were too distant from folk tradition to be considered genuine; and Mrs. Maggie Lee Hayes, who gave so much of her time and energy during three years in singing and coaxing other persons to sing. I should like to thank the three ladies who transcribed the music from the tapes, Joyce Schultz, Viola Fuehr, and especially Imelda McNamee, who gave unselfishly two years of her time as she could spare it, her only recompense being the enjoyment of her task. Professors Leon Howard and Wayland Hand were always helpful and understanding; to them my gratitude. Finally, I should like to remember my wife, Olwyn, (killed in an automobile accident in 1964), who helped me collect and who enjoyed the work as much as I did.

Introduction

I

Alabamians have always been a singing people. The settlers who moved into the various sections of the state brought with them songs which reflected their national origins and geographical backgrounds, and as they spread into the hills and over the lowlands they created new songs out of the conditions under which they lived. Also, they absorbed songs from outside sources whenever these pieces could be adapted to their sentiments and ways of life. Thus, by a process of memory, composition and recreation they developed a rich body of folk songs. The following collection is a part of my effort to discover and preserve these songs.

The effort of collecting and editing involved me in the problem of definition. This problem, as every folklorist knows, is both serious and crucial, for, too narrow and arbitrary a definition would be more representative of one's own approach to the subject than of the actual living tradition of the folk. On the other hand, too generous an impulse in classification would break down all distinction between "folk songs" and art songs. From the outset, then, I tried to formulate and use a definition elastic enough to include all *genuine* folk songs yet rigid enough to exclude all others.

This attempt at definition was primarily concerned with two questions: that of origins and that of the relative importance of folk transmission in establishing authenticity. Two schools of thought have developed through the years on these questions and may persist in the minds of some folklorists to today. For that reason I have decided to retrace in some detail at least parts of the arguments.

One, for a time the more influential, was the "communal composition" school fathered by Grimm with his famous dictum: "das Volk dichtet" — the people compose.[1] The romantic notions in these words intrigued Gummere, Kittredge and many others into the belief that a ballad, or folk song, has no individual author. "Rather is it the group product of a whole community, or folk, under the sway of a strong common emotional stimulus,"[2] said Reed Smith, in outlining the beliefs of this group. Under such a situation, Kittredge theorized, "Different members of the throng, one after another, may chant each his verse, composed on the spur of the moment, and the sum of these various contributions makes a song.

This is communal composition, though each verse, taken by itself, is the work of an individual. A song made in this way is no man's property and has no individual author. The 'folk' is the author."[3]

This insistence on communal composition has been modified through the years, and the stress has shifted to "communal transmission" — unwritten folk tradition — as being of greater importance than communal origin. Perhaps Kittredge best stated the modified position of this school:

It makes no difference whether a given ballad was in fact composed in the manner described [improvisation in company of sympathetic group,] or whether it was composed (or even written) in solitude, provided the author belonged to the folk, derived his material from popular sources, made his ballad under the inherited influence of the method described, and gave it to the folk as soon as he had made it, — and provided, moreover, the folk accepted the gift and subjected it to that course of oral tradition which, as we have seen, is essential to the production of a genuine ballad.[4]

But even this modified position differs from that held by scholars who could not agree with the Grimm-Gummere-Kittredge school.

These scholars (who constituted a "school" only insofar as they were non-believers in the "communal composition" school) have recognized that many genuine folk songs come originally from sources outside the folk. From this point of view have evolved most of the presentday efforts at definition, even though no single one of them has been satisfactory to everybody. They have presented me, however, with material for my own set of criteria, and therefore I should like to outline the development of this point of view and base my own definition upon it.[5]

As early as 1836 Freiherr von Erlach suggested a category between art songs and folk songs which he called "volksthümliche Lieder" that must be studied in connection with the origins of genuine folk songs.[6] In 1859 Hoffmann von Fallersleben, the German poet and scholar, compiled a convenient finding list of songs by known authors which have passed more or less as "genuine" folk songs.[7] Franz Magnus Böhme, summarizing the work of his predecessors, moved significantly toward the new definition of "folk song":

The folk sings not only its old traditional songs — songs by unknown authors, which are known in the narrower sense as folk songs — but sings in addition a number of songs in the simple manner of the folk songs, whose authors in the main can be established; these are the so-called popular songs ("volksthümliche Lieder") or folk songs in the more liberal sense.

We are concerned here with "volksthümliche Lieder." That is what we call art songs written by known or unknown poets, which have gone over into popular tradition with little or no change, having become old favorites ("Lieblingslieder") without really becoming genuine folk songs. These songs, which are eagerly sung by cultivated and uncultivated alike, stand midway between art song and folk song. Let us therefore consider the relationship between the two somewhat more closely.

The "volksthumliche Lied" derives from the realm of the cultivated; in content and language, however, it is composed according to generally understood expressions and modes of speech, and is therefore sung by the masses. There appealing songs become real folk songs, however, as soon as the folk has thoroughly worked them over in its own way and utilized them ("sobald das Volk sie in seiner Art 'verarbeitet' hat").[8]

To Böhme, then, genuineness in folk song was a matter of degree, full status of any piece, regardless of its origin, being achieved when it came into complete possession of the folk. Any song can become a "folk song," as he conceived the process, by being thoroughly worked over by the folk and adapted to their own needs.

William Wells Newell, writing about the origins of games and songs of American children, insisted that folk songs and games, far from being folk creations, *"invariably came from above, from the intelligent class.* If these uses seem rustic, it is only because the country retained what the city forgot."[9] In 1909 Moses Gaster, President of the London Folk-Lore Society, said in his Presidential Address:

No less interesting is it, then, to follow downwards the further development of the discarded literature of the classes. It does not disappear; it only filters downward slowly to the masses . . . .There can be no doubt that much of the popular literature of the day — in the widest sense of the word — was the literature of the upper classes of the preceding centuries remodelled by the people in accordance with the innate instincts and dispositions of each nation.[10]

Twelve years later Hans Naumann said essentially the same thing:

We know today that the best loved "folk songs" of 1900 were art songs that had sunk from a higher stratum and had been changed by continuous singing ("herabgesunkene und zersungene Kunstlieder"). . . .In my view this is the basis upon which the different notions concerning the origin of folk song may be reconciled. It is correctly said that the bearers of folk poetry are the lower stratum of national culture, and that the taste of this lower stratum ("Unterschicht") lags behind the upper stratum ("Oberschicht") by an extended period of time. . . .Folk songs derive from the art song, but from the art songs of former days ("vergangener Tage").[11]

With this statement about the origins of songs few presentday scholars would disagree, except with the insistence that the art songs must be "of former days."

Phillips Barry, one of America's ablest ballad scholars, early recognized that folk songs might originate outside the folk tradition and still become "genuine" folk songs. At the end of a thirty-year crusade for a more liberal, and a more practical, definition he wrote:

It matters little where the folk-singer learns his songs. Ancient ballads, some of them centuries old; later ballads, in part based on world-old themes, in part celebrating events yet unforgotten; traditional lyrics, popular and vaudeville songs, — *all* are to be found in his repertory. . . .He takes them as he finds them, and makes them his own, shaping them according to the subconscious dictates of his own fancy.[12]

This "shaping them according to the subconscious dictates of his own fancy" is "communal recreation" at work. In explaining what he meant by the term "communal recreation," a controversial point in American folk song criticism, Barry wrote:

We see in a folksong, a communal song in the sense only that the author who made the text and the composer who made the music are *not its sole author and composer*. On the contrary, into its being has gone the collective labor — collective only in the sense of *cumulative through tradition in time and space* — of an indefinite number of authors of poetry and composers of music. . . .[13]

The main difference between folk song and art song, he concluded, is that in the former there is no one text or music; the folk change as they please. In the latter, however, there *is* one text and one music, and the song is not changed.

Louise Pound, a close student of folk song origins who single-handedly vanquished the romantic notions of the Gummere-Kittredge school, defined a folk song in these terms:

Genuine folksongs are not static, but are in a state of flux; they have been handed down through a fair period of time, and all sense of their authorship and origin has been lost.[14]

Essentially her definition is the same as Barry's, except for the stipulation that the songs must have been "handed down through a fair period of time." It is this requirement of "aging," as it were, that present-day scholars are likeliest to modify.

The above scholars, then, would accept as a genuine folk song one which, regardless of origin, had (1) undergone certain textual and musical changes and had (2) become so much a part of folk culture that the members felt free to sing it as they had learned it without any self-conscious concern for its origin or its "correct" version. Most later scholars would agree on these conditions but would perhaps be more tolerant of other origins and of the time required for "aging."

A late effort at definition is that of John Greenway.[15] Trying to liberalize the conception of folk songs, he makes, in general, incisive remarks. After belaboring the implications of the theory that it is anonymity of authorship which is important in folk songs, Greenway says: "It is impersonality of authorship, not anonymity of authorship, that is a requisite of genuine." Several of his passages deserve quoting:

A new definition must be made which will include evanescent Negro songs, hillbilly songs like Jimmie Rodgers' blue yodels which the folk have accepted, sentimental pieces like "The Fatal Wedding," and songs of social and economic protest.[16]

A folksong, therefore, is a song concerned with the interests of the folk, and in the complete possession of the folk. All other qualifications, such as the requirement of transmissional changes, are to be considered only as helpful tests in establishing either or both of the basic conditions of the definition.[17]

If an individual is the sole author of a folksong he must speak not for himself but for the folk community as a whole, and in the folk idiom; he must not introduce ideas or concepts that are uncommon, nor may he indelibly impress his own individuality upon the song. His function is not that of a consciously creative artist, but that of a spokesman for the community, an amanuensis for the illiterate, or, to put it more precisely, for the inarticulate.[18]

If we do not accept people like. . .Woody Guthrie as the folk, then we have no folk, and we have no living folksong.[19]

With most of Greenway's statements present-day scholars will agree. Yet in stretching his definition to include all his songs of protest he undermines his own thesis. For people like Guthrie and Rodgers do not, *can not* in fact, *compose* folk songs. All they can do is compose songs that *become* folk songs. A folk song is a piece which has been sung by the people over a period of time and taken fully into their possession. Guthrie composes a song. Then, because his background is so much a part of the folk, the piece he writes affects a guise close to the folk, in theme, sentiment and diction. This song will, therefore, undergo little or no alteration when it is adopted by the folk and taken wholly into their possession. Nonetheless when such songs are written, they are *art songs* and some of them remain so.

From this point of view, Stephen C. Foster must be considered

with the men Greenway mentions. Were Foster's songs at the time of
their composition folk or art songs? They were undoubtedly *all* art
songs. But some were so close to the folk, were so "folksy," that
they appealed to them, were therefore adopted, and became the
full and unconscious possession of the folk. The Frank C. Brown
collection of North Carolina ballads and folk songs (III, 488-491)
includes several pieces by Foster which without doubt must be
considered "genuine" folk songs. "Nelly Bly" was collected with
verbal differences in stanza and chorus from the original. "Oh,
Susanna" is reported in nine versions, most of them differing mark-
edly from the original, and it has been reported, too, from Pennsylvania and Tennessee. Brown also collected (III, 504) what is
obviously a folk version of "Camptown Races":

I gone down town wid ma pockets full o' tin,
    Dudah! Dudah!
I come back home wid my hat caved in,
    Dudah! Dudah day!
    Dudah! Dudah day!
I boun' ter run all night,
I boun' ter wuk all day,
I bet ma money on de bob-tail horse —
    Dudah! Dudah day!

But these Foster pieces had *become* folk songs.[20] Others by the
same author — "I Dream of Jeanie with the Light Brown Hair,"
for instance — were not sufficiently close to the folk to become
folk songs. Therefore they remained art songs. Thus, we can only
conclude that Foster, Guthrie, Rodgers, and all individual authors,
do not, per se, compose folk songs.[21]

In attributing folk song composition today exclusively to such
composers as Guthrie and Rodgers, Greenway is as extreme in his
way as the members of the "communal school" were in theirs. The
present-day collector is therefore obliged to be "open-minded"
rather than merely "modern" in his approach to his material. Folk
songs have undergone and are now undergoing great change. Many
of the old ones have died our or are disappearing. Taking their place
are art songs of various kinds — "popular," literary and others.
The collector must always ask himself the question: Are these
really "genuine" folk songs? The answer is that some are and some
are not; the real test is whether the songs have been taken fully

into the possession of the folk. Two illustrations will help clear up this point.

The person who sings "Froggy Went A-Courting" very likely sings "The Fatal Wedding" and "America The Beautiful." "The Fatal Wedding," though probably written by W.H. Windom and Gussie L. Davis in 1893, is generally accepted as a genuine folk song. It has come fully into folk possession. It has been altered unconsciously — sometimes not so unconsciously — until it now speaks in a familiar way about things close at hand. Each person sings her own version; and usually nothing anyone can do will change a particular singer's rendition. If she should see the song in print or hear in on the radio in a version different from her own, she would still insist tht she was going to sing it "the way I leaned it." One singer, in fact, told me that she had been hearing the people over Nashville's "Grand Ole Opry" singing some of the old songs *wrong* and she was going to write and tell them so.

With "America The Beautiful," however, different forces are at work. When a folk singer sings it she does not feel free and uninhibited. She learned it, probably, in school. She still hears it on radio, she probably has a book around which includes it, and she sings it at school functions, at meetings of the Home Demonstration Club, and doubtless on other occasions. And these versions are always the same — the "correct" one. If she should forget the words, she would not recreate them but would look them up. It is precisely this authoritative, stabilizing force of the printed page, radio, TV, motion pictures, and various other media, which prevents this type of song from becoming a "genuine" folk song. As long as it is being constantly corrected, it cannot become the full and unconscious possession of the folk and thus cannot become a genuine folk piece. Could "America The Beautiful" ever become a genuine folk song? Not unless there were removed all the stabilizing and correcting forces now operating to keep it in one "correct" version. If this were to happen, and the song continued to be sung by the folk, it would cease maintaining its identity and would become a genuine folk song.

The answer to our question of whether or not the songs now being sung by the folk are genuine folk songs is that the test of genuineness of any piece is not whether there exist forms of it in both art and folk tradition, but rather whether these forms are independent, or whether the art form stabilizes and "corrects" the folk version. A piece can have both art and folk existences and the former exercise no influence on the latter. Foster's songs existed in art and folk forms concurrently. Many persons, undoubtedly, were so "art" conscious that they wanted to sing the songs as they were written; to such persons the art form would act as a stabilizing force. But the vast majority of the folk surely took liberties with the pieces they liked to sing. Probably these liberties were not so much in conscious alteration, that is, folk re-writing, though there was much of this, as they were in forgetting, and the consequent filling in of forgotten parts. But either way the pieces were changed, and the end products were versions which were genuine folk songs.

There is much further evidence of how songs can have concurrent art and folk existences, and the study of them throws light on the whole process of folk recreation of art songs. The passage from *The Passionate Pilgrim* (by Shakespeare and others, published 1599) beginning "Crabbed age and youth" (XII, authorship unknown), for instance, has had a long tradition in the two forms. It was referred to in Beaumont and Fletcher's *The Woman's Prize* (1615) and in several other works of the first half of the seventeenth century.[21] In Ford's *Fancies Chaste and Noble* (1638) there was quoted one, variant, stanza:

Crabbed age and youth
    Cannot jump together;
One is like good luck,
    T'other like foul weather.

In Thomas Deloney's *Garland of Good Will* (c. 1690) there was included a version running to ninety-seven lines. The first stanza was nearly exactly like the original. I quote enough of the second stanza to give the flavor:

Here I do attend,
    Arm'd by love and Pleasure:
With my youthful friend,
    Joyful for to meet:
Here I do wait,
    For my only treasure,
Venus sugared habit,
    Fancy dainty sweet:
Like a loving wife,
So I lead my life,
    Thirsting for my heart's desire,

Come sweet youth, I pray,
Away old man, away,
   Thou can'st not give, what I require;
For old age I care not,
   Come my love and spare not.

Percy *(Reliques of Ancient English Poetry,* 1767) gave a version exactly like that in *The Passionate Pilgrim.* Evidence indicates, therefore, that soon after the first published versions, variant folk versions were being sung. During the eighteenth and nineteenth centuries, this particular poem was used as an art song at least seven times.[22] Apparently all followed the original closely. One copy, therefore, will illustrate them and the art version:

Crabbed age and youth cannot live together,
Youth is full of pleasance, Age is full of care;
Youth like summer morn, Age like winter weather,
Youth like summer brave, Age like winter bare.

Youth is full of sport: Ages breath is short;
Youth is nimble; Age is lame;
Youth is hot and bold; Age is weak and cold;
Youth is wild, and Age is tame.

Age, I do abhor thee! Youth, I do adore thee!
O, my love, my love is young!
Age, I do defy thee! Oh sweet shepherd, hie thee!
For me thinks thou stays too long.

This song has been published at least once as a "popular" song, in one of the widespread songbooks of the nineteenth century called "songsters."[23] Many pieces in such books were "folk" songs or becoming "folk" songs:

Crabbed age and youth
Cannot live together;
Youth like summer morn,
Age like winter weather.

Age is full of care.
Youth is full of pleasure;
Age like winter bare,
Youth like summer weather.

Age I do abhor thee,
Youth I do adore thee;

O sweet husband, hie thee,
Me think'st thou stay'st too long.[24]

The tune for this piece is not indicated, but obviously it was intended to be sung. Textually it differs sharply from the original
and from the art versions, as also the version in Ford varies from
all others. In both "popular" versions we have evidence of how the
song was adapted to suit folk taste. Words were made more familiar,
and the art form was shortened and reduced to its important ele-
ments. The art and "popular" versions existed concurrently, but
the art version apparently exercised no stabilizing or corrective
influence on the others. The version in Ford evidently was taken
from current oral tradition. That in the songster may have been
either collected from tradition or composed by someone indifferent
to the correct text. The interesting fact is that art and non-art versions could exist side by side.

Poems other than Shakespeare's were published as songs in the
nineteenth century songsters. *Grigg's Southern and Western Songster* (1846), for instance, included among its more than 450 songs of
all kinds twenty-seven by Thomas Moore, sixteen by Burns, seven
by Scott, and six by Byron, as well as some by other well-known
authors. Often a particular piece appeared in several, or many, collections — Byron's "Maid of Athens," for example. This poem
appeared in *The Universal Songster, or, Museum of Mirth,*[25] where
the only change from the original was that the refrain was translated.
In *The English Minstrel*[26] it had the following chorus:

Oh, hear my vow before I go,
Oh, hear my vow before I go.
My dearest life, I love you!

It appeared too in *The American College Songster,*[27] under the
section entitled "Harvard College," where the last two lines of each
stanza were repeated as a chorus, the Greek being untranslated:

Hear my vow before I go
Zoe mou sas agapo.   bis

I have also collected this item as a folk song from a person who
learned it originally from a piece of printed music given as a part
of the instruction book for the organ. In this version there is a kind

of chorus much longer than any of the above (No.

Then hear my vows before I go.
Oh! hear my vows before I go.
My life, my soul, I love you.
My dearest maid, I love you.
Then hear my vows before I go.
My life, my soul, I love you.

These four versions, all of which derive from print, are different one from another, and two differ from Byron's original. The liberty taken by at least two persons — the editor of the popular songbook and the publisher of the music instructions — shows that literary works were not safe from pirating and alteration.

More evidence of the non-art treatment accorded literary works can be derived from the songsters. In the fifteen hundred such songbooks I have examined, poems of many American poets were published: Whittier had nineteen different poems which appeared for a total of twenty-eight times in the various songsters; one tune for his "Up for the Conflict," to mention only one poem, was "Gayly the Troubadour."[28] Holmes had fifteen poems which appeared thirty-three times; his "Parting Hymn" was sung, at least sometimes, to the air "Dundee."[29] His "The Ballad of the Oysterman" illustrates even better how a literary piece can become a full-fledged folk song. This poem was written in 1830, but, as explained in a book of Maine folk songs, did not long remain Holmes' own:

The ballad-sheet printer and the cheap songbookmaker promptly pirated it and bore it off, without bow to copyright or acknowledgment of any sort; it became anonymous immediately and the Folk adopted it joyously, and still are singing it occasionally. We have picked up one copy of it fitted out with a comic ending and a "tol-de-rol-de-riddle-de-ride-o" refrain which would have grieved the fastidious soul of Dr. Holmes. . . . Hardly more than six years after he had written "The Ballad of the Oysterman" it was well on its way to alteration. In the John Hay Library of Brown University we have found a local broad-side with the imprint of "42 North Main Street, Providence," which by its black latticed border shows that it must have been printed about 1836. It has eight stanzas, one having been added to meet the popular taste, and in various ways it has been revised. Evidently the word "Metamorphosed" proved difficult, for it is changed into "metamphrosed" — which in later copies is dropped out entirely, together with the classical reference to Leander and the Hellespont. Holmes' delicately diffusive opening, "It was a tall young oyster-man," becomes the direct, "There was a tall young oysterman"; the young lady, instead of being "wide awake," declares herself "up to snuff" and "chucks a brickbat," instead of "throws a pebble," into the water; and the notable changes in the sixth stanza of the orig-inal are begun — all this probably within six years of the composition of the poem.[30]

It appeared in at least two songsters, once with the "tol-do-rol-de-riddle-de-ride-o" chorus mentioned above, and once with another, comic, chorus:

With a Rock-chee-took, che-took-che-took-che, Whack! Fal-lal-diddle-lol-la-day.[31]

A work of art which has undergone as many changes by the folk as has this poem is obviously a folk song; the art form exercises absolutely no restraining or stabilizing force.

In the songsters Longfellow had six poems, published nine times, with the "Psalm of Life" being rendered, at least once, with the following chorus:

Co-ca-che-lunk, che-lunk, che-laly,
Co-ca-che-lunk, che-lunk, che-la;
Co-ca-che-lunk, che-lunk, che-laly,
Hi! oh, chick-a-che-lunk, che-la![32]

The freedom with which people — sophisticated as well as unsophisticated — use literary works is illustrated by a college students' parody of the "Psalm of Life" which was also sung to the tune "Cocachelunk":

Tell me not in mournful numbers,
Of long nights of weary toil;
Broken and uneasy slumbers,
And the wasted midnight oil.

Chorus:
Cocachelunk chelunk chelaly,
Cocachelunk chelunk chela,
Cocachelunk chelunk chelaly,
Hi! O cocachelunk chela.

Tell me not of unshorn whiskers,
Of each gloomy Sophomore,
Contemplating *Sophroniscus,*
Cramming Euclid o'er and o'er.

Tell me not of old *Alcestis,*
How she carried on of yore:
She forever now at rest is
Though she was a precious bore.

Tell me not of fearful pleasures

Of the new Alumni Hall,
How the tutors brought forth treasures
Hidden till Biennial.

For Biennials are fleeting,
And our hearts are stout and brave;
And today, together meeting,
Stand we o'er our tyrants grave.[33]

Bryant was represented by six poems, published eight times; Lowell had three, appearing once each; and Emerson had two, which were published once each. Various other American poets and poetasters furnished over 100 poems for songs in these popular songbooks. These included such persons as Joseph Rodman Drake, Timothy Dwight, Bayard Taylor, E. C. Stedman, William Gilmore Simms, David Humphreys, George H. Boker, R. H. Stoddard, Robert Treat Paine, Samuel Woodworth, Thomas Bailey Aldrich, Paul H. Hayne, J. T. Fields, Orpheus C. Kerr, Horatio Alger, Jr., B. P. Shillaber, Harriet Beecher Stowe, William Lloyd Garrison, Horace Greeley, and others. Bret Harte had at least four poems set to music and one songster[34] named for one of his works.

Louise Pound recognized literary pieces sung by the folk as genuine folk songs and reported seven: Thomas Moore's "Main of the Dismal Swamp" and "Ossian's Serenade" — "The Burman Lover" — (from *Lalla Rookh*), Longfellow's "The Bridge," Holmes' "One Hoss Shay" ("The Deacon's Masterpiece"), a song based on Tennyson's "Enoch Arden," Elizabeth Akers Allen's "Rock Me to Sleep, Mother," and "All Quiet on the Potomac" ("The Picket Guard"), by Ethel Lynn Beers.[35]

I have collected in folk tradition five literary pieces: Byron's "Maid of Athens," mentioned above, Wordsworth's "The Little Cottage Girl," Longfellow's "The Bridge," Robert Louis Stevenson's "Time to Rise," and Eugene Field's "Little Boy Blue." An examination of these pieces (see below) will reveal to what extent they have been altered in oral transmission.

The fact that literary songs have an existence frozen in art form, as we have seen above, does not alter their status as genuine folk songs. Their inclusion in a songster or other popular songbook, furthermore, would not act as a corrective or stabilizing force. On the contrary, the fact that they were included in these cheap books would probably be license enough for the folk to take liberties with them. Songsters were too ephemeral to be regarded as sacrosanct. They probably served rather to introduce songs into a community than to stabilize those which they brought in. School texts doubtless introduce other literary poems. But these, too, served little if any as stabilizing forces, since the folk usually did not see the text copy after their grade-school days. Nowadays, the old text books have been discontinued, and the new books do not contain nearly so much poetry as did McGuffey's and Barnes' texts, which were used almost exclusively in the South. Thus even the potential correcting force of an occasional re-perusal of a text which was used by one's children has been removed. These literary pieces have become, therefore, genuine folk songs.

According to the above evidence, then, any art song can become a genuine folk song in one of two ways: (1) by the art form's being forgotten, thus leaving the song entirely to the folk; (2) by the art form's being ignored by the folk. Both these conditions imply that folk songs come from discarded art material. To a certain extent such is the case, especially with the so-called "popular" songs which become folk songs. But not all folk songs are discarded art songs. Literary songs, the pieces of Stephen C. Foster, and certain works of such people as Guthrie as have been taken over by the folk regardless of the author's own version are evidence that a song or poem can have two totally independent existences, being at the same time both "art" and "folk" song.

The International Folk Music Council, meeting in 1955, passed the following resolution about the definition of folk music:

Folk music is the product of a musical tradition that has been evolved through the process of oral transmission. The factors that shape the tradition are: 1) continuity which links the present with the past; 2) variation which springs from the creative impulse of the individual or the group; and 3) selection by the community, which determines the form or forms in which the music survives.

The term can be applied to music that has evolved from rudimentary beginnings by a community uninfluenced by popular and art music and it can likewise by applied to music which has originated with a individual composer and has subsequently been absorbed into the unwritten living tradition of a community.

The term does not cover composed popular music that has been taken over ready-made by a community and remains unchanged, for it is the re-fashioning and re-creation of the music by the community that gives it its folk character.[36]

These criteria are, generally speaking, good, provided they are not interpreted too narrowly. The past which is linked to the present is not necessarily distant; one generation, or even a half-generation, must be considered sufficient. Nor can one be too strict in his insistence on point number two. Greenway is undoubtedly correct when he says that different versions of a song are evidence of popularity but not of authenticity. Therefore such a requirement should be used only as a useful test. If the collector finds one folk singer who gives him a song which fulfills the other requirements of genuineness, then he should accept it as authentic. Perhaps his one version means simply that he has not been able to find other singers who know the piece. Every collector knows the experience of collecting a fragment and then searching for days, weeks, months, or even years before finding someone else who knows it. To assume that the piece exists in only one version because no other has been collected is concluding from negative evidence, which is always dangerous.

But the existence of a folk piece in only one version at any given time does not necessarily invalidate it as a genuine folk song. It obviously is not widespread, but it still can be genuine. The "community" or "group" possession criterion of genuineness should be loosely interpreted to mean its possession by only one member of a folk "community" or "group."

In arriving at a satisfactory working definition, then, we can say that a folk song is any piece, regardless of authorship or date of origin, which is sung by a member or members of the folk and is not subject to the corrective and stabilizing influences of an art form or any non-folk medium of communication. Often, if it comes from an art form it will be "outmoded" or "discarded," but this does not matter; all it needs is an independent existence among the folk.

II

The songs in this volume are part of a collection made in the summers of 1951, 1952 and 1953, when I traveled through every section and nearly every county of Alabama and talked with more than a hundred informants. During this time I obtained some 2500 ballads and songs — the largest collection ever made for Alabama, and, indeed, one of the biggest made for any state.

The folk song heritage of Alabama, in general, is the result of the state's geographical and historical position — modified by more recent additions. The state was settled by people with varying backgrounds, and every group brought the songs of its class and geographical origin.

Generally speaking, the wealthy slave-holding planters of Virginia and South Carolina, most of whom had first stopped off in Georgia, pre-empted the rich bottom lands of the Tennessee Valley and the Black Belt in the south-central part of the state. The poorer Scotch-Irish and English from the mountains of western Virginia, North Carolina and Tennessee and South Carolina and Georgia were forced to accept the hill country of the northern part and the sandy plains south of the Black Belt.

In general, then, the English and the Scotch-Irish — aided tremendously by Blacks — shaped the folk singing and the folklore of the state. There were other ethnic groups there, to be sure. The Tombigbee River section around what is now the town of Demopolis was originally settled by a group of French. But this effort to turn part of the New World into a French vineyard was abortive, and the only remains of the effort are to be seen in the town names. French and Spanish traditions around Mobile persist in legends and folktales. Cajun folk songs are still sung south of Mobile, in Mobile County, but are of limited circulation, and practically none have been recovered. Small Russian and Scandinavian settlements in Baldwin County, the Russian community around Brookside, and the German colony in Cullman have contributed little to the folk songs of the state.[37]

In pioneer Alabama lines were sharply drawn, socially as well as geographically, between the rich and poor. The gentry despised the poor hill folk. Even as late as the Civil War, Colonel S.A.M. Wood echoing of words of William Byrd of a hundred year earlier, wrote to General Bragg about these folk: "They are the most miserable, ignorant, poor ragged devils I ever saw."[38]

Although the lines between the wealthy and the poor, the "respectable" and the "non-respectable," were well defined, there was still some intercommunication. Ballads and songs were indispensable to all classes of people. Traditionally we think that the poor Scotch-Irish were the singing folk in any community. Perhaps they did bring into Alabama many or most of the ballads. But undoubtedly the well-to-do and poor families of English descent came into their communities with rich stores of songs and ballads.

Soon these songs and ballads were jumping barriers of economy and geography and becoming a part of the lives of both classes. And they continued to be rather freely interchanged until the stirring of the crucible of war. During the years immediately preceding the Civil War, however, class conflict between the poor highlanders and the wealthy lowlanders became intense. Because of blood, economic differences, and political and social affinities, the chasm between the poor and the rich widened. Most of the northern counties were unenthusiastic about the conflict. The causes did not touch them. Not owning slaves, and being less dependent on cotton, these hill folk wanted only to be left alone to pursue life as they chose. And when not allowed to remain neutral, they threatened to join with certain similar Tennessee counties and form the independent state of Nickajack. At the present time, a folk tradition holds that one northern county threatened to secede and set up the Free State of Winston County.

When these reluctant counties were eventually forced into the Confederacy, their people displayed much bitterness about the war which was not of their choosing. During this time, when feelings ran high, the folk songs of the rich and the poor were most sharply separated. To this day, in the land of the almost-consummated state of Nickajack, the collector finds traces of songs — especially ballads — which express resentment against "the rich man's war and the poor man's fight."

Aside from a small number of anti-Confederacy songs and ballads, however, nowadays it is impossible to identify the part of the state from which a particular type of song came. All sections sing the same kinds. In the hills of Cullman County, for instance, except for a few anti-War pieces, the songs I found were no different from those I collected farther south in the foothills, or in the Black Belt, or in the southern part of the state. The kind of song sung in any particular community depends not on the geography but upon the individual. From an eighty-year old lady in Cullman County I collected old war ballads — Civil War and earlier — fiddle tunes, and old comical songs. Her sixty-four year old daughter sang love and sentimental songs. A neighbor lady, around fifty, provided modern love songs and parodies. From two other women in the neighborhood — around forty years old — I obtained mostly love songs. Their father sang two or three funny songs, including the relatively new comical fifth version of "Springfield Mountain."

Farther south, in Lamar County, I again collected all kinds of ballads and songs. One informant's repertory ranged all the way from the silliest songs to the most dignified Child ballads. Another's consisted only of love songs. A fine ninety-six year old lady gave me only Civil War ballads. Her daughter, some sixty-five years old, sang love songs and sentimental pieces, which she had learned from her mother, and other songs of later vintage. In the Black Belt — the former home of the wealthy slave-holders — I found Child ballads, and funny and love songs. In the extreme south — in Baldwin County — I collected mostly love songs and a few American ballads. These experiences in the field indicate that no section sings any particular variety of songs. All divisions along lines of geographical provenience, social descent and political attitude have almost completely disappeared.

The 2500 songs and ballads in my complete collection represent, therefore, all classes and geographical sections of the state. In it there are 800 ballads of all kinds — both English and American — and 1700 folk songs of various types. From this larger collection I chose for this volume a relatively small number — 192 pieces (328, counting variants), all of which are lyrics. I selected lyrics and excluded ballads for three reasons:

(1) Judging from the fact that I have twice as many lyrics as ballads in my total collection, lyrics are more representative of the kinds of folk songs people sing at the present time.

(2) I wanted to include in this study as many songs as possible which have not been reproduced in other collections. Ballads, since they have been worked on so much, have been widely reprinted. It is surely important to show how widespread songs are in tradition, as has been done by the constant reproduction of the same songs in sectional studies, but it is more important, perhaps, to indicate the

wide variety of songs sung. In this volume, therefore, I have excluded all ballads and many of the widely known lyrics to make
room for those not hitherto reported or not so well known. Nearly
half of the songs in this volume — eighty-four out of a hundred and
ninety-two — have not been found in other collections and are
therefore "unique." A breakdown of the various types is revealing,
as the following list shows:

	Number Included	Number "Unique"
Love Songs[39]	89	37
Sentimental Songs[39]	37	8
Comical Songs[40]	23	12
Songs About Animals[40]	8	4
Pseudo-Hegro Songs[40]	14	6
Satiric Songs	12	6
Social Commentary Songs	6	3
Parodies[41]	7	5
Literary Songs[41]	5	4

(3) My third reason for selecting only lyrics was that they are
less stabliized in and by tradition than are ballads and therefore
change more as culture changes. Thus they are better reflections of
Alabama folk culture of 1950.

Lack of space has precluded from this volume many songs and
several types which I would have liked to use. The omission of Negro songs, for instance, is regrettable, although this type receives some
representation in the "Pseudo-Negro Songs" which are included.
Most of the types excluded here, however, receive rather full treatment in other Southern collections, so the omission is more apparent
than real.

In reproducing these songs I have tried to simplify the dialect
as much as possible. Everybody knows, or thinks he knows, how
Southerners, and Alabamians, talk. Therefore I have made no effort
to reproduce speech peculiarities except in a few instances where
the singers were exaggerating for effect, as in the case of several
pseudo-Negro songs. These extremes I have retained in order to give
a truer picture of the song. Obsolete, archaic and dialect terms I
have retained as they were sung, and except where they were unin-
telligible to the general reader I have not clarified the meanings.

This volume of folk lyrics is a fair example of the most important
kinds of folk songs represented in my larger collection. A more
comprehensive study of the folk's total musical repertory would

have included specimens of all types of folk songs, not just those I have treated, and of the several types of ballads, that is, in fact, my entire holdings. But reproduction of such a large quantity was impossible at the present time. All are in the orchives of the center for the Study of Popular Culture, Bowling Green State University, Bowling Green, Ohio.

The presentation of a group of folk lyrics, as opposed to ballads, creates a problem of identification which has not yet been solved by collectors. For there is no standard collection of lyrics like the Child collection of ballads which can be used for making likely distinctions between the old and the new or the known and the unknown. In certain important respects, too, the means of dissemination of the lyrics were different from those of the ballads, for they seem to have been more quickly and more easily transferred from the art to the folk tradition. For these reasons I have felt obliged to give some account of their most probable means of dissemination in order to provide a background for the identifying notes with which I have prefaced each selection in this volume.

Unfortunately there have not been enough studies in the cultural history of Alabama to provide basic materials for research in the dissemination of songs through the actual regions of my collecting. The main channels through which "popular" and folk music spread, however, probably did not differ in kind from one section of the country to another, and a general survey which directs attention to certain specific sources is therefore possible. Since "popular" songs so often were taken into the "folk" tradition, we shall begin with the means of their dissemination.

The hawking of songs — one of the earliest and commonest methods of selling them — persisted into the 1880's in New York. Known as "song sheet men," hawkers sold sheets of popular music for from one to five cents apiece.[42] Their techniques were apparently little changed from those of their seventeenth and eighteenth century counterparts in England. William Dean Howells, in *A Hazard of New Fortunes* (1890), gives a good description of such a man:

[The hawker] had his ballads strung singly upon a cord against the house wall, and held down in piles on the pavement with stones and blocks of wood. Their control in this way intimated a volatility which was not perceptible in their sentiment. They were mostly tragical or doleful: some of them dealt with the wrongs of the workingman,[43] others appealed to a gay experience of the high seas; but vastly the greater part to memories and associations of an Irish origin; some still uttered the poetry of plantation life in the artless accents of the end-man. Where they trusted themselves, with syntax that yielded promptly to any exigency of rhythmic art, to the ordinary American speech, it was to strike directly for the affections, to celebrate the domestic ties, and, above all, to embalm the memories of angel and martyr mothers whose dissipated sons deplored their sufferings too late . . . .[This was] literature, popular in a sense which the most successful book can never be. (Ch. XI)

Outside the largest cities, to which the song hawkers were necessarily limited, there were many ways of bringing songs to the people.
One of the most important was the Negro minstrel shows, which, as
Robert C. Toll has demonstrated, reached a large percentage of the
American public from the middle 40's past the end of the nineteenth
century.[44] Such minstrel groups as Edwin P. Christy's (perhaps the
biggest name in Negro minstrelsy, and probably because of his close
association with Stephen C. Foster) and the Ethiopian Serenaders
were amazingly successful. Both groups toured England with great
success, the Serenaders appearing by royal command before Queen
Victoria. As late as 1915 there were thirty minstrel groups touring
the U.S.[45] Judging from the large number of minstrel songbooks
still extant, these shows popularized hundreds of songs.

Quartets, too, were so popular that they literally covered the
country, especially in the 1880's. They sang many "old" and many
not so old songs, particularly funny and ridiculous ones. These singing groups persisted in Southern tradition longer than in other sections of the country. They are, in fact, still singing there, and apparently getting more popular. Amateurs, semi-professionals, and
professionals, they sing all kinds of songs today, but they specialize
in religious, harmonizing, and, to a less extent, comic songs.

Contemporary with the minstrels, another kind of singing group,
the family group, was becoming well established. Of the several singing family groups touring the country, perhaps the most successful
were the Hutchinsons of New Hampshire, the father and mother
being joined by sixteen children, all of whom assisted by singing or
playing instruments. Other such groups included the Baker, also
of New Hampshire, the Barker and the Reiner (or Rainer). These
organizations did much to spread popular songs throughout the land.

There were many other ways songs were popularized: songsters
(to be discussed in detail below), variety shows, circuses, the "Museum" show — a combination of side-show and variety-hall — special-
ties of all kinds, caravan shows of such performers as the Lingards,
Tony Pastor himself (one of the great showmen of his era), Sol
Smith Russell, William J. Scanlon, and many others.

Traveling shows provided a good means for getting songs throughout the country. "After The Ball," for instance, was popularized by
May Irwin and other singers in Hoyt's farce *A Trip to Chinatown*,

as well as by the daily playing of it at the Columbian Exposition, in 1893, by John Philip Sousa; in all over five million copies of the sheet music were sold. Songs of a "religious or moralizing character," says Louise Pound, "were popularized by Moody and Sankey and other revivalists, and some were floated into general currency at temperance gatherings."[46] Itinerant patent medicine vendors and other wandering bands of entertainers spread songs. Chautauqua singers helped. A very important minor singer in the spreading of songs was the busker, a latter day minstrel who traveled wherever crowds were likely to be — conventions, picnics, political gatherings— with his guitar or fiddle. He entertained with his songs and received in return donations for his art. Such shows as these outlined above were respectable enough to be attended by all members of a family, and they doubtless provided many a song to be whistled and sung long after the entertainment was over.

On another level, taverns and free-and-easies provided good outlets, though their clientele was somewhat more restricted. Because of the nature of the situation, customers participated rather closely with singers. Gilbert gives an interesting account of how an entertainer, Matt O'Reardon for instance, would sing such a piece as:

Love, it is such a very funny thing
And it catches the young and the old.
It's just like a plate of boarding house hash,
And many a man it has sold.
It makes you feel like a fresh water eell (sic)
And it causes your head to swell.
It turns your mind
For love it is blind
And it empties your pocketbook as well.

Chorus:
Boys keep away from the girls I say,
And give them lots of room.
For when you are wed
They will polish up your head
With the bald headed end of a broom.

"And at this the audience clinked glasses," Gilbert continues, "scuffed their feet, chucked their Mamies and Betsies under their chins and . . .shouted 'Another, Mr. Funnyman. Give us "Her Age is Was Red',"...the highspot of the evening."[47]

Newspapers and magazines, also, constituted an important means of disseminating songs. Those designed primarily for farm folk usually had a kind of free forum where subscribers asked and answered questions and made contributions of various sorts. One of the most frequent queries was whether any reader knew such and such a song or ballad. Usually the next issue contained the desired information. Hundreds — or thousands — of songs were popularized in this way. Today the collector frequently finds an old book with its leaves pasted over with these newspaper songs, or an old jar in the kitchen stuffed full of these forgotten clippings of songs now remembered and preserved in an oral tradition.

Amidst the avalanche of songs that poured from the popular song mills of the last half of the nineteenth century, traditional ballads and folk songs were not forgotten. Many people liked them best. In the repertories of the traveling entertainers there were usually a few traditional ballads and songs. Furthermore, many genuine ballads such as "Gypsy Davy" and "The House Carpenter" were sung in the taverns and free-and-easies in the 60's and 70's under the name of "antiques."[48] Thus, traditional songs were disseminated along with the popular pieces.

The above mentioned media for getting songs to the people were doubtless not all. Sheet music, singing schools, church singings, and other relatively less important means were instrumental. Once introduced into a community, songs were passed from one person to another by several folk devices. In country communities singers learned many songs from their parents and the older generations. Many others they learned from other members of their own age group, frequently writing them down as "ballets" so that they would not forget them. Before and after church meetings, girls and boys frequently sang and exchanged songs. Occasionally there were socials, at which time all the new songs were likely introduced and sung until everybody learned them.

Townspeople learned songs in the same way as did the country people, but frequently with an important difference. Town families were more likely to own organs and, later, pianos. These instruments, in either town or country, were undoubtedly the means by which a large number of songs was popularized in a community. Frequently on Friday and Saturday nights, young ladies and young men congregated around an organ or piano and sang until they had run through all the new songs and everybody's repertory of old ones.

Thus, word of mouth, "ballets," socials, individual exchanges, and group exchanges around the organ or piano seem to have been the main ways among the folk for passing on songs that had been introduced into a community.

One can only speculate about some of the lost chords of the various popularizers of songs in the nineteenth century, since much concrete evidence is not extant. But there is one medium available, though hitherto largely neglected, which casts much light on the dissemination. This is the so-called "songster," mentioned above. Collections of songsters, which contain lyrics primarily, though unwieldy in bulk and form, constitute an accumulation of songs most nearly comparable to the standard ballad collections. Because of their importance, these songsters should be discussed at rather great length.

The "songster" was the popular songbook of the eighteenth and nineteenth centuries, somewhat similar to the numerous "fireside" books of "familiar" songs of today. The idea behind them was to provide collections of songs at minimum prices. Nineteenth century songsters ranged from very small to large. The smallest contained from twelve to twenty songs and sold for a nickel. Beadle and Adams (publishers of dime novels) printed some fifteen pages of songs and sold them as "Half-Dime Songsters." The largest works of this sort, well bound though usually on rather cheap paper, contained up to five hundred songs and sold for a considerable a-mount. The usual size, however, contained seventy-five to a hundred items and sold for a dime. Ordinarily they were small enough to fit into a person's pocket and were therefore frequently called "pocket songsters."

According to Irving Lowens, the leading authority on early songsters, the earliest songster published in America was *The constitutions of the free-masons,* "London printed; Anno 5723. Re-printed in Philadelphia by special order, for the use of the brethren in North-America. In the year of Masonry 5734, Anno Domini 1734." The printer was Benjamin Franklin. Judging from extant titles, there were some 650 songsters published in America by the end of 1820, though only 542 have actually been located by Lowens in a fifteen year search. In the early years they were published in such cities as Philadelphia, New York, Boston, Baltimore, and in numerous smaller towns, especially along the eastern seaboard.

They were even more widespread in the nineteenth century, though it is impossible to establish exact numbers because many such ephemera have been lost. But basing my count on a total of about 1500,[49] I can establish some kind of pattern which will serve to demonstrate parameters. For the first three decades the numbers were comparatively small, only a few score for each decade. The rise in numbers thereafter, however, was sharp, roughly paralleling the development and growth of Negro minstrelsy. At least 100 were published from 1840 to 1850; at least 150 during the next decade. But, as would be expected, the beginning of the Civil War brought large numbers; at least 200 were published during the Sixties. After the War the number continued to increase; at least 500 were published during the 70s, at least 400 during the 80s.[50] But thereafter apparently the volume decreased astonishingly, with only a couple of dozen brought out during the 90s. In the twentieth century they are still being published, though in small numbers. *Elton's Out-and-Out Comic Songster* (1938) and the *4-H Club Song Book* (c. 1950) are recent examples. Labor Unions still occasionally use them: *Amalgamated Song Book*[51] and *CIO Song Book*,[52] being two examples.

The songs in these books were of great variety. Selections apparently were based on popularity of individual songs and editors' memories. Sometimes all the pieces in a particular songster were supposedly composed by the editor of person whose name it bore — *Sig. Abecca's Sentimental Songster* (1864), for instance. Often the collection consisted of songs sung by a particular man or group, such as the various Hutchinson songsters or *Ben Cotton's Own Songster* (1864). Usually, however, the contents were the editor's choice, and they were divided roughly into the following ratio: one-third to one-half definitely "popular" songs (the publishers and dates of copyright were given when known), a few that might have been derived from Tin-Pan Alley, several (sometimes many) minstrel pieces, and a considerable number of popular ballads and folk songs. Frequently these ballads and folk songs were not old but were well established in the folk tradition: "Mollie Darling," "Dearest Mae," and "Old Rosin the Beau" were favorite pieces, as were Foster's songs. Sometimes songs were falsely attributed to authors, as Foster's were usually assigned to Christy. Often pieces by known composers were published anonymously.

Ordinarily music was not included in the songsters. Sometimes, though much less than half the time, the name of the intended air was indicated. For instance, such and such a song might be sung to the tune of "Dearest Mae," or "Old Rosin the Beau." Where no tune was indicated presumably a person could fit the song to any known tune or make up one of his or her own.

Nineteenth century songsters were published all over the country. New York was by then the largest center; Philadelphia was apparently second. Boston, Baltimore, Washington, New Haven, Cincinnati and Providence were other important centers. Southern cities and towns, too, were sites of publication, especially during the Civil War, with Richmond, New Orleans, Augusta and Savannah apparently the most important. On the West Coast, San Francisco was the publishing center of such songbooks. Santa Barbara, too, saw at least one, a free advertising songster that contained the latest songs, a few stories and suggestions as to where one should do his or her shopping.

Such, then, is a brief description of the songster. It is now impossible to determine the full role it played in the transference of songs from the "popular" to the "folk" tradition, but that the role was great there is little reason to doubt. Of the 192 songs in this volume, for instance, forty-two were found in the songsters I have consulted and are probably in other I have not seen. An additional fifty pieces are similar and may well be in songsters not available, or they are definitely of unconventional "folk" origin. Some songs appeared in the songsters scores of times, "Old Rosin the Beau" and Barney McCoy," for example. Therefore it is safe to assume that of the straight and obvious "pure" lyrics sung by the folk of Alabama during the early 1950s about half were obviously brought into the "folk" canon from outside, non-folk origins, and approximately one-fourth to one-half were introduced and/or popularized by the songster, sheet music or some other printed source. There is another important indication of the role played by the songster in popularizing songs: of the forty-two pieces in this volume appearing in such books, twenty-one have been reported in other collections of folk songs — "The Arkansas Traveller (No. I)," (No. 137, below), for example, is included in twenty-six such collections; "Old Rosin the Beau," in sixteen, and others in lesser numbers; only six appear just once.

Though in some cases songs were included in the songsters because they were already favorites with the people, undoubtedly publication made them even more popular; and, more important, other pieces were introduced to the people for the first time, and were subsequently transferred from the printed to the oral tradition.

In the headnotes for the following collection I have not only indicated if and where the songs appear in other folk song collections but also shown the extent to which they appeared in songsters. This area of investigation is new, and my exploration of it has demonstrated that more songsters must be examined by scholars if the full story of folk song dissemination is to be clearly told.

IV

My basic collection was made, of course, in an effort to record what the people of Alabama were actually singing during the early 1950s, and it includes a great variety of material ranging from English and American ballads to fiddle tunes. The relatively large group contained in the following pages represents an arbitrary selection of only nine categories from among the twenty-one into which the whole collection is organized.

The twelve categories not represented here are mostly, like the two groups of ballads, types which are independent of each other and susceptible perhaps to separate presentation at some future time. "Cowboy Ballads and Songs," "Work Songs," and "Play-Party Songs," for example, are recognized categories of folk music, and "Negro Songs," "War Songs and Ballads," "Prohibition and Drinking Songs," "Prison Songs," "Lullabies and Nursery Songs," "Fiddle Tunes," and "Religious Songs" are equally distinctive groups. The nine categories I have used here are somewhat more coherent and seemed to me particularly interesting because they provide a better insight into the folk culture of the state than do those of any other substantial group.

At first glance there may seem to be little coherence in a collection which includes "Love Songs" and "Sentimental Songs" on the one hand and one the other such material as that contained in the categories of "Comical Songs," "Songs About Animals," "Pseudo-Negro Songs," "Satires," "Social Commentaries" and "Parodies," as well as "Literary Songs." But in the actual process of collecting I found that a relationship did exist between all these groups except "Literary Songs," which group I included because of its general interest. The first two groups are held together by their common treatment of love, and the other categories, regardless of subject, by their bond of humor. Women, generally speaking, preferred songs of sentiment, and men preferred those with a humorous slant. In order to get a cross section of folk culture in these songs, therefore, I had to balance the feminine propensity for sentimentality with the masculine bias toward humor. Each category in the two larger groups and "Literary Songs" will be discussed in detail.

The subject matter of "Love Songs" is, naturally, love. But since love is a large subject and susceptible to varied treatments I have divided this category into five types based upon treatment: "Court-ing Songs," "Happy Love Songs," "Unhappy Love Songs," "Anti-Marriage Songs," and "Humorous Love Songs."

The six "Courting Songs," although not numerous, are quite interesting. They deal with the troubles of meeting and marrying the person of one's choice. The subject is not so popular as more advanced stages of love, but the songs reveal much about the atti-tudes toward and techniques of courting.

One of the largest and most important groups of love songs is concerned with "Happy Love," as the thirty pieces in this category indicate. These songs sing of the joys of being in love — and some-times of the exquisite pain. The songs in this category are related through the general treatment of the subject. Love is grand and the world a song.

In love, however, things do not always come out as planned. Folk singers recognize this sad fate and enjoy singing about it. In the "Un-happy Love" category the world is shown filled with broken and breaking hearts, and this is the theme holding together the fifteen songs in this category. Although the songs in this category are nearly always sad, they are not overly sentimental.

Another kind of love song which is more artistically satisfactory deals with a definite rejection of love, the "Anti-Marriage Songs." More cynical in their treatment of life, these songs face up to life's situations. Throughout this group the tone is light and the pieces are always sung with a smile, or with mock tears.

Of the love songs, undoubtedly the most interesting and amusing are the forty-three "Humorous Love Songs." These pieces do not take life and love seriously. As a result their approach, emotion, and language are pleasing.

The treatment of the subject in the "Sentimental Songs" is at times unduly saccharine. This group is large in my collection, though I have included only twenty-six in this volume. These songs cloy the appetite. All animals, birds, nature and life feel for the broken heart of each individual. With all their sentimentality, however, they are little if any worse than many current popular songs.

Though the songs in this category are not favorites with anybody but folk singers, among whom they are cherished, they are important as an index to folk sentimentality. They show in folk feeling a hold-over of the sentimentality of the sixties and seventies of the nine-teenth century.

Another important category in this volume is the "Pseudo-Negro Songs." Alabamians in the past enjoyed Negro-like songs and Negro-like singing, as the thirteen pieces in this group indicate. In every case but one the songs in this section were sung by whites. Usually the white singer rendered the piece with a reasonable imitation of Negro delivery. And in every case he was aware of what he was doing. He was consciously imitating — and occasionally caricaturing — the Negro. This imitation and caricature is evidence of the peculiar quirk in Southern behavior which throughout history has allowed a white Southerner himself to make fun of the Negro at the same time that he would fight any non-Southerner for doing the same thing.

These songs are of two kinds: love songs and comic songs. In both cases they are easily identified as pseudo-Negro by their idiom and treatment of subject. In language there is a liberal sprinkling of bad grammar and of "des" and "dos" for "these" and "those." In treatment of subject matter, the songs use stylized Negro references: to 'possums and 'coons, jaybirds, cotton picking, mules, and the like. Many of these pieces have minstrel origins, and their treatment and idiom are obviously of that medium.

The pseudo-Negro love pieces perhaps belong with the more general group of "Love Songs." But I have kept them here because they use the Negro more or less as a point of reference. The majority of the songs in this category, however, are humorous. At times they are nothing but nonsense. The degree to which they sound like Negro songs varies, but, again, for convenience I have put into this group all those songs with any Negro blood, as the whites of the South do with people. These pieces are often delightfully humorous. Exagerative, nonsensical, often ridiculous, they nevertheless are nearly always amusing.

The category identified as "Social Commentary" comprises one of the most interesting and information groups in this volume. These songs date back to the latter part of the preceding century. They indicate well what people did not like in the "old days." Pretentiousness, trying to get ahead of one's fellows — these two unfavorable traits were especially disliked.

In many ways, however, the most interesting songs in this section and indeed in the whole book, are the two "Booker T. Washington" and "Climbing Up The White House Stars." The former shows how the people of Alabama, and the South, reacted against the famous Negro educator's popularity in the North and at the National Capital.

And the romantic possibilities of the White House are treated in the second piece. These two songs illustrate how topical pieces can persist in tradition long after the events on which they are based have passed away. The whole category shows how the folk continue to sing songs which no longer have any real reason for existing.

Satires — as distinguished from social commentaries — include the inevitable lampoons on Arkansas and its inhabitants, satires on marriage ("Tommy and Jack") and the mother-in-law problem, which is given a half-serious, half-comic treatment in "My Mother-In-Law." Included also are accounts of the expense of women — how they say they are not hungry, then eat everything in sight ("I Had But Fifty Cents").

The eleven pieces in this section indicate definite points of view, but the treatments are usually humorous. They are good songs.

In many ways the degree of sophistication of a people can be gauged by the number of parodies found among them. Parodies show the degree of detachment people exhibit in their view of life. If this is a worthwhile yardstick, then the Alabama folk are rather mature, for this volume contains a sizable collection, nine, in fact. The popular Tin-Pan Alley hit "Down On The Farm," for instance, rankled in the breasts of the folk, who knew from bitter experience what life is like on the farm. Therefore a wholesome and uncomplimentary satire rose against the sentimentality of the false picture of the old homestead:

For I'd rather go to jail and no one to go my bail
Than to go and spend one hour on the farm.

"In the Shade of the Old Apple Tree" receives its humorous treatment in "Maggie Jones," a story of falling apples, broken limbs, and fighting parents. "You Wore A Tulip" is turned into a comparison of the merits of a Model T Ford and a Buick ("You Drove A Buick"). The sentimentality of Paul Dresser as shown in "Just Tell Them That You Saw Me" is nicely parodied in a treatment of lost legs and lonely oysters ("Oyster Stew"). But of this group perhaps the most satisfying is the parody of "Home Sweet Home." In a land where nearly every home has its "Home Sweet Home" motto, this treatment of not-so-sweet-home comes as a fresh breeze:

The little baby cries just on one track,

And you step on the point of a rusted carpet tack.
Your wife sticks her cold feet in the middle of your back.
There's no place like home.

All in all, this is a pleasurable section for both scholar and general reader.

The "Comical Songs" have been divided into two sections: "Comical Songs" and "Songs About Animals." Though both categories are in effect the same, they differ in emphasis, and for that reason have been separated. In the "Comical Songs" the accent is on being funny. So it is in the second; but here the subject and treatment are almost exclusively of animals. Animals appear also in the former category, but not to such a great extent. The basis for division, then, is strictly one of emphasis.

Sometimes the "Comical Songs" are nonsense; nearly always they are ridiculous. The twenty-three songs in this section are definitely amusing.

The "Songs About Animals" are even more nonsensical. They place greatest emphasis on animal and fowl. Their avowed purpose is humor, and they never fail. The eight animal songs in this group show how close Alabama folk are to the soil and nature; and how they find humor in the aspects of life nearest them.

"Literary Songs," the final category in this volume, have not been widely reported by collectors. Perhaps this failure stems from the belief that these songs are not true "folk songs." But, as we have seen above, such an attitude is not tenable, for such songs must be included in a collection that is truly comprehensive of the songs the folk sing.

My collection includes only five such pieces, but they illustrate the absorption of formal literature into the folk tradition. One informant sang Wordsworth's "The Little Cottage Girl" and said that people "used to sing all those old poems." She cited as another example Poe's "Annabel Lee." She might have been referring to the version of "Poe's 'Annabelle Lee' (sic)" which "was changed by a writer to fit a pop tune."[52] Another informant sang Byron's "Maid of Athens" and recounted how the song — words and music — had been included in the back of a book of instructions with an organ her family bought around the turn of the century. This same informant sang Longfellow's "The Bridge." Robert Louis Stevenson's "Time to Rise" was sung by another person, who was surprised that anybody else had ever heard of the piece. She thought it was unique with her family. Another singer gave me Eugene Field's "Little Boy Blue." Examination of this rather small, though significant, group of songs will reveal to what extent they were altered in oral transmission.

The nine categories, and seven sub-categories, outlined above illustrate the range and depth of the folk lyric. Each group casts light on the lyric as a genre and upon the Alabama folk singer. These categories do not comprise the total lyric of Alabama. Because of lack of space some groups had to be excluded. Their inclusion would have enriched this volume and made it more nearly representative. Enough have been included, however, to show that the lyric is a rich field of study for both folklorists and general scholars.

NOTES

[1] Kittredge pointed out that this phrase is a summary of Grimm's views, not a direct quotation *(English And Scottish Popular Ballads,* ed. Kittredge and Sargent, Boston, 1904, p. xviii, n. 1.

[2] For a full discussion of the matter of "communal composition" see Reed Smith, *South Carolina Ballads* (Cambridge, Mass., 1928).

[3] Kittredge, *op. cit.,* p. xix.

[4] *Ibid.,* p. xxvii.

[5] In this Introduction I am primarily concerned with showing that the definition of folk songs must be enlarged. Therefore I do not discuss songs obviously of folk origin. This collection contains many such pieces.

[6] Friedrich Karl Freiherr von Erlach, *Die Volkslieder der Deutschen* (Mannheim, 1834-1836), V. 23.

[7] Hoffmann von Fallersleben, *Unsere volkstumlichen Lieder,* 4th ed., ed. Karl Hermann Prahl (Leipzig. 1900).

[8] Franz Magnus Bohme, *Volksthumliche Lieder der Deutschen im 18. und 19. Jahrhundert* Leipzig, 1895), p. iii. In addition to Joffman and Bohme, John Meier should be mentioned for his basic work in the field of folk song origins. Beginning his researches with a brilliant essay on the literary background of Schnaderhupfel ("Volksthumliche und Kunstmassige Elemente in der Schnaderhupfelpoesie," Beilage zur Allgemeinen Zeitung, Oct. 6, 1890), Meier went on in 1906 to write his standard work, *Kunstlieder im Volksmunde* (Halle, 1906).

[9] W.W. Newell, *Games and Songs of American Children* (New York, 1883 and 1903), p. 7. The italics are mine.

[10] Moses Gaster, "Presidential Address," *Folk-Lore,* 20 (1909), 25-29.

[11] Hans Naumann, *Primitive Gemeinschaftskultur* (Jena, 1921), pp. 4-5.

[12] Phillips Barry, "The Transmission of Folk-Song," *JAFL,* XXVII (1914), 67.

[13] Phillips Barry, "American Folk Music," *SFQ,* I, No. 2 (1937), 44.

[14] Louise Pound, *American Ballads and Songs* (New York, 1922), p. xiii.

[15] John Greenway, *American Folksongs of Protest* (Philadelphia, 1953).

[16] *Ibid.,* pp. 7-8.

[17] *Ibid.,* p. 9.

[18] *Ibid.,* p. 8.

[19] *Ibid.,* p. 10.

[20] Newman I. White *(American Negro Folk-Songs,* Cambridge, Mass., 1928, pp. 164-167) says that "Uncle Ned" has long since gone into oral tradition among Negroes. Everyone is familiar with the several tunes composed by Foster which have been used innumerable times as tunes for other songs. Foster's tunes, in fact, became more widely used than his words.

[21] *A New Variorum Edition of Shakespeare, The Poems,* ed. Hyder E. Rollins (Phila., and London, 1938) notes: "Malone (ed. 1790): This song is alluded to in *The Woman's Prize* (c. 1615). . .by B[eaumont] and Fletcher (IV.I; *Works,* ed. Walter, 1910, VIII, 58). Lee (ed. 1905, p. 39n) notes references to it in Rowley's *Match at Midnight,* 1633, sig. I 2^v; Ford's *Fancies Chaste and Noble,* 1638, IV. I *(Works,* ed. Dyce, 1869, II, 291). There is another in *Lady Alimony,* 1659, sig. B3, II. i)."

[22] See J. Greenhill, *A List of All the Songs and Passages in Shakespeare which have been set to Music* (London, 1884), p. 100.

[23] In *The Songster's Library and Museum of Mirth, Being Volume one of the most extensive collection of Ancient and Modern songs in the English Language* (Cambridge, [England] : Manson, Emerson, and Co. 1834), p. 80.

[24]There were three real Shakespearean pieces in the same songster and another falsely attributed to him.

[25]Songsters had full and comprehensive titles. The full name of this one was: *The Universal Songster, or, Museum of Mirth, forming the Most Complete, Extensive, and valuable Collection of Ancient and Modern Songs in the English Language* (London, 1846), I, 98.

[26]*The English Minstrel: Containing a Selection of the Most Popular Songs of England* (Glasgow, 1850), p. 39.

[27]*The American College Songster, A Collection of Songs, Glees, and Melodies, sung by American Students: Containing also popular American, English, Irish and German Songs, Negro melodies*, etc. (Ann Arbor, Michigan, 1876), p. 62.

[28]*The Wide-Awake Vocalist; or Rail-Splitters Song Book* (New York, c. 1860), p. 62.

[29]*Patriotic Songs and Hymns* (New York, c. 1864), p. 19.

[30]Fannie H. Eckstorm and Mary W. Smyth, *Minstrelsy of Maine* (Boston, 1927), pp. 266, 267. Quoted in Reed Smith, *South Carolina Ballads,* where there is an interesting discussion of the changes in several other pieces.

[31]In the *Forget-Me-Not Songster* (New York, c. 1842), p. 207, it had the chorus mentioned by Eckstorm. In *The American College Songster* (in the "Songs of Dartmouth" section), p. 71, it had the other chorus.

[32]*Popular Songs Printed for the Use of the New York Commandery of the Military Order of the Loyal Legion* (New York, n.d.), no page number.

[33]*American College Songster* ("Songs of Yale College" section), p. 36. The popularity of the tune "Cocacheluck" is illustrated by the fact that two other songs were sung to it: "Osseous Philosophy" (p. 83) and "Our Maidens Far Away" (p. 120).

[34]*The Heathen Chinee Songster* (New York, c. 1871).

[35]Louise Pound, *Folk-Song of Nebraska and the Central West, A Syllabus,* Nebraska Academy of Sciences Publication, Vol. 9, No. 3 (Lincoln, 1915), pp. 67-68.

[36]*Journal of the International Folk Music Council,* VII (1955), p. 23.

[37]For a brief study of Alabama folklore see *Alabama, A Guide to the Deep South,* Compiled by W.P.A. (New York, 1941).

[38]A.B. Moore, *History of Alabama* (University, Ala., 1934), p. 439, This is the best history of the state.

[39]These proportions probably derive from the fact that editors have not felt some of these pieces sufficiently "genuine." But they should be reported, for they are sung.

[40]Songs from these groups are so evanescent in character that they do not maintain their identity; often two singers in the same locality sing them differently. Such songs are "floaters." Individual stanzas frequently appear in other songs and in other collections, but not these songs *in toto.*

[41]Parodies are by nature local. Literary songs have not been widely reported as folk songs, perhaps because editors did not accept them as "genuine."

[42]Douglas Gilbert, *Lost Chords: The Diverting Story of American Popular Songs* (New York, 1942), pp. 40-42.

[43]Gilbert says *(Ibid.,* p. 85) that not until the seventies did popular songs begin referring to the condition of labor and the socially underprivileged.

[44]*Ibid.,* p. 90.

[45]Louise Pound. *Syllabus,* pp. 6-7.

[46]Gilbert, *op. cit.,* p. 105. See the folk version of this song below.

[47]*Ibid.,* p .105.

[48]See Oscar G.T. Sonneck and W. T. Upton, *A Bibliography of Early Secular American Music* (Washington, 1945), pp. 533-535. They list 110 for the period 1760-1800.

[49]The largest collections are in the Library of Congress and the New York Public. There are numerous other important collections of varying sizes.

[50]Establishing exact numbers is impossible. Many songsters were published with the date 18--, a good number had no city and no date of publication. The general date of 18-- was widely used during the 1870s and 80s, as internal evidence indicates.

[51]Published in New York by the Amalgamated Clothing Workers of America, CIO (c. 1948).

[52]Published in Washington, by CIO Department of Education and Research (c. 1949).

[53]Gilbert, *op. cit.,* p. 294.

I
LOVE SONGS

A
COURTING SONGS

1

Sweet Lily

This song, like so many folk lyrics and ballad-like songs, consists of fragments which float from one piece to another. Several songs begin with the line, "My foot's in the stirrup," which has become in the Alabama version, "My horse to my buggy." The concluding stanza of my A text is a common motif for disappointed love. The "It is love," stanza is common in funny songs. For references and an interesting comment see Brown (II, 373). The one North Carolina text reported there is a six-stanza song which tells a more complete story than do the Alabama versions. Randolph (IV, 205) has one text and several references.

A

"Lily," sung by Miss Drucilla Hall, Millport, Lamar County, 1952.

My horse to my bug-gy, my lines in my hand. I'm

court-ing fair Li-ly and I'll mar-ry her if I can. Oh,

Li-ly, sweet Li-ly, Li-ly, fare you well. I'm sor-ry

to leave you, I love you so well.

My horse to my buggy, my lines in my hand,
I'm courting fair Lily and I'll marry her if I can.
Oh, Lily, sweet Lily, Lily, fare you well.
I'm sorry to leave you, I love you so well.

She wrote me a letter that she's lying low.
I wrote her an answer; she didn't get it, I know.
Go dig up sweet Lily and bury her by my side.
The last word that was spoken was, "Lily, be my bride."

It is love, it is love,
It is love on my mind.

And if love don't kill me
I'll live a long time.

Your parents don't like me; they say that I am poor.
They say that I'm unworthy to enter your door.
Some say I drink whiskey; my money is my own.
And if they don't like me they can let me alone.

B

"Sweet Lily," sung by Mrs. Della Collins, Vernon, Lamar County, 1952. She lived in the country close to Miss Hall some twenty years ago, and possibly she learned the song at this time.

My horse to my bug-gy, my lines in my hand. I'm court-ing fair Li-ly, and I'll mar-ry her if I can.

Chorus

Oh, Li-ly, oh, Li-ly, Li-ly, fare you well. I'm sor-ry to leave you, I love you so well.

My horse to my buggy, my lines is in my hand.
I am courting sweet Lily to marry her if I can.

Oh, Lily, sweet Lily, oh, Lily, fare you well.
I am sorry to leave you, I love you so well.

Her people don't like me; they say I am poor.
They say I am not worthy to enter her door.

They say I drink whiskey: my money is my own,
And if people don't like me, they can let me alone.

She wrote me a letter that she was lying low.
I wrote her an answer, she did not get it, I know.

Go dig up sweet Lily, come bury her by my side.
The last word was spoken was, "Lily, be my bride."

2
Katy Did

This song was probably originated in the music hall or songster. In *Beadle's Dime Song Book,* No. 13 (1864, p. 8) there is a song entitled "Katy Did, Katy Didn't," but the words are totally different from those in this song. The chorus, however, is similar. I have found no other record of the song. It apparently was rather popular in Alabama. I have three texts, all fragments.

A

"Katy Did," sung by Mrs. Ramie Hankins, Vernon, Lamar County, 1952. She has known it some thirty years.

Tell me, pretty little elven, (elf)
In your corsage green,
Have you seen my Katy pass
This way since yestere'en?
Did she have a stranger with her
Whisp'ring words of love?
Did she sigh, and did she answer
Murm'ring words of love?

Chorus:
   Yes, she did, Katy did.

Katy did, she did, she didn't.
Katy did, Katy didn't.
Katy did, she did.

B

"Have You See My Katy Pass?" sung by Mrs. Nola Browne, Millport, Lamar County, 1952. She has sung this song for forty years. A fragment.

Have you see my Katy pass this way since yester-

day? Did she have a stranger with her whisp'ring words

of love? Yes she did, Katy did, Katy did, Katy did-n't,

Katy did, Yes she did, Katy did, Katy did, she did-n't.

Have you seen my Katy pass this way since yesterday?
Did she have a stranger with her whisp'ring words of love?
Yes she did, Katy did, Katy did, Katy didn't.
Katy did, yes she did, Katy did, Katy did, she didn't.

C

"Tell Me, Pretty Little Miss," sung by Mrs. L.A. Mac Donald, Vernon, Lamar County, 1952. A four-line fragment.

3
Lonesome Seems The Winter

This piece is similar in theme to the widespread "Lonesome Scenes of Winter" reported in Brown (II, 302) but is a different song. Henry *(Still More Ballads and Folk-Songs*, p. 111) reports a text very close to mine, as does Belden *(Ballads and Songs*, p. 195, with references). See also Dean *(The Flying Cloud and 150 Other Old Time Poems and Ballads*, p. 108) and Wyman and Brockway *(Twenty Kentucky Mountain Songs*, p. 94).

"Lonesome Seems The Winter," sung by Miss Drucilla Hall, Millport, Lamar County, 1952. She thinks she has been singing it for some forty years.

Lone-some seems the win-ter, The kind-ly frost and snow; The storm-y clouds of sor-row, The storm-y winds did blow.

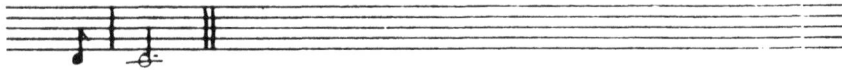

Lonesome seems the winter,
The kindly frost and snow,
The stormy clouds of sorrow,
The stormy winds did blow.

I went to see my love last night,
And she proved most scornfully.
I asked her if she'd marry,
And she would not answer me.

The little birds sung sweetly
On every bush and vine.
My joys they would be doubled
If you were only mine.

There I sat the livelong night,
Till near the dawn of day.
I'm waiting for an answer, say,
Love, what do you say?

Kind Sir, if I must answer you,
I'd choose a single life,
For I never thought it suitable
For me to be your wife.

Now take this for your answer,
And for yourself advice
I found another lover
While you were lying aside.

In the course of three weeks after,
This maiden's mind did change.
She wrote to me a letter
Saying: Kind Sir, I'm ashamed.

Oh, since my mind has changed me
I hate to see you mourn,
Oh, here's my heart, Love, take it,
And claim it as your own.

I wrote to her an answer,
And sent it on my speed,
Saying: Since your mind has changed you
I've looked another way.
Upon a more fair damsel
More suitable than thee.

Upon a more fair damsel,
Where love can have its fill.
This world it is too wide.
If one don't suit, another will.

4
Why Don't You Try?

This humorous treatment of flirting on vacation is obviously no folk composition. It probably originated in the music-hall or song-ster. I have not, however, found any record of it. I have not found it in any other collection of folk songs, and I have only one text.

"Why Don't You Try?" sung by Mrs. Guy J. Johnson, Oneonta, Blount County, 1953. She has sung it for some thirty years.

Did you every see a maiden in a little rolling chair?
Room for two, me and you,
Hear the salty breezes whistle through her curly locks of hair?
Ocean's blue, so are you.
For another lucky fellow is attending at her side,
There to stay if he may.
And she whispers in his ear, "Don't be quite so distant, Dear,
Though we first met yesterday."

Chorus:
    Do you think you'd like me better,
    If you thought that I liked you?
    Do you think that I'd be angry
    If you stole a kiss or two?
    Do you think that you could love me
    In the sweet, sweet by-and-by?
    If you think that you can learn to,
    Why don't you try? Why don't you try?

Just another season later in another rolling chair,
There is Sue, so are you.
But you don't remember Susan and her curly locks of hair,
Nor does Sue think of you.
So at last you get acquainted, and you thing you've made a hit.
But you're wrong all along.
For there'll be another year, and there'll be another dear
Who will hear the same old song.

5
Flirting

Perhaps a take-off or parody of Longfellow's poem which begins, "I stood on the bridge at midnight, when the clocks were striking the hour," this song is more probably merely a result of the sentiment of the 70's and 80's. There are many similar items. This piece has not been widely recorded. Randolph (IV, 272) reports two texts. Owens *(Texas Folk Songs,* p. 166) reports one. I have only one Alabama text.

"Flirting," sung by Mrs. O.C. Powell, Titus, Elmore County, 1952. She has sung it fifty years.

> There stood on the bridge in the evening,
> Under the moonbeams fair,
> A youth in the pride of manhood,
> A maid of beauty rare.
> His face was pale with passion,
> Now flushed with a sunset glow.
> His head was bent in listening
> To a voice so sweet and low.
>
> "Oh, I never knew you loved me,
> Never thought you really cared,"
> And her beautiful head drooped sadly
> Beneath her dark brown hair.
> For she was only flirting,
> Only playing a part.
> Only a man's life blighted,
> Only a broken heart.
>
> "Oh, I'm to be married next winter."
> With a sigh she offered her hand,
> Then drew her light robe around her,
> And left him alone on the strand.
> For she was only flirting,
> Only playing a part.
> Only a man's life blighted,
> Only a broken heart.
>
> She sits by her carriage window,
> A beautiful haughty face,
> An elegant stately women
> All dressed in satin and lace.
> He walks the halls of passers,
> Always silent and cold.
> It's a head too soon grown silvery,
> A heart to soon grown cold.

6
Anna Lee

This song has not been frequently recovered. It has been found in North Carolina, southern Illinois, New York, Tennessee, Missouri, Arkansas, and perhaps Kentucky. It was probably more widespread in Alabama one generation ago. For references see Brown (II, 376).

"Anna Lee," sung by Mrs. Mary Drake, Huntsville, Madison County, 1953. She got it from her mother, who she says composed it.

Ev-'ry bod-y in the vil-lage knows that he's

been court-ing me. But this eve-ning he was driv-

Chorus

ing with that hate-ful An-na Lee. Now I al-most

wish I'd nev-er wrote to him that he was free,

For per-haps it was a sto-ry that he rode with

An-na Lee.

Everybody in the village
Knows that he's been courting me,
But this evening he was driving
With that hateful Anna Lee.

Chorus:
    Now I almost wish I'd never
    Wrote to him that he was free,
    For perhaps it was a story
    That he rode with Anna Lee.

I declare, out in the moonlight,
There is someone coming there.
Can it be? Yes, it is his figure,
Just as sure as I am here.

He is coming through the gateway
And I'll meet him at the door,
And I'll tell him that I'll love him
If he'll court Miss Lee no more.

B
HAPPY LOVE SONGS

7
Wait Till the Clouds Roll By

This song was composed by J.J. Fulmer (real name Charles E. Pratt), words by himself or J.T. Wood, in 1881. Fulmer's purpose, apparently, was to foist this piece off as an older and unavailable number (Spaeth, *History of Popular Music,* p. 224). It was copyrighted by T.B. Harms, N.Y. in 1881, and became a popular stage song which was widely disseminated through the songsters. For example: *The Bicycle Crank Songster* (N.Y. 1884, p. 11); *J.H. Conroy's Tipperary Christening Songster* (N.Y. 188-, p. 21); *Charles Diamond's Milanese Minstrel Songster* (N.Y. 1877, p. 58); *Dupres & Benedict's Famous Minstrels Songster* (N.Y. 18--, p. 4); *Harrigan & Hart's Blackbird Songster* (N.Y. c. 1882, p. 13); *Harrigan & Hart's "Muddy Day" Songster* (N.Y. 188-, p. 44); *J.H. Haverly's New Mastodons Minstrel Songster* (N.Y. 188-, p. 60); *Harrigan & Hart's Mordecai Songster* (N.Y., 1882, p. 8); *Minnie Lee's Serio-Comic Queen Songster* (N.Y. c. 1881, p. 9). The popularity of the song generated numerous parodies. For instance: "I'll Wait Till the Clouds Roll By. Answer to: Wait Till the Clouds Roll By'" *(Wehman's Universal Songster, No. 16,* N.Y., 1883, p. 124); *The Kernell's Miss Fogarty Christmas Cake Songster* (N.Y. 188-, p. 12); "Wait Till the Cash Runs Dry," ("Sung by Tony Pastor," *The American 4 Songster,* N.Y. 1884, p. 45); "Wait Till the Keg Runs Dry," ("Sung with Haverly's Mastadons by the King of Banjoists, E.M. Hall," *George Jarvis's Boats A-Going Over Songster* (N.Y. 18--, p. 37).

Though this song has not been reported in other collections, my two versions indicate a certain popularity in Alabama.

A

"Wait Till the Clouds Roll By," sung by Mrs. R. Van Iderstine, Daphne, Baldwin County, 1953. She did not remember when she had learned it.

Jen-ny, my own true loved one, I'm go-ing far from thee, Out on the bound-ing bil-lows, Out on the dark blue sea. How I will miss you, my dar-ling, There when the storm is rag-ing high. Jen-ny, my own true loved one,

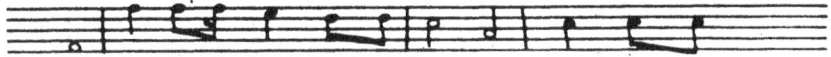

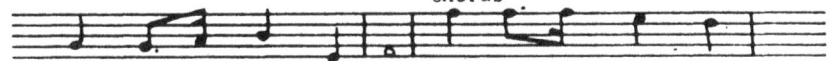

Chorus

Wait till the clouds roll by. Wait till the clouds roll by, Jen-ny, Wait till the clouds roll by. Jen-ny, my own true loved one, Wait till the clouds roll by.

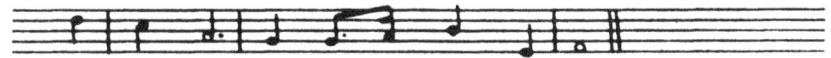

Jenny, my own true loved one,
I'm going far from thee,
Out on the bounding billows,
Out on the dark blue sea.
How I will miss you, my darling,
There when the storm is raging high.
Jenny, my own true loved one,
Wait till the clouds roll by.

Chorus:
    Wait till the clouds roll by, Jenny,
    Wait till the clouds roll by.
    Jenny, my own true loved one,
    Wait till the clouds roll by.

Jenny, when far from thee, love,
I'm on the ocean deep.
Will you then dream of me, love?
Will you some promise keep?
And will I come to you, Darling?
Take courage, Dear, and never sigh.
Gladness will follow sorrow.
Wait till the clouds roll by.

Jenny, I'll keep your image
Within my heart so true.
Each thought of mine forever
Still, Love, shall be of you.
Dry, then, your teardrops, my darling,
Soon will the night of sorrow fly.
Cheer up and don't be lonely.
Wait till the clouds roll by.

B

"Wait Till the Clouds Roll By," contributed by Mrs. Ada Vail, Millport, Lamar County, 1952, from a newspaper clipping, where the song is attributed to J.T. Wood. Same version as A.

8
Venus, My Shining Star

This piece is obviously not of folk origin. Yet I have not been able to find where it did originate. Probably it is a music-hall production.

"Venus, My Shining Star," sung by "Mother" Daisey Key, Florence, Colbert County, 1952. She does not remember when she learned it, but probably upwards of fifty years ago.

Some think to love an-oth-er is vain, But with them
I dis-a-gree. None has ev-er come .... 'Twixt Ve-nus,
my lov-er, and me. Ve-nus, my star-kind-led lov-er, Like
doz-ens to me you are seen. But when I com-pare with some
oth-ers Ve-nus my shin-ing star, None shall e'er come between us, sweet Ve-nus mine. None as bright as my dar-ling

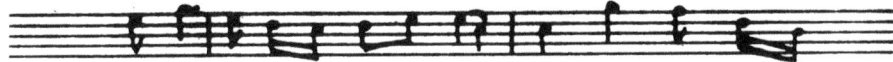

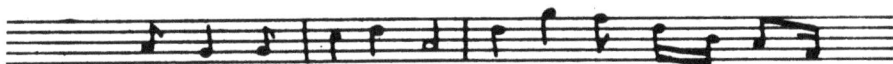

Chorus

so far, far a-bove. Ve-nus, beau-ti-ful Ve-nus, my shin-ing
love. Stars do twin-kle, I love that beau-ti-ful star. I

think how dear I love you. I know you love me too. Ve-nus,

beau-ti-ful Ve-nus, How bright you shine. None shall e'er

come be-tween us, sweet Ve-nus mine.

Some think to love another is vain,
But with them I disagree.
None has ever come. . . . . . .
'Twixt Venus, my lover, and me.
Venus, my star kindled lover,
Like dozens to me you are seen.
But when I compare with some others,
Venus, my shining star,
None shall e'er come between us,
Sweet Venus mine.
None as bright as my darling,
So far, far above.

Chorus:
    Venus, beautiful Venus, my shining love,
    Stars do twinkle. I love that beautiful star.
    I think how dear I love you.
    I know you love me too.
    Venus, beautiful Venus, how bright you shine.
    None shall e'er come between us, sweet Venus mine.

9
Pretty Saro

This piece, as Randolph (IV, 224) points out, seems made up of fragments from several songs. It is widespread in the South and Midwest. For references see Randolph and Brown (III, 285). The L.C. Checklist (pp. 11; 166; 324-325) reports texts from Kentucky, New York, Ohio, Tennessee, Mississippi and Indiana. I have two texts, both fragments.

A

"Lonesome," sung by Miss Drucilla Hall, Millport, Lamar County, 1952.

I came to this country in eighteen forty nine. I

saw all their true loves but I did not see mine. I looked

all around me and I was alone; Me a poor stranger and

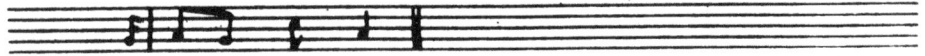

a long ways from home.

I came to this country in eighteen forty nine.
I saw all their true loves but I did not see mine.
I looked all around me and I was alone.
Me a poor stranger and a long ways from home.

B

"Pretty Molly," from a manuscript copy in the possession of Mrs. Flora Phillips, Cullman, Cullman County, 1953. It was written down about twelve years ago.

I came to this country 1849,
I saw many pretty fair maids
But I did not see mine.

When I look around me and see that I'm alone —
A poor lonely stranger and a long ways from home.

I wish I was some pensman,
Could write a fine hand,
I'd write my love a letter
That she could understand.
I would send it by the waters
When the waters overflow,
And think of pretty Molly
Wherever I may go.

10
The Bachelor's Prayer

Most bachelor folk songs praise the freedom of bachelorhood. This piece, however, sings of a wanted end to the state. Apparently this song was never popular. I have only one text and have not found it reported from elsewhere.

"The Bachelor's Prayer," sung by Mrs. Maggie Lee Hayes, Vernon, Lamar County, 1952. She probably learned it in Fayette County.

It's Ma-ry my dar-ling in her blue ging-ham dress.

Of all the girls ev-er I love her the best. She's as fair

as a li-ly that blooms in the dell. Oh, Ma-ry, oh, Ma-ry,

I love thee so well.

It's Mary, my darling, in her blue gingham dress.
Of all the girls ever I love her the best.
She's as fair as a lily that blooms in the dell.
Oh, Mary, oh, Mary, I love thee so well.

Chorus:
    I love her, I love her in her bonnet of blue.
    Oh, Mary, oh, Mary, will she ever be true?
    I love her, I love her, I love her, I do.
    My darling, my darling, I'll be true to you.

Her hair is all curls, her eyes are so blue.
Her lips are like roses that's wet with the dew.
Her voice is the sweetest that ever I heard
When it echoes, "I love you," in every word.

If only some day she will be my bride,
I'll cherish and love her, the girl of my pride.
I'll build her a home, a mansion so fair,
And that will be the answer to a bachelor's prayer.

11
Charming Little Girl

This piece is probably from the music-hall or songster. It is lighter in mood than the usual folk song on the same subject. I have not found it in any other collection, and I have only one text.

"Charming Little Girl," contributed by Mrs. Guy J. Johnson, Oneonta, Blount County, 1953, from a manuscript she wrote some thirty years ago.

There's a charming little girl,
Just the sweetest in the world,
And I love her, for she's pretty and refined.
If she would let me take her hand,
I would be a happy man.
I would kiss the little girl and call her mine.
When you see her on the streets,
Oh, she looks so nice and neat,
And her eyes they are so very bright they shine.
If I knew that she loved me,
What a different man I'd be.
I would kiss the little girl and call her mine.

Chorus:
    I would kiss the little girl and call her mine,
    I would kiss the little girl and call her mine.
    If she would only be my wife I would live a happy life.
    I would kiss the little girl and call her mine.

There are many other girls,
With their dimples and their curls,
But no one is near so gentle and so kind.
There's no other girl I've known
That I want to call my own.
I would kiss the little girl and call her mine.
There's no troubles would occur,
For I'd be so good to her.
I would love her with a love that is divine.
And I'd keep my promise true
To her pretty eyes so blue.
I would kiss the little girl and call her mine.

How I love this little girl.
She's the sweetest in the world.
I can see her in my visions all the time.
With this little girl so sweet,
All my life would be complete.

I would kiss the little girl and call her mine.
When this life on earth is done,
Our two hearts be made as one,
Then I know we would be happy all the time,
For I'd keep my promise true
To her pretty eyes so blue.
I would kiss the little girl and call her mine.

12
I Have A Sweetheart

This love song, typical of many in Alabama, seems to have been popular in the state. It sounds like a music-hall production. I have not found it in other collections.

A

"I Have A Sweetheart," sung by Mrs. A.J. Shea, Sheffield, Colbert County, 1953. She probably learned it in Mississippi forty years ago.

I have a lit-tle sweet-heart, and you can't guess

his name Or the town he lives in; he lives there just the

same. He won't let me kiss him but I can call him dear,

Put my arms a-round his neck and whis-per in his ear:

Chorus

"Give me your heart and let it be true, For I'm in love

and I don't know what to do. An-swer me now ere we shall

part, For I'm in love and give me your heart."

I have a little sweetheart,
And you can't guess his name,
Or the town he lives in;
He lives there just the same.
He won't let me kiss him
But I can call him dear,
Put my arms around his neck
And whisper in his ear.

Chorus:
    Give me your heart,
    And let it be true,
    For I'm in love
    And I don't know what to do.
    Answer me now,
    E'er we shall part,
    For I'm in love,
    And give me your heart.

                    B

"Give Me Your Heart," sung by Mrs. O.C. Powell, Titus, Elmore
County, 1952. She has sung it more than fifty years. First stanza
and chorus are same as A. Second stanza continues:

Now, my little rose-bud,
I know how you feel.
Don't you mean you love me,
Your heart as true as steel.
Let me tell you something,
I'll tell it soft and low.
I have a wish for you to grant,
I want to be your beau.

13
Sweet Birds

This song seems to undergo more changes in folk treatment than the usual folk song. Nearly every singer alters his version rather sharply. At least such seems to be the tendency in Alabama, judging from the three texts I have. It is a favorite in North Carolina. See Brown (III, 350). Davis *(Folk-Songs of Virginia,* p. 103) reports it. See Brown for a short headnote.

A

"Sweet Bird," sung by Miss Drucilla Hall, Millport, Lamar County, 1952.

Spring-time is com-ing, sweet lone-some bird, Your

ech-o in the wood-land I hear. Down in the mea-dow so

lone-some you sing; The moon-light is shin-ing so

clear. I know he's a-way in a far dis-tant land, In

a land that's ov-er the sea. Go fly to him sing-ing

this sweet lit-tle song, And tell him to come back

to me. Sweet bird, sweet bird, Oh, tell me that my

lov-er's still true. Sweet bird, sweet bird, Then I'll

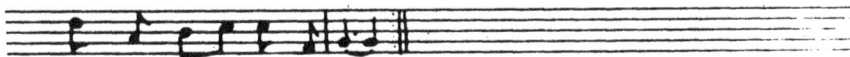

be just as hap-py as you.

Springtime is coming, sweet lonesome bird;
Your echo in the woodland I hear.
Down in the meadow so lonesome you sing,
The moonlight is shining so clear.
I know he's away in a far distant land,
In a land that is over the sea.
Go fly to him singing this sweet little song
And tell him to come back to me.

Chorus:
    Sweet bird, sweet bird, oh tell me that my lover's still true.
    Sweet bird, sweet bird, then I'll be just as happy as you.

Upon my finger he placed a ring
On the day he was leaving his home.
I promised him I'd be his dear little girl
And love him wherever he roamed.
I'd give all of this world for the clasp of his hand
And I know that his heart is still true.
Sweet bird, sweet bird, then I'll be just as happy as you.

B

"Sweet Birds," sung by Mrs. Velma Dean, Kennedy, Lamar County, 1951.

Oh tell me, sweet birds, is he thinking of me,
Of the promise that he made long ago?
If he was to come now how happy I'd be.
Oh tell me why the years roll so slow.

Chorus:
    Sweet birds, sweet birds,
    Oh tell me if my lover is still true.
    Sweet birds, sweet birds,
    And I'll be as happy as you.

He promised at parting he loved none but me,
He called me his darling, his pride.
He promised when he came from over the sea
He would make me his own happy bride.

Perhaps he has found in that far distant land
Some face that is fairer to see.
I would give all the world for the clasp of his hand
And to know that he is thinking of me.

I'm tired and heartsick of waiting so long
For my lover that's over the sea.
So fly to him now, singing your beautiful song,
And tell him to come back to me.

C

"Sweet Bird," sung by Mrs. Mary Drake, Huntsville, Madison County, 1953. She says her mother wrote this song.

Sweet birds returning their sweet notes of spring
O'er woodland and meadow I hear.
Far down in the vale where they joyously sing
And the silver brook sparkles so clear.
I sit me and dream in the shadows so deep
Of my darling far over the sea,
And I just ask the birds as they fall off to sleep
If they think that he truly loves me.

Chorus:
Sweet birds, sweet birds, oh tell me is my lover still true?
Sweet birds, sweet birds, and then I'll be as happy as you.

Oh tell me, sweet birds, is he thinking of me,
And the promise he made long ago?
If he would renew them how happy I'd be.
Oh why do the years roll so slow?
I'm weary and heartsick with waiting so long
For my darling far over the sea.
Oh fly to him singing a beautiful song
And tell him to come back to me.

He told me at parting he'll love none but me.
He called me his darling, his bride,
And said when he came from far over the sea
He'd make me his own happy bride.
But if he has found in some far distant land
A face that is fairer to see.
I'd give all this world just to clasp his hand
And to know that his heart still beats true.

14
Willie, Oh, Willie

This English piece I have not found reported anywhere else. Yet it seems to have been rather popular in Alabama. My two texts differ so widely that there must have been much oral tradition between them and the original.

A

"Johnny, Oh, Johnny," sung by Mrs. Ercelle Hand, Saragossa, Walker County, 1953. She has sung it for at least thirty years.

John-ny, oh, John-ny, you are my dar-ling. You look like a rose from yon-ders gar-den. I'd rath-er have you with-out a for-tune Than to have my mate ten thou-sand for-tunes.

Johnny, oh, Johnny, you are my darling.
You look like a rose from yonders garden.
I'd rather have you without a fortune
Than to have my mate ten thousand fortunes.

My father has given me house and land,
If I will stay at his command.
But if command I disobey,
I'll follow my Johnny both night and day.

The rose is red, and the violet's blue,
The sugar is sweet, and so are you.
As sure as the grape grows on the vine,
I'll be yours if you'll be mine.

B

"Willie, Oh, Willie," sung by Mrs. Clemmie Kyles, Millport, Lamar County, 1951. She has known it probably fifty years.

Oh, Willie, Oh, Willie, you are my darling.
Red roses grows in yonders garden.
I'd rather have you than a thousand starlets,
Or any other boy with a thousand dollars.

It ain't the wind that blows so cold,
Nor it ain't the rain that makes me cry.
But the whitest frost that ever fell,
I love you, Willie, 'tis death to tell.

My father he blames me for my kindness.
He says I'm all wrapped up in blindness.
But he may set and fret at leisure.
By the side of you, Willie, I'll take my pleasure.

So fare you well, Father, fare you well, Mother.
So fare you well, Brother, likewise, Sister.
Oh, fare you well, friends, I fear no danger.
I've forsakened you all for the love of a stranger.

15

The Merry Girl

This lighthearted love song is less usual than the unhappy type.
It came straight from the songsters. I quote the entire song from
one *(Robert Jones Songster*, N.Y. 18--, p. 6) for comparison:

Goodbye Darling

What a jolly girl am I.
And I'll tell you the reason why,
Because I'm engaged to something sweet;
And it seems as every day,
When he goes away,
To whisper something sweet at the door.

Chorus:
Goodbye darling, I must leave you:
One more kiss before I go.
I'll be back tomorrow night:
If I cannot I will write a line or two
To let my darling know

Ladies, if you want to find
Some gents that's good & kind;
You can be no happier I'm sure,
Ain't it nice to have a beau,
That when he comes to go
To whisper something sweet at the door?

And his teeth are white like pearl
And his darling little curl;
And his name is Lilly Dusky Moore.
He's the joy of my life,
And I soon will be his wife,
Then he need not whisper at the door.

Another interesting version, sung by Eddie Norwood, has an interesting verse *(Birch & Backus Songs of San Francisco Minstrels*,
N.Y. 187-, p. 141):

Goodbye, Darling, I Must Leave You

Oh I love a charming girl
And to her I never shall
Say or do anything that's wrong.
Now tis my great delight
To bring her here each night
Just to hear a quiet little song

Chorus:
    Goodbye, darling, I must leave you.
    One more kiss before I go.
    I'll be here tomorrow night.
    If I cannot come I'll write
    Just a word or two to let my darling know.

This same version appeared in the *There's Millions in it Songster* (N. Y. 18--, p. 35); and in *Jennie Engel's Bouquet of Melodies Songster* (N.Y. 1873, p. 27).

This song has been popular in Alabama but apparently not elsewhere. Owens *(Texas Folk Songs,* p. 164) prints one stanza (roughly the second of my A) and a parallel chorus. I have not found the piece elsewhere.

A

"Such a Happy Girl Am I," sung by Mrs. Mary Drake, Huntsville, Madison County, 1953. She claims her mother wrote it.

Such a hap-py girl am I, and I'll tell you the rea-

son why. It's be-cause I'm en-gaged to such a dear. He comes

near-ly ev-'ry day and when he goes a-way, These words he al-

Chorus.

ways whis-pers in my ear: "Good-night, dar-ling, I must

leave you. One more kiss be-fore I go. I'll be here to-mor-

night. If I can't come I will write, Just a word or two to

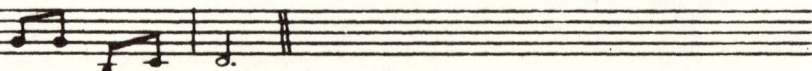

let my dar-ling know."

Such a happy girl am I and I'll tell you the reason why.
It's because I'm engaged to such a dear.
He comes nearly ev'ry day and when he goes away,
These words he always whispers in my ear:

Chorus:
    "Goodnight, Darling, I must leave you,
    One more kiss before I go.
    I'll be here tomorrow night.
    If I can't come I will write
    Just a word or two to let my darling know.

Oh, he has teeth as white as pearls and such darling little curls.
His name is Harry Martin. . . . .
He's the pleasure of my life, for I'm soon to be his wife,
And these words I'll no longer have to hear:

Oh, young ladies, when you find a young lover true and kind,
You cannot be more happy, I am sure,
For it's nice to have a beau who will love and pet you so,
And kiss you when he leaves you at the door.

To the gentlemen I say, "When obliged to go away
From the lady that is dearest to your heart,
You had best remember this, she'll expect a sweeter kiss,
And a word or two like this."

B

"Merry Girl," sung by Mrs. Nettie Coleman, Tucson, Arizona, 1952. She learned it in Greene County, Alabama, around forty years ago. Essentially first two stanzas and chorus of version A.

C

"The Merry Girl," from a manuscript copy in the possession of Mrs. J.V. Tarwarter, Fayette, Fayette County, 1952. She has known the song for more than fifty years.

16
Love Me Now

This frank, common-sense, and realistic picture of making the
most of time is unusual in folk songs. I have not found this song
in any other collection. Yet, judging by my two Alabama texts, it
seems to have, or have had, a certain popularity in the state.

A

"Love Me Now," contributed by Mrs. E. E. Agee, Thomasville,
Clarke County, 1953.

        If you are ever going to love me,
        Love me now that I may know
        All the sweet and tender feelings
        Which from real affection flow.
        Love me now while I am living.
        Do not wait till I am gone,
        And carve upon my tomb in grieving
        Warm words on marble stone.

        If your dear thoughts are about me,
        Why not whisper them to me?
        They will make me glad
        And as happy as can be.
        If you wait till I am sleeping,
        Never more to wake again,
        There will be walls of earth between us.
        I cannot hear you then.

        If you knew some one was thirsting
        For a drink of water sweet,
        Would you be so slow to bring it,
        Would you step with laggard feet?
        There are tender hearts all round us
        Who are thirsting for our love.
        Why withhold from them
        What God has sent from above?

        I won't need your fond caresses
        When the grass grows over my face.
        I won't need your love and kisses
        In my last love's resting place.
        So if you're ever going to love me,
        If 'tis but a little bit,
        Won't you love me now while I am living,
        That I may know and treasure it?

B

"Love Me Now," contributed by Mrs. Mattie Dewberry, Wedowee, Randolph County, 1953, from a manuscript copy in her possession. Four stanzas indentical with A.

17
Little Julie

This piece might originally have been a play-party song. If so, all vestiges have fallen away. It was sung to me as a love song. I have not found it elsewhere, and have only one Alabama text.

"Little Julie," sung by Miss Drucilla Hall, Millport, Lamar County, 1952.

Lit-tle Ju-lie, lit-tle Ju-lie, I love you. Lit-tle

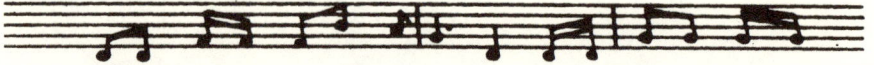

Ju-lie, lit-tle Ju-lie, I love you. Lit-tle Ju-lie, lit-tle

Ju-lie, I love you. Swing o-pen your win-dow for me.

Little Julie, little Julie, I love you,
Little Julie, little Julie, I love you,
Little Julie, little Julie, I love you,
Swing open your window for me.

I'll pick my guitar at your window,
I'll pick my guitar at your window,
I'll pick my guitar at your window,
Swing open your window for me.

Brick walls are built all around me,
Brick walls are built all around me,
Brick walls are built all around me,
Swing open your window for me.

Six months on the ocean I'll grieve me,
Six months on the ocean I'll grieve me,
Six months on the ocean I'll grieve me,
Swing open your window for me.

Six months on dry bread and cold water,
Six months on dry bread and cold water,
Six months on dry bread and cold water,
Swing open your window for me.

18
I'll Do Anything, Dear

The following fragment is typical of many Alabama folk songs in having little material to develop and little development. It is pure lyric, sung only to provide singer with some excuse for singing. I have only one text of it, and I have not found it reported elsewhere.

"Song," sung by Mrs. Nola Browne, Millport, Lamar County, 1952. She has sung it for at least forty years, and as far as she remembers never knew any more.

I'll do anything, Dear, that you tell me to.
I won't do much for Mary,
For Sarah, Sal, or Sue.
But I'll do anything that you tell me to.

I'll do anything, Dear, that you tell me to.
I won't do much for Nancy,
Mary Jane, or Sue.
But I'll do anything that you tell me to.

19
Dewdrops Are Falling On Me

This song is typical of many that ask girls if they will not be boys' sweethearts. The song is typical, too, in having a verse, this time the first, which bears little or no relevance to the song except in carrying on the melody. The L.C. Checklist (p. 76) reports one text from South Carolina and another from New York City. I have not found it elsewhere.

"Dewdrops are Falling on Me," sung by Miss Drucilla Hall, Millport, Lamar County, 1952. She has sung it around forty years.

Dew drops are fall-ing on me, Dew drops are fall-ing on me, Dew drops are fall-ing on me at once. Say, Dar-ling, won't you love me once more?

Dewdrops are falling on me,
Dewdrops are falling on me,
Dewdrops are falling on me at once.
Say, Darling, won't you love me once more?

I'll ask your papa for you,
I'll ask your papa for you,
I'll ask your papa for you at once.
Say, Darling, won't you love me once more?

I'll buy the license for you,
I'll buy the license for you,
I'll buy the license for you at once.
Say, Darling, won't you love me once more?

20

Over the Garden Wall

The words of this music-hall piece were written by Harry Hunter,
the music by G.D. Fox, and it was probably published in 1879.
The words were essentially those that became the folk version, as
the first verse and chorus of the text sung by Cool Burgess demonstrate *(Cool Burgess' I'll Be Gay Songster*, N.Y. 1880, p. 7):

Oh, my love stood under the walnut tree
Over the garden wall.
She whispered and said she'd be true to me
Over the garden wall.

Chorus:
    Over the Garden Wall,
    The sweetest girl of all.
    There were never yet such eyes of jet.
    And you may bet I'll never forget
    The night our lips in kisses met
    Over the garden wall.

This text appeared also in *Hitchcock's Collection of Old And New
Songs*, N.Y. c. 1883, book 7, p. 122).

The sentimental (not to say absurd) words and the sprightly tune
unleased a virtual torrent of parodies, the flavor of which can be
tasted in this songster stanza *(Pullman Car Songster*, N.Y. 18--,
p. 30) as sung by W.E. Burke, with the Barnum and London Circus,
with this note: ("The music of this song will be sent upon receipt
of 10 cents."):

One day I jumped down on the other side,
Over the garden wall.
And she bravely promised to be my bride
Over the garden wall.
But she screamed in a fright,
"Here's my father, quick
"I have an impression he's bringing a stick."
But I brought the impression of half a brick
Over the garden wall.

The popularity of the parodies can be seen from a sampling of the
songsters they appeared in: *Birch & Backus' Songs Of The San Francisco Minstrels* (N.Y. 1881, p. 93); *Callender's Original Colored*

Minstrel Songster (N.Y. 18--, p. 20); *Ley Drew's Great Banjo Song-ster* (N.Y. 1882, p. 10); *Duprez & Benedict's Famous Minstrels Songster* (N.Y. 18--, p. 10); *Harrigan & Hart's Squatter Songster* (N.Y. 1878, p. 14); *James Gray's There's Nobody Knows What I Know Songster* (N.Y. 1880, p. 40); *Gems Of Minstrels Songs No. 2* (N.Y. 1882, n.p.); *Lester & Williams Empty Is The Stable, Davy's Gone Songster* (N.Y. 1882 p. 28); *Frank McNish & Leland Sisters' Jolly Three Songster* (N.Y. 1881, p. 60); *The Monarch Collection of Music* (Springfield, Mass. 1883, n.p.); *One Hundred Charming Songs Of The Day* (Boston, 1884, p. 8); *100 Gems Of Songs, Words And Music* (St. Louis, 1890, n.p.); *Over The Garden Wall Songster* (N. Y. 1881, p. 3); *Dan Rice's Old Time Circus Songster* (N.Y. 188-, p. 8).

Randolph (IV, 392) reports only the chorus of this piece. One person told him that he had heard it as a child in England, saying that the song was regarded as old in 1890. Brewster reported it from Indiana *(Southern Folklore Quarterly, IV,* 1940, pp. 175-203). Pound *(Syllabus,* p. 58) lists the title,. My one Alabama version dates from about 1900.

"Over The Garden Wall," sung by Mrs. Jenny Weathers, Millport, Lamar County, 1951. This song was learned in a way usual to certain groups in Alabama. At night teenage girls — and often older and younger — would get together to sing around a piano, or, more usual, an old organ. At such a singing all new songs would be played and sung over and over until they were learned.

I'd like to tell of a girl I met o-ver the gar-den

wall. With eyes of blue and hair of jet, o-ver the gar-den

wall. O-ver the gar-den wall, The pret-ti-est lit-tle girl

of all. And you can bet I'll nev-er for-get the night our

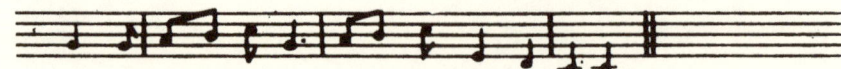

lips in ki-ess-es met, O-ver the gar-den wall.

I'd like to tell of a girl I met,
Over the garden wall.
She had eyes of blue and hair of jet,
Over the garden wall.

Chorus:
    Over the garden wall,
    The sweetest little girl of all.
    And you may bet I'll never forget
    The night our lips in kisses met
    Over the garden wall.

I asked her then to be my bride,
Over the garden wall.
She answered quickly with a smile,
Over the garden wall.

"Yes, dear, I'll go away with you,
Over the garden wall.
I'm sure there's room enough for two,
Over the garden wall."

21
When The Stars Above Are Shining

The sentiments in this song — as well as the references — are typical of much Alabama folk lyric. The song, however, seems not have been popular. I have only one text. I have not seen it reported elsewhere.

"When The Stars Above Are Shining," sung by Mrs. Nola Browne, Millport, Lamar County, 1952. She has been singing this song for at least forty-five years.

When the stars above are shining,
And the moon is sinking low,
I will call to see my darling,
Who will welcome me, I know.

We'll be merry, we'll be happy,
Floating down the stream of time.
We'll be merry, we'll be happy,
Floating onward with the tide.

22
When I Left The State Of Georgia

Undoubtedly this song does not refer to the actual migration from Georgia to Alabama, but is rather just a love song. Stories of departing lovers are common in folk songs. I have only one text of this song and have not found it listed in other collections.

"When I Left the State of Georgia," sung by Mrs. Ercelle Hand, Saragossa, Walker County, 1953.

When I left the state of Georgia, To Al-a-bam-er
I did go. There I spied a pret-ty fair girl, Al-though
her age I did not know.

When I left the state of Georgia,
To Alabamer I did go.
There I spied a pretty fair girl
Although her age I did not know.

Your mama says that she's not willing
For you to go with me.
But, Sweetheart, if you are willing,
I will run away with you.

23
Midnight Serenade

Many folk love songs use a nature setting. The present one is a good example. Though the type is common I have not found this song reported from elsewhere. I have two Alabama texts.

A

"Serenade Song," sung by Mrs. Mary Drake, Huntsville, Madison County, 1953. She claims her mother wrote it.

The voices of the night, Love, are singing their lullaby.
The little stars so bright, Love, are peeping through the sky.
The insects are sleeping beneath the hawthorne tree,
While I, my love, am singing a serenade to thee.

Chorus:
    Then awake, my love, and listen,
    Open your eyes so blue.
    Awake to the notes of my guitar
    And listen to your lover true.

Thou art my star of gentleness setting up the long life's way.
Thou art my hope of happiness, the sunshine of my day.
I know you do not love me. I fear you'll ne'er be mine.
While heaven's skies shine over me this heart shall e'er be thine.

The pale moon is sinking, the stars begin to fade.
While I, my love, am thinking to end my serenade.
So now, my love, I bid you goodnight to let you dream again.
Forgive me for awaking you to listen to my strains.

Then sleep, Love, and dream and close your eyes and dream.
Forgive me for awaking you to listen to my strains.

B

"Midnight Serenade," sung by Mrs. A.J. Shea, Sheffield, Colbert County, 1953.

The voi-ces of the night, Love, Have hushed their

lull-a-by. The lit-tle stars so bright, Love, Are peep-ing

Chorus

through the sky. A-wake, my love, and lis-ten. O-pen thine

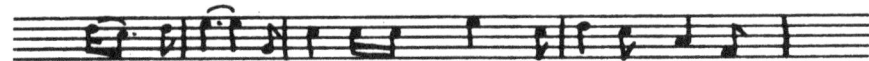

eyes so blue. A-wake to the strings of my gui-tar And

lis-ten to your lov-er true.

The voices of the night, Love,
Have hushed their lullaby.
The little stars so bright, Love,
Are peeping through the sky.

Chorus:
  Awake, my love, and listen.
  Open thine eyes so blue.
  Awake to the strings of my guitar,
  And listen to your lover true.

The insect chirps are ringing
Throughout each leaf and tree.

While at your window singing,
Oh, listen, Love, to me.

Thou art the star of brightness,
The sunshine of my day.
Thou art the sky of loveliness,
The blessing of my day.

24
Why Can't We Wed?

Pleading for a true love is, of course, common in folk songs. Stanza two is probably to be taken for its surface meaning, and not for its implication of illicit relations, a topic rare in Alabama folk songs. I have not found this song elsewhere, and I have only one Alabama text. The song is a little too sophisticated for folk origin. I suspect it is a music-hall production.

"Why Can't We Wed?" sung by Mrs. Nola Browne, Millport, Lamar County, 1952. She learned it as a girl in Lamar County, some fifty years ago.

You know I've loved you man-y long years. Vain thoughts have struck me, Caused me sad tears. Then did my heart ache, Oh, how it bled. Why can't we wed? Why can't we live to-geth-er? Why can't we have a name?

You know I've loved you many long years.
Vain thoughts have struck me, caused me sad tears.
Then did my heart ache, oh, how it bled.
Why can't we wed?
Why can't we live together,
Why can't we have a name?

Living in true affection,
Who cares for wealth or fame?
Why do you make me plead so?
Think of the times you said,
Some day I could have you.
Now, why can't we wed?

25
Paul Vane

Songs in the form of love letters are popular with the folk. Around 1857 "Lorena," a song written supposedly by a Confederate soldier to his love, was published. Dolph *(Sound Off,* p. 335) calls it "the best known and most popular of the many lovesongs of the boys in gray." For an interesting headnote on the song see Randolph (IV, 257). "Paul Vane" is Lorena's answer to her soldier boy. This song, like "Lorena," was popular in the war song books and songsters in the mid sixties. "Paul Vane, or Lorena's Reply" was in the *Jack Morgan Songster* (Raleigh, N.C., 1864, p. 19), *Songs of Love and Liberty,* "Compiled by a North Carolina Lady" (Raleigh, 1864, p. 26); *The Beauregard Songster* (Macon and Savannah, Georgia, 1864, p. 22); *Beadle's Dime Song Book,* No. 16 (1865, p. 50); and the *New Confederate Flag Song Book,* No. 1 (n.d., p. 62). Judging from these Southern songsters, the piece was popular in the South. But I have only one text.

"Paul Vane," contributed by Mrs. R. Van Iderstine, Daphne, Baldwin County, 1953. She has forgotten when and how she learned it.

> The years are creeping slowly by, dear Paul.
> The winters come and go.
> The wind sweeps by with mournful cry, dear Paul,
> And pelts my face with snow.
> But there's no snow upon the heart, dear Paul.
> 'Tis summer always there.
> The early love throws sunshine over all,
> And sweeter memories dear.
>
> I thought it easy to forget, dear Paul.
> Life glowed with youthful hope.
> But now the future gleameth near, dear Paul,
> And bids us slumber on.
> They, frowning, said it must not, cannot be.
> Break now those hopeless bonds.
> And, Paul, you know how well that bitter day
> I bent to their commands.
>
> I've kept you ever in my heart, dear Paul,
> Through years of good and ill.
> Our souls cannot be torn apart, dear Paul.
> They're bound together still.

I never knew how dear you were to me
Till I was left alone.
I thought my poor, poor heart would break
The day they told me you were gone.

Perhaps we'll never, never meet, dear Paul,
Upon this earth again.
But there where happy angels greet, dear Paul,
You'll meet Lorena there.
Together up the ever-shining way
We'll tread with hoping hearts;
Together through the bright eternal day,
And never more to part.

26
Loved You in the Days of Joy

Love songs in the form of letters are rather common in folk tradition. This sentimental piece is typical too in using the same figures of speech, the same kind of sentiment as many such songs. I have not found this particular song reported from elsewhere, and I have only one text. Apparently it was not very popular.

"Loved You in the Days of Joy," contributed by Mrs. Guy B. Johnson, Oneonta, Blount County, 1953, from a manuscript in her possession. She has known the song for perhaps forty years.

    I loved you in the days of joy,
    When you was but a slender boy.
    I loved you when your heart was light,
    When youth's gay charms were fond and bright.

    Thine eyes' sweet flash I'll never forget,
    And those sweet smiles whenever we met.
    If I was sad your smiles would cheer.
    You always smiled when I was near.

    Your memory on me cast a spell.
    On those loved bowers, oh, let me dwell.
    And at the dawn of thy sweet voice,
    My cheeks would blush and my heart rejoice.

    But times have changed since then and now.
    The stamp of manhood is on your brow.
    Though you may soon sadly change,
    My true love is gone and my heart deranged.

    Though you may wish a fairer flower,
    And bless the mutual happy hour,
    Still your thoughts sometimes stray
    To me, perhaps, though I am far away.

    Though I may be another bride,
    And the dark seas may us divide,
    Still I see that happy day,
    When we shall meet though far away.

    Farewell to you; I would rather make
    My bowers on some icy lake
    Where thawing sun refuse to shine
    Than to trust such false heart as thine.

I'll cling to you as clings the vine
Upon some lofty forest tree,
And when my strength of death regains,
I too will fall and rise with thee.

To you, my love, I will impart
The dearest object of my heart.
If I am wrong, oh teach me right,
For you are my own heart's delight.

Could I you a welcome find
Here's my heart, oh take my hand,
To live, to cherish, and to bless,
Until we part to go to rest.

Now if this offer you do slight,
A long farewell, my heart's delight.
Farewell, my friends, my love is gone.
My heart is almost broken for you.

So now I lay my pen at rest,
But not the love within my breast.
Until I see that happy day,
When we shall meet through far away.

And when I am gone and far away,
I hope you will remember me.
Remember all the words that passed
When we were altogether last. (sic)

27
Riding In A Sleigh

This song was written by Will Hays in 1871. It sold some three hundred thousand copies of sheet music. (See Spaeth, *History of Popular Music,* p. 159.) I have not found it reported as a folk song. I have two Alabama texts, indicating a certain popularity.

"On a Certain Night Next Winter," sung by Mrs. Nola Browne, Millport, Lamar County, 1951.

Snowflakes glisten in the moonlight
Falling everywhere.
Sleigh bells ring their merry voices
On the wintry air.
Every gallant has his lassie,
Dashing down Broadway.
I had mine and we were happy
Riding in a sleigh.

Chorus:
    Whip-a-roo, hold your horses,
    Don't they'll get away.
    Ain't it pleasant with your sweetheart,
    Riding in a sleigh?

On a certain night next winter,
I'll not name the day.
But there'll be a preacher with us,
Riding in a sleigh.

B

"Riding In A Sleigh," sung by Miss Malissa Richardson and Mrs. Pluma Stewart, Kennedy, Lamar County, 1951. They say this is "one of the old ones."

28
Kitty Clyde

This song derives partially from a popular piece in the songsters, though the composer was never identified. For comparison I quote the songster piece *(Rollin Howard's Dramatic Songster* (N.Y. 1875, p. 42):

O, who has not seen Kitty Clyde
Who lives at the foot of the hill,
In a sly little nook by the babbling brook,
That carries her father's old mill.

O, who does not love Kitty Clyde,
That sunny eyed, rosy-cheeked lass,
With a sweet dimpled chin
That looks roguish as sin,
With always a smile as you pass.

Chorus:
     Sweet Kitty, dear Kitty, my own sweet Kitty Clyde
     In a sly little nook by the babbling brook
     Lives my own sweet Kitty Clyde.

This version was published in *Christy's Plantation Melodies, No. 5* (N.Y. c. 1851, p. 33); *J.S. Berry's Flying Trapeze Songster* (N.Y. 1868, p. 62); *Harry Bennett's Charley Flynn Songster* (N.Y. 1878, p. 48); *Billy Courtright's Flewy, Flewy, Flew Songster* (N.Y. 1875, p. 22); *Willie E. Lyle's Great Georgia Minstrels Songbook* (N.Y. 1975, p. 38); *Gus Williams Famous Banjo Songster* (N.Y. 1882, p. 27).

This song is reported by Brown (II, 476) and the editors give three references, from Pennsylvania, Virginia and Nebraska. The Alabama text is a fragment, mixing the stanzas as reported in the two Brown texts. The chorus is a stranger, brought in from some other song.

"Kitty Clyde," sung by Mrs. Nettie Coleman, Tucson, Arizona, who learned it in Greene County, Alabama, forty years ago.

Oh! who would not love Kitty Clyde,
A fair brown-eyed, rosy-cheeked lass
With a soft dimpled chin as roguish as sin,
And always a smile as you pass.

Chorus:
    Take me, take me home,
    To the fair sunny South take me home
    Where the mocking bird sings me to sleep every night.
    To the bright sunny South take me home.

I wish that I were a little bee.
I would not gather honey from the flowers.
I'd steal one sip from my sweet Kitty's lips,
And I'd build my hive in her bower.

Oh! how I wish I were a little bird.
I would not build my nest in a tree.
I'd stay close by the side of my own Kitty Clyde,
Where the bad boys would never bother me.

29
Swinging, Swinging

This fragment is a good example of pure lyric sung by the folk. Loosely speaking, the subject is love, but the words make little effort to develop it. Both words and music attempt to imitate a swinging motion. I have not found this song reported anywhere else. I have only one Alabama text.

"Swinging, Swinging," sung by Mrs. Nola Browne, Millport, Lamar County, 1952. She learned it about sixty years ago in Lamar County.

Swinging, swinging, swinging, swinging,
Swinging 'neath the old,
'Neath the old apple tree.
Swinging, swinging, swinging, swinging,
Swinging 'neath the old apple tree.

How my heart is beating thinking of the greeting,
Swinging 'neath the old,
'Neath the old apple tree.
Swinging, swinging, swinging, swinging,
Swinging 'neath the old apple tree.

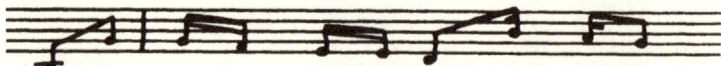

30
Mollie Darling

This piece was written in 1871 by Will S. Hays, published by J.L. Peters, N.Y., and is generally considered his most popular song (Spaeth, *History of Popular Music,* p. 159). It was widely disseminated by the songsters, one being named for it (N.Y. 1871). For example: *Diamond & Ryan's Irish Hod Carriers Songster* (N.Y., 1874, p. 60); *Don't Go Mollie Darling Songster* (N.Y. 1872, p. 4); *Jennie Engel's Favorite Songster* (N.Y. 1873, p. 44); *Erin-Go-Brach Songster* (N.Y. 1890, p. 80); *Foy Sisters' Branigan Band Songster,* (N.Y, 1876, p. 30); *Harrigan & Hart's When the Soup House Comes Again Songster* (N.Y. 1874, p. 93); *Irish Song and Dance Book* (N.Y. p. 23).

The song was so susceptible to parody and comic versions that an almost uncountable number arose sung by Tony Pastor, Billy Andrews, E.D. Gooding, Billy West and others. For comparison I give the first stanza of two: "Parody on Molly Darling, written for Tony Pastor, by Ned Harrigan" *(Harrigan's Mulcahey Songster,* N.Y. c. 1871, p. 14):

I met Molly in the garden,
   I believe twas after tea.
She had on her Dolly Varden,
   She completely dazzled me.

Chorus:
   Molly, fattest, fairest, hugest,
      Look up, darling, tell me that
   You still love me, Molly darling,
      Don't despise me cause I'm fat.

This version appeared also in *Billy Andrews' Comic Songster* (N.Y. 1873, p. 17). Another comic version was written by E.D. Gooding for Billy West, a take-off in the 19th century style of inflated rhetoric (*West's Banjo Soloes Songster,* N.Y. c. 1873, p. 45):

Ah how many times must I expressly desire you to communicate to me, Molly Darling,
That you never placed your affections on any other snoozer in the world but me.

The text has not been widely reported as a folk song. Shearin *(Syllabus,* p. 29) reports it from Kentucky. Arnold *(Folksongs Of*

Alabama, p. 82) gives one text. The song is one of the most popular in Alabama, however, as my five texts show. It has undergone much alteration in oral transmission.

A

"Mollie Darling," sung by Mrs. Mary Drake, Hunstville, Madison County, 1953. She says her mother wrote it.

Will you tell me, Mollie darling,
That you love none else but me,
For I love you, Mollie darling,
You are all this world to me.

Winter comes upon the flower,
And though they hang their head in shame,
They seem modest, Mollie darling,
When they hear me call your name.

Stars are shining, Mollie darling,
Through the misty veil of night.
They seem hiding, Mollie darling,
When fair Luna gives her light.

Look up, Mollie, look up, loved one.
Look up, Mollie, tell me this.
If you love me, Mollie darling,
Let your answer be a kiss.

Farewell, Mollie, farewell, loved one.
Happy may you ever be.
In your dreams, Mollie darling,
Don't forget to dream of me.

B

"Mollie Darling," sung by Mrs. Ercelle Hand, Saragossa, Walker County, 1953.

Won't you tell me, Mollie darling,
That you love none else but me,
For I love you, Mollie darling.
You are all the world to me.

Tell me, darling, that you love me.
Put your little hand in mine.
Take my heart, sweet Mollie darling.
Say that you will give me thine.

Mollie, fairest, dearest Mollie,
Little darling, tell me this:
Do you love me, Mollie darling?
Let your answer be a kiss.

No one listens but the flowers,
While they hang their heads in shame.
They are modest, Mollie darling,
When they hear me call your name.

C

"Mollie Darling," sung by Mrs. Mary Rouse, Titus, Elmore County, 1953. Two stanzas, one and two of B.

D

"Mollie Darling," contributed by Miss Lena Roberts, Florence, Colbert County, 1953. Five stanzas, similar to B. Concluding stanza is a variant:

Oh, no one listens but the flowers,
While they hang their heads unashamed.
They are modest, Mollie darling.
Happy will you ever be.
When you're dreaming, Mollie darling,
Don't forget to dream of me.

E

"Mollie Darling," sung by Mrs. Herring, Gordo, Pickens County,

1952. A two-stanza fragment.

Will you tell me, Mol-lie dar-ling, th .t you love none

else but me? For I love you, Mol-lie dar-ling; you are all

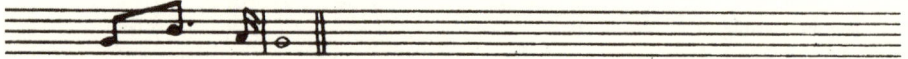

tai: or.d to me.

Will you tell me, Mollie darling,
That you love none else but me?
For I love you, Mollie darling;
You are all this world to me.

31
Dan Kelly

Feud songs are practically non-existent in Alabama. This one is
the only one I have found. It has also been reported from Mississippi
(Hudson, *Folksongs of Miss.*, p. 247). The L.C. Checklist (p. 456)
reports a text from Virginia. The events in the song, according to my
informant, supposedly took place in Hickman County, Tennessee.

"Dan Kelly," sung by Miss Drucilla Hall, Millport, Lamar County,
1952.

A-way on the Ten-nes-see moun-tains, A-way from the

scenes of the world, Old Dan Kel-ly's son, there he leaned

on his gun, A-think-ing of Zeb Tur-ney's girl.

Away on the Tennessee mountains,
Away from the scenes of the world,
Old Dan Kelly's son, there he leaned on his gun,
A-thinking of Zeb Turney's girl.

Dan was a hot blooded youngster,
His pap raised him sturdy and right,
But he had him sworn from the day he was born
To shoot every Turney on sight.

Powder and shot for the Turneys;
Don't save a hair on their head,
Old Dan Kelly cried, as he lay down and died,
With young Danny there by his side.

Dan made a vow to his pappy,
He swore he would kill every one.
Defying the world with his love for the girl,
He loaded his double barrel gun.

Over the mountains he wandered,
The son of a Tennessee man,
With fire in his eye and his gun at his thigh,

A-looking for Zeb Turney's clan.

Shots ringing out on the mountain,
Shots ringing out on the breeze.
Young Dan Kelly run with the smoke in his gun.
The Turneys fall down on their knees.

The story of Dan Kelly's movements
Has spread far and wide o'er the world,
How Dan killed the clan, shot them down to a man,
And brought back old Zeb Turney's girl.

32
Somebody Loves Me

The words and music to this piece were probably written by H. Starr. I have not seen the song reported in any other collection, but apparently it was rather popular in Alabama. I have two texts, both seemingly fragmentary.

A

"Somebody Loves Me," sung by Miss Malissa Richardson and Mrs. Plumer Stewart, Kennedy, Lamar County, 1952. They have sung it for forty years.

Some-bod-y loves me; how do I know? Some-bod-y's eyes

have told me so. Some-bod-y loves me; how do I know? Some-

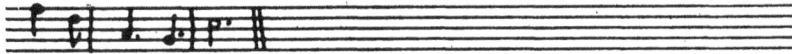

bod-y told me so.

Somebody loves me; how do I know?
Somebody's eyes have told me so.
Somebody loves me; how do I know?
Somebody told me so.

B

"Somebody," sung by Mrs. Nola Browne, Millport, Lamar County, 1952. She has sung it some fifty years. Two stanzas. The first is exactly like A. The second continues:

Somebody loves me; how do I know?
Somebody loves me; I know this is so.
Somebody loves me; this I know.
That somebody is you.

33
Somebody

This song in all probablility worked into the folk tradition from some other source. The Brown Collection (III, 323) suggests that it was "perhaps originally a parlor song." I have not run across it in the songsters. See Brown and Randolph (III, 94) for several references. Sandburg *(American Songbag* p. 464) has two stanzas reported from Nebraska in the 80's. The L.C. Checklist (p. 373) reports a text from Texas. The song is old in Alabama. One informant reported singing it in the 90's if not before. The three Alabama texts are approximately complete, but each informant treats the material a different way.

A

"Somebody Loves Me," from a manuscript book in the possession of Mrs. Mattie Dewberry, Wedowee, Randolph County, 1953. She has had it at least thirty years.

Somebody loves me dearly.
Somebody loves me well.
Somebody loves me with all his heart.
Tis more than tongue can tell.

Somebody's tall and handsome.
Somebody's brave and true.
Somebody's hair is very dark.
Somebody's eyes are blue.

Somebody writes me letters.
Somebody writes me few.
Somebody asks me to answer them.
Of course you know I do.

Somebody comes to see me.
Somebody came last night.
Somebody asked me to marry him.
Of course I said, "All right."

There's something on my finger.
That you might easily guess.
He placed it there one moonlight night,
The night I answered, "Yes."

Somebody has a cottage
With flowers all around the door.
Somebody's going to carry me there
To dwell forevermore.

B

"Somebody," sung by Mrs. Nola Browne, Millport, Lamar County, 1952. She sang it around Kennedy, Lamar County, at least as early as the 1890's.

Chorus:
    Somebody's tall and handsome.
    Somebody's brave and true.
    Somebody's hair is very dark.
    Somebody's eyes are blue.

Somebody came to see me,
Somebody came last night.
Somebody asked to marry me
And of course I said, "All right."

I've something on my finger.
What it is you cannot guess.
It was given to me one moonlight eve,
The eve I answered, "Yes."

C

"Somebody's Tall and Handsome," sung by Mrs. Flora Phillips, Cullman, Cullman County, 1953, from a manuscript copy in her possession. Copied from the manuscript.

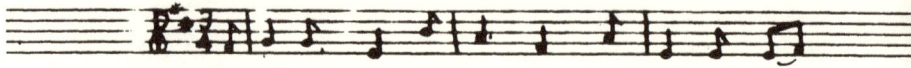

Some-bod-y's tall and hand-some. Some-bod-y's brave
and true. Some-bod-y's hair is ver-y dark. Of course his
eyes are blue. Some-bod-y loves me dear-ly, Some-bod-y
loves me well. Some-bod-y loves me with all their heart.
It's more than tongue can tell.

Somebody's tall and handsome
Somebody's brave and true.
Somebody's hair is very dark
Of course his eyes are blue.

Chorus:
    Somebody loves me dearly,
    Somebody loves me well.
    Somebody loves me with all their heart
    It's more than tongue can tell.

Somebody came to see me
Somebody came last night.
Somebody asked me to marry him,
Of course I said all right.

There's going to be a wedding
One day in the fall,
The happy bride to be is I
And that's the best of all.

I've something on my finger
Something you can't guess,
Was placed on there that moon-light night,
'Twas the night that I said yes.

34
On The Tombigbee River So Bright

This song was apparently written by S.S. Steele (*Ethiopian Seren-aders Own Book*, N.Y. 18--, p. 160), where it appeared in dialect which apparently needed to be "cleaned up for some singers." I quote the original version for comparison, if Steele's is the original:

On Tombigbee river, so bright I was born,
In a hut made of husks ob de tall yeller corn.
An dar I fust met wid my Jula so true,
An I row'd her about, in my Gum Tree Canoe.

Chorus:
    Singing row away, row, oer de waters so blue.
    Like a feather we'll float, in my Gum Tree Canoe

All de day in de field de soft cotton I hoe,
I think of my Jula an sing as I go.
An I catch her a bird, wid a wing of true blue,
An at night sail her round im my Gum Tree Canoe.
                    * * * * *
But one night de stream bore us so far away,
Dat we couldn'nt cum back,
so we thought we'd just stay.
Oh we spied a tall ship wid a flag of true blue,
And it took us in tow in my Gum Tree Canoe.

Though the Tombigbee is an Alabama river, apparently the song was not popular in that state. The L.C. Checklist (p. 132) reports it from Texas. It was widely disseminated by the songsters: *Cool Burgess In The Morning By The Bright Light Songster* ("Music published by Russel & Tolman, Boston." N.Y. 18--, p. 29); *Christy's Plantation Melodies* No. 1 (N.Y. 1851, p. 41); *Rosalie The Prairie Flower Melodist* (Boston, c. 1859, p. 39); *White's New Illustrated Melodeon* ("As sung by B.F. Stanton in White's Band of Serenaders at the Melodeon Concert Saloon, N.Y. c. 1859, p. 34); *Wehman's Universal Songster, No. 11* (N.Y. 1882, p. 86).

Randolph (IV, 302) cites this song as appearing in *Heart Songs* (1909, pp. 250-251) with words and music attributed to S.S. Steele, as they are in *The Modern Choral Hour*, ed., by Hall & McCreary (1941, pp. 129-132). For a few other references see Randolph. The piece is apparently not popular in Alabama. The L.C. Checklist (p. 132) reports it from Texas.

"On The Tombigbee River So Bright," from the Alabama Archives with this note: "Sung by the Carlan family during ante-bellum years."

On the Tombigbee River so bright, I was born,
In a hut mid the pastures of tall yellow corn.
It was there that I met with my Julia so true,
And took her to ride in my gum tree canoe.

Chorus:
    Sing and row away, row away,
    Waters so blue.
    Like a feather we'll float
    In my gum tree canoe.

One night the steamboat was so far away
We couldn't get back, so we thought we'd just stay.
But at last I spied a ship of true blue,
And she took us in tow in my gum tree canoe.

35
The Ohio

There are several songs in folk tradition about the Ohio River. This one, however, seems not to have been reported before. It probably dates back to the days of migration to Texas. The confused geography has no significance.

"The Ohio," sung by Mrs. Fannie Lewis, Tucson, Arizona, 1952. She learned it in Greene County, Alabama, some fifty years ago.

Just as soon as we get mar-ried to Tex-as we will go.

Set-tle on the banks of the O-hi-o, Where there's bear and

buf-fa-lo, And all sort of game, Creep-ing through the

cane on the O-hi-o. Come a-long here, my true love, and go

a-long with me, For I will take good care of thee.

Just as soon as we get married to Texas we will go.
Settle on the banks of the Ohio,
Where there's bear and buffalo and all sort of game
Creeping through the cane on the Ohio.
Come along here, my true love, and go along with me,
For I will take good care of thee.

36
The Twelve Days of Christmas

It is important to show this song in Alabama tradition. The head-note to the Brown Collection (II, 208) gives a brief indication of the song's age (it goes back at least to Shakespeare's *Twelfth Night* and probably further), and says that the piece seems "more widely known in the North than in the South." Without doubt my informant learned it from Alabama tradition.

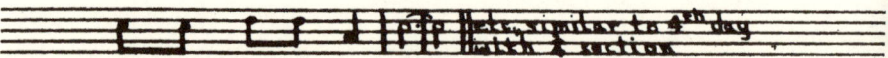

"Partridge on a Pear Tree," sung by Miss Drucilla Hall, Millport, Lamar County, 1952.

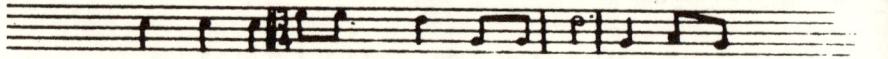

On the first day of Christ-mas my truest love said to me: Par-tridge on a pear tree. On the sec-ond day of Christ-mas my tru-est love said to me: Two tur-tle doves, par-tridge on the pear tree. On the third day of Christ-mas my tru-est love said to me: Three......, two tur-tle doves, par-tridge on the pear tree. On the fourth day of Christ-mas my tru-est love said to me: Four blue pig-eons, three........., two tur-tle doves, par-tridge on the pear tree.

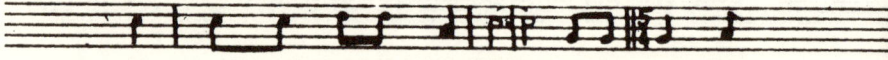

On the first day of Christmas my truest love said to me:
Partridge on a pear tree.
On the second day of Christmas mv truest love said to me:

Two turtle doves, partridge on the pear tree.
On the third day of Christmas my truest love said to me:
Three . . . ., two turtle doves, partridge on the pear tree.
On the fourth day of Christmas my turest love said to me:
Four blue pigeons, three . . . ., two turtle doves, partridge on the pear tree.
On the fifth day of Christmas my turest love said to me:
Five gold rings, four blue pigeons, three. . . . . ., two turtle doves, partridge on the pear
   tree.
On the sixth day of Christmas my turest love said to me:
Six men singing, five gold rings, four blue pigeons, three. . . . ., two turtle doves, part-
   ridge on the pear tree.
On the seventh day of Christmas my turest love said to me:
Seven swans swimming, (etc. back through the list)
On the eighth day of Christmas my truest love said to me:
Eight hens cackling, (etc.)
On the ninth day of Christmas my truest love said to me:
Nine geese waving, (etc.)
On the tenth day of Christmas my turest love said to me:
Ten mules braying, (etc.)

C
UNHAPPY LOVE SONGS

37
Swinging in the Lane

The words and music of this song were composed by Charles Carroll Sawyer. It appeared from the beginning in numerous songsters: *Beadle's Dime Song Book No. 15* (N.Y. 18--, p. 24); *The Clown's Shoo Fly Songster* (N.Y. 1870, p. 27); *Daisey Deane Songster* (Albany, N.Y. 18--., p. 56); *De Witt's Forget-Me-Not Songster* (N.Y. 1872, p. 154); *Greenback Club Songster* (Gettysburg, Pa., 1877, p. 59); *Hooley's High Daddy Songster* (N.Y. c. 1865, p. 69); *Leavitt's Song Book* "Consisting of songs sung by the Green Mountain Minstrels at their Popular Concerts" (Montpelier, Vt., 1868, p. 8); *The "Nobby" Songster* (Baltimore, 1869, p. 67); *Parisian Can Can Songster* (N.Y. 1869, p. 122); *Sol Smith Russell's Comic Songster* (N.Y. 1871, p. 120); *Sol Smith Russell's Goose and Injuns Songster* (N.Y. 1870, p. 39); *Swinging In The Lane Songster* (N.Y. 1868, p. 1); *Tony Pastor's Song Of The Flags Songster* (N.Y. 1874, p. 71).

There were, of course, numerous parodies, under such names as "Sliding on the Cellar Door" (*Pulling Hard Against The Stream Songster*, N.Y. 1868, p. 47); "Swinging on the Grape-Vine Swing" (*Wehman's Popular Songs No. 29*, N.Y. 18--, p. 16) and various songs sung to the same tune, such as "The Drunkard's Appeal" (*Capt. Kelly's Songster*, N.Y. 1874, p. 9); and "Such a Foot is Mine" (*Kelly & Leon's Grand Dutch Songster*, N.Y. c. 1868, p. 14).

The piece has not been widely reported as a folk song. Randolph (IV, 397) has one text. Pound (*Syllabus*, p. 49) lists it. Sandburg (*American Sogbac*, pp. 114-115) prints it with a different chorus, saying it was sung in Oklahoma in the late 80s. Fuson (*Ballads Of The Kentucky Highlands*, p. 99) and Shoemaker (*North Pennsylvania Minstrelsy*,] ; 132) include it. This is one of the most popular folk songs in Alabama. I have six texts.

A

"Swinging in the Lane," from the Alabama Archives. Collected by John Proctor Mills, Montgomery.

We often talk of childhood hours,
Of tricks we used to play
Upon each other while at school

To pass the time away,
And, oh, how often I have longed
For those bright days again,
When little Rosy Nell and I
Went swinging in the lane.

Chorus:
    Oh yet I'd give this world to be
    With Rosy Nell again.
    I never, never can forget
    Our swinging in the lane.

The boys and girls would often go
A-fishing in the brooks
With spools of thread for fishing lines
And bended pins for hooks.
They often wished me to go with them,
But always wished in vain,
For I'd rather be with Rosy Nell
A-swinging in the lane.

At last a cloud of sorrow came.
A strange young man from town
Was introduced to my Rosy Nell
By Aunt Jemima Brown.
She stayed away from school next day.
The truth to me was plain:
She'd gone off with that city chap,
A-swinging in the lane.

Now all young men with tender hearts,
Come take advice from me.
Don't be so quick to fall in love
With every girl you see.
For if you do you soon will find
That you have loved in vain.
She'll go off with some other chap
A-swinging in the lane.

B

"Rosa Nell," sung by Mrs. Mary Crowder, Sulligent, Lamar County, 1952. She has sung it fifty years. Seven stanzas essentially the same as A.

I of-ten think of child-hood days and pranks we

used to play. I think of tricks we used to play to pass

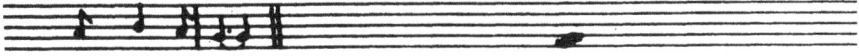

the time a-way.

C

"Swinging in the Lane," sung by Miss Lena Roberts, Florence, Colbert County, 1953. Three stanzas essentially the same as A.

D

"Rosy Nell," contributed by Mrs. Mattie Dewberry, Wedowee, Randolph County, 1953. A fragment. Stanza 3 of A, chorus, and stanza 2 of A.

E

"Rosa Nell," sung by Miss Malissa Richardson and Mrs. Jenny Geer, Kennedy, Lamar County, 1952. Five-line fragment.

I'd rath-er be with Ro-sa Nell Swing-ing in the

lane. Swing-ing in the lane, Swing-ing in the lane; I'd

rath-er be with Ro-sa Nell Swing-ing in the lane.

F

"Swinging in the Lane," sung by Mrs. Ruth Clements, Holt, Tuscaloosa County, 1952. Four stanzas essentially same as A.

38
My Pretty Quadroon

This piece, very much in the Stephen Collins Foster tradition, was published by the H.M. Higgins Co., around 1865. It appeared in *Beadle's Dime Song Book,* No. 16 (1865, p. 40), with no author given. Beck *(Lumberjack Songs,* p. 217) reports it. My informant did not sing it as a Negro song. It is probably a pseudo-Negro creation. Possibly it is a song about a white man's love for a mulatto, in the same spirit as "The Little Mohea." Mesalliance is not widespread in American folksongs, but when found it is sung without self-consciousness. My informant seemed unaware of any implications in the situation she was singing about. This piece bears no resemblance to Longfellow's "The Quadroon Girl."

"My Pretty Quadroon," sung by Mrs. Leila Robertson, Millport, Lamar County, 1952.

I'll nev-er for-get when I met sweet Co-ra, my pret-ty quad-roon. I can see her dear eyes shin-ing yet and her cheeks like the wild rose in bloom. Her form was ex-ceed-ing-ly fair And her voice was the drift of the moon. And the ring-lets of bright glos-sy hair were the curls of my

Chorus

pret-ty quad-roon. Oh, my pret-ty quad-roon, my flow-er that fad-ed too soon. My heart's like the strings of my ban-jo, All broke for my pret-ty quad-roon. My heart's like the strings of my ban-jo, All broke for my pret-ty quad-roon.

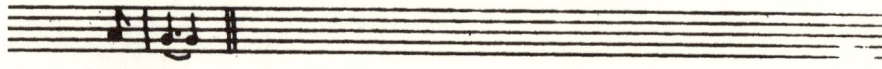

I'll never forget when I met sweet Cora, my pretty quadroon.
I can see her dear eyes shining yet and her cheeks like the wild rose in bloom.
Her voice was exceedingly fair, and her voice was the drift of the moon.
And the ringlets of bright glossy hair were the curls of my pretty quadroon.

Chorus:
    Oh, my pretty quadroon, my flower that faded too soon.
    My heart's like the strings of my banjo,
    All broke for my pretty quadroon.
    My heart's like the strings of my banjo,
    All broke for my pretty quadroon.

Farewell to Kentucky's bright shade, farewell to Kentucky's bright hills.
Farewell to the rocks and the rills where Cora and I often strayed.
My voice shall be gone with the wind, my thoughts shall find rest pretty soon.
But my spirit shall linger up here and keep watch o'er my pretty quadroon.

39
The Sailor Boy

This English song, printed by Catnach and Such and probably other ballad printers in the nineteenth century, is known variously as "Moment's River Side," "Down by the River Side," "The Lost Lover," "The Sailor's Sweetheart," and the above title. It is a widely known song. For references see Brown (II, 323) and Randolph (I, 296). The L.C. checklist (p. 101) reports two texts from Mississippi, one from Vermont, one from Indiana. My two texts are about as long as the usual versions.

A

"Father, Father, Go Build Me a Boat," sung by Mr. Andrew Aldrich, Hubbertville, Fayette County, 1953. He has sung it perhaps fifty years.

Fa-ther, Fa-ther, go build me a boat, And on this

o-cean I will float. And ev-'ry ship that I pass by I'll

stop and in-quire for my sweet sol-dier boy.

Father, Father, go build me a boat,
And on this ocean I will float,
And every ship that I pass by,
I'll stop and inquire for my sweet soldier boy.

As I sailed out one morning in May,
I spied a ship a-coming from Spain.
I hailed my captain; he drew near.
I stopped and inquired for my sweet soldier boy.

"Oh, tell me quick, oh, tell me joy,
Oh, does sweet Billy sail with you?"
"Your sweet Billy he's not here.
He's drownded in the . . . . .that said my. . . . . ."

B

"Go Bring Me Back the One I Love," sung by Mrs. R. A. Dunham, Fairhope, Baldwin County, 1953.

Oh, Cap-tain, Cap-tain, tell me true, does my

true lov-er sail with you? Oh, no, he does not sail with

me. He's with the mer-maids in the sea.

"Oh, Captain, Captain, tell me true
Does my true-lover sail with you?"
"Oh, no he does not sail with me.
He's with the mermaids in the sea."

Bring back to me the one I love.
Oh, bring, oh, bring him back to me.
They say he loves another now.
Oh, he's not keeping all his vows.

40
The Blackest Crow

This fragment is representative of the kind of stanza that floats from one song to another. At times any such stanza may be sung as a complete song. The singer of the folk lyric enjoys singing these fragments as much as he does a complete song. For a brief note, references and an example of how this stanza may become part of a song, see Brown (II, 423, stanza 2).

"The Blackest Crow That Ever Did Fly," sung by Mrs. Belle Soury Jackson, Nauvoo, Walker County, 1952.

Don't you hear that tur-kle dove a-fly-ing from

pine to pine, A-weep-ing for her own true love, and

why not I for mine? The black-est crow that ev-er did

fly will sure-ly turn to white; If ev-er I prove false

to you, bright days will turn to night.

Don't you hear that turkle dove
A-flying from pine to pine,
A-weeping for her own true love,
And why not I for mine?
The blackest crow that ever did fly
Will surely turn to white.
If ever I prove any false to you
Bright days will turn to night.

41

Barney McCoy

This song supposedly was copyrighted in 1881 (Mark Sullivan, *Our Times*), although Ozark singers told Randolph that it was widespread in the 70s (Randolph, IV, 291). It was immensely popular in the songsters. One lists it "as sung by Charles Konollman, published by Frank P. Anderson, Brooklyn" *(The Dayton's Songster, N.Y., 18--, p. 23)*; another lists somewhat a different version as "words by Harry Miller, Music, F.D. Murphy, Music published by T.B. Harms, N.Y." *(Bob Slaven's "Over The Neighbor's Fence" Songster, N.Y. 18--, p. 14)* I quote the first of two stanzas of the version:

We'll bid all our dear friends goodbye,
We're leaving old Ireland today;
But long for our sweet home we'll sigh
And weep in the land far away.
The sod of my birth still I love,
It's memory no pain can destroy.
And true as the stars up above
We'll be, dear, your Barney McCoy.

Chorus:
Then Dry all your tears, Norah dear,
Oh come with your own darling boy,
There's nothing but misery here.
You'll be happier with Barney McCoy.

This piece appeared in many other songsters. For example: *Billy Mendel & Bertha Trent Ireland vs Germany Original Songster* (N.Y. 1882, p. 46); *Blossom & Roach's Wooley Heads Songster* (N.Y. 1882, p. 11); *Billy Burke's Barnum & Great London Circus Songster* (N.Y. 1880, p. 10); *Charles H. Duprez's & Benedict's Famous Minstrels Songster* (N.Y. 18--, p. 7); *Charles Glidden Banjo Songster* (N.Y. 1881, p. 27); *Charles A. Gardner's Yust So Sure As You Lif Songster* (N.Y. 1882, p. 37); *Crosby & Martin's Footsteps In The Moonlight Songster* (N.Y. 1881, p. 27); *Dooley & Tenbrooke's Black Diamond Songster* (N.Y. 1881, p. 27); *Ferguson & Mack's Tony Pastor Star Troupe Songster* (N.Y. 1881, p. 11); *Flynn & Susan's Erin's Eccentrics Songster* (N.Y. 1881, p. 24); *Fred Somers' 250 Songs* (Chicago, 1887, p. 20); *Gallagher & West's Nonsense Song-*

ster (N.Y. 1881, p. 25); *Harrigan & Hart's Squatter's Sovereighnty Songster* (N.Y. 1882, p. 23); *Harry Hill's Greatest Songster* (N.Y. 1882, p. 29); *I'm Just Going Down To The Gate Songster* (N.Y. 18--, p. 22); *John Hogan's Pretty Little Black-Eyed Kitty Songster* (N.Y. 1881, p. 27); *Leavitt & Allen's God Bless Our Boy Songster* (N.Y. 1882, p. 44); *Maggie Cline's Mary Ann Kehoe Songster* (N. Y. 18--, p. 20); *Minnie Lee's An Irishman's Toast Songster* (N.Y. 18--, p. 60); *Morris Weston's Minstrel Boy Songster* (N.Y. 1882, p. 43); *The Murphy's Paddy & Ella Ma-Ma Songster* (N.Y. 1882, p. 42); *The Only B.C. Hart Songster* (N.Y. 1882, p. 35); *Palles & Cusick's Sunburst Of Ireland Songster* (N.Y. 1882, p. 54); *Pat Rooney's Is That You Mr. Reilly Songster* (N.Y. 18--, p. 26); *Sheeran's America, Ireland & Germany Songster* (N.Y. 1882, p. 29); "As sung by Charles Konollman," *Thatcher, Primrose & West's Consolidated Mammoth Minstrels Songster* (N.Y. 1885, p. 30); *Toothless Murphy's Get There Ely By Gum Songster* (N.Y. 1882, p. 49); *Wehman's Universal Songster* No. 8 (N. Y. 1882, p. 61); *Wheatley & Traynor's Dublin Boys Songster* (N.Y. 1883, p. 59); *Wm. C. Cameron's Volks Theatre Songster* (N.Y. 1882, p. 9).

Brown (II, 346) has a copy and several references. Spaeth *(History of Popular Music)* and Gilbert *(Lost Chords)* do not list it. The L.C. Checklist (p. 19) reports texts from Virginia and New York City. My one text indicates lack of popularity in Alabama. My informant sang the first stanza and chorus from memory. Later she found a manuscript copy of the whole song. I reproduce both versions to show how even one person can alter a song from the manuscript in singing.

A

"Barney McCoy," sung by Mrs. R. Van Iderstine, Daphne, Baldwin County, 1953.

I am go-ing far a-way from you, my dar-ling, and

my ship is now an-chored down the bay. It would break my

heart far a-part from you to part, And in oth-er kind

Chorus

and true. Then come to my arms, No-rah dar-ling. Bid

your friends in dear old Ire-land good-bye. And it's

hap-py we will be in the dear land of the free, Liv-ing

hap-py with your Bar-ney Mc Coy.

I am going far away from you, darling,
And my ship is now anchored down the bay.
It would break my heart
Far apart from you to part
And no other one so loving, kind and true.

Chorus:
    Then come to my arms, Nora darling.
    Bid your friends in dear old Ireland goodbye.
    And it's happy we will be
    In the dear land of the free,
    Living happy with your Barney McCoy.

B

"Barney McCoy," from a manuscript owned by Mrs. Van Iderstine, Daphne. It was found and given to me after she had sung the above fragment.

I am going far away, Nora darling.
And I'm leaving such an angel far behind.

It would break my heart in two
Which I fondly gave to you,
And no other one so loving kind and true.

Chorus:
> Then come to my arms, Nora darling.
> Bid your friends in dear old Ireland goodbye.
> And it's happy we will be
> In the dear land of the free
> Living happy with your Barney McCoy.

I would go with you, Barney darling,
But the reason I have told you long ago.
It would break my mother's heart
If from her I had to part
And go roaming with you, Barney McCoy.

I am going far away, Nora darling,
Just as sure as there's a God that I adore.
But remember what I say,
That until the Judgment day,
You will never see your Barney any more.

I would go with you, Barney darling,
If my mother and the rest of them were there.
For I know we would be blessed
In the dear land of the free,
Living happy with you, Barney McCoy.

I am going far away, Nora darling,
And the ship is now anchored down the bay.
And before tomorrow's sun
You will hear the signal gun.
So be ready, it will carry us away.

42
I'm Sitting by the Stile, Mary

This song is Lady Dufferin's "Lament of the Irish Emigrant." According to the Brown Collection (II, 369) it was widely known and sung, although the editor refers only to Dean *(The Flying Cloud,* p. 81), who says it was sung in the Northwest, and was in "various song collections." It was in literally dozens of songsters; for example: *The American Vocalist* (N.Y. 1853, p. 88); *Barney The Jarvey's Hibernicon Songster* (N.P., 1869, p. 17); *The Broth Of A Boy Songster* (N.Y. c. 1870, p. 39); *Daisy Deane Songster* (N.Y., 1869, p. 41); *Erin-Go-Brach Songster* (N.Y. 1890, p. 65); *Irish Song And Dance Book* (N.Y. c. 1873, p. 59).

"I'm Sitting By The Stile, Mary," from the Alabama Archives, collected at Eufaula, Barbour County. It is called a "song of the Irish immigrant."

I'm sitting by the stile, Mary,
Where we sat side by side,
On a bright May morning long ago,
When first you were my bride.
The corn was spring fresh and green,
And the lark sang loud and high,
And the red was on your lips, Mary,
And the love light in your eye.

The place is little changed, Mary,
The day is bright as then.
The lark's loud song is in my ear,
And the corn is green again.
But I miss the soft clasp of your hand,
And the breath warm on your cheek.
And I still keep lis'ning to the words
You never more will speak.

43
Woe Unto Me When The Time Draws Near

This parting song is so typical of farewell sentiment that one is surprised that it has not been reported frequently. Randolph (IV, 262) has five texts. The L.C. Checklist (p. 288) lists texts from North Carolina, Kentucky, Virginia and New York City.

A

"Woe Unto Me When The Time Draws Near," sung by Mrs. Cora Lee Pennington, Fernbank, Lamar County, 1952. She learned it from her father.

It's woe un-to me when the time draws near   When

you and I must part.   Your let-ter of the griev-ing woe

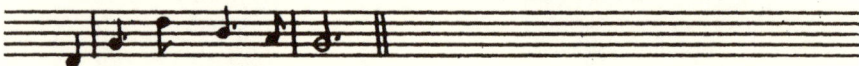

of my poor ach-ing heart.

It's woe unto me when the time draws near
When you and I must part.
Your letter of the grieving woe
Of my poor aching heart.

It's woe that I suffered and it's for your sake,
It is you that I loved so dear.
I wish that you could go with me
Or I could linger here.

Your cheeks they are of the rosy red,
Your lips are the rose . . . . . .
There's no one fault within your love
That ever I could see.

Your eyes they are of the sparkling blue,
Like diamonds they do shine.
Your disposition it is so true
That it charms this heart of mine.

I wish your breast was made of glass,
Wherein I might behold
Your name engraved upon my breast
In letters lined with gold.

I wish I were ten thousand miles,
Upon some lonesome shore,
Upon the rocks and mountains high,
Where the wild beasts cry and roar.

There is a crow and it is so black.
It surely will turn white;
If ever I prove false to you
Bright days will turn to night.

B

"Farewell," sung by Miss Drucilla Hall, Millport, Lamar County, 1952. Six stanzas, essentially same as A. The tune is somewhat different.

It's woe on you, the time draws near when you and

I must part. There's no one knows the grief and woe of

my poor ach-ing heart.

44
I Cannot Be Your Sweetheart

This song contains all the sentiment that would endear it to the folk — the girl who is going to marry another, the sad farewell, and the heart that will ever love her despite her marriage to someone else. It was written by Abbie L. Ford, copyrighted 1899 by S. Brainard's Sons Co. and entered Stationers Co. London. The first stanza is almost like my version, the chorus is exactly like mine. The second stanza I shall quote for comparison. Was it dropped as being inappropriate, inadvertently, or why?

We bade farewell in the moonlight,
My heart is turned to stone,
One blissful hour I was happy,
But now I am sad and alone.
Empty my life is forever
She will go far away.
Yet while I love I will love her
E'en tho I still hear her say.
Chorus

Shearin *(Syllabus,* p. 29) reports the song from Kentucky. I have not found it elsewhere. My three full texts indicate a considerable popularity in Alabama.

A

"Love Song," sung by Mrs. Della Collins, Vernon, Lamar County, 1952.

Last night I told my heart's love Un-der the deep

blue sky. Ea-ger-ly wait-ing an an-swer I on-ly saw pain

in her eye. Soft-ly I whis-pered I loved her, Asked her

to be my bride. Her face grew pale as she trem-bled and

Chorus

sad-ly to me re-plied: "I can-not be your sweet-heart.

How can I stay by your side, For there is one wait-ing

o'er yon-der, One who should call me his bride? My heart

is al-most bro-ken, Your vows on-ly add to my pain. My

dar-ling, my dar-ling, I love you, Though we may ne'er

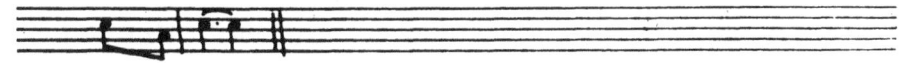

meet a-gain."

Last night I told my heart's love,
Under the deep blue sky.
I eagerly waited an answer,
I only saw pain in her eyes.
Softly I whispered I loved her,
Asked her to be my bride.
Her face grew pale and she trembled,
And sadly to me replied:

Chorus:
    I cannot be your sweetheart,
    How can I stay by your side
    When there is another one waiting,
    One who would claim me his bride?
    My heart is almost broken,
    Your vows will answer my pain.
    I love you, my darling, I love you,
    Though we may ne'er meet again.

We bade farewell in the moonlight,
My heart was turned to a stone.
That blissful hour I was happy,
Now I am sad and alone.
This is my life forever.
She may go far away,
But as long as I live I will love her.
But still I can hear her say.

B

"I Cannot Be Your Sweetheart," sung by Mrs. Susie Bell Hankins, Vernon, Lamar County, 1952. Two stanzas and chorus. Practically identical with A.

C

"We May Never Meet Again," sung by Miss Drucilla Hall, Millport, Lamar County, 1952. Two stanzas and chorus. Practically identical with A.

45
You Went and Courted Nancy

Jealousy is not unusual in folk songs. I have not found this song elsewhere, and I have only one text.

"You Went and Courted Nancy," sung by Miss Drucilla Hall, Millport, Lamar County, 1952.

John, you told me a story,
You told me so before.
You told me you'd come to see me,
But you haven't come no more.
You went and courted Nancy
With the black and roving eye.

John, she is your fancy,
This here you can't deny.
If I had all the gold and silver
That ever crossed the sea,
I freely now would give it
For your sweet company.

But if I am forsaken
I know I'm not forsworn.
I'll spend my days a-roving
This lonesome valley through.

46
I Once Had A Sweetheart

Although somewhat similar to the present versions of the old English love song "Green Grows the Laurel," this song seems distinct. Compare with Brown (III, 328). The figures of speech and emotions are typical of many folk love songs.

"I Once Had A Sweetheart," sung by Miss Drucilla Hall, Millport, Lamar County, 1952.

I once had a sweetheart but now I've got none.
He's gone to old Kentucky to never return,
To never return, to never return.
He's gone to old Kentucky to never return.

I once was a snowbird but now I'm a lark.
Oh, boys, if you aim to marry, now's the time to spark.
I went to sleep the other night, I dreamed an awful dream.
I dreamed I saw my true love a-smiling at me.

But when I awoke I found it was not so,
The tears from my eyes like some ocean did flow,
Some ocean did flow, some ocean did flow.
The tears from my eyes like some ocean did flow.

We once had a parting, but now we've come to meet.
We'll lock our love together and throw away the key,
And throw away the key, and throw away the key.
We'll lock our love together and throw away the key.

47
Dark Blue Eyes and Raven Hair

This song has been rather widely reported from the southern Appalachian area. See Brown (II, 417) for a short bibliography. Randolph (IV, 283) reports one text. The L.C. Checklist (p. 38) lists texts from New York City and Tennessee. My two texts adhere rather closely to the usual texts.

A

"Dark Blue Eyes and Raven Hair," sung by Mrs. Guy J. Johnson, Oneonta, Blount County, 1953, from a ballad book in her possession. She has sung the song for thirty years.

They were stand-ing by the win-dow, And the night

wind kissed their cheeks, As he wait-ed long in si-lence,

Wait-ed long for her to speak. When at last she mur-

mured sad-ly, As she raised her tear-ful eyes, "ith a

look so flush of an-guish That it filled him with

sur-prise.

They were standing by the window,
And the night wind kissed their cheeks
As he waited long in silence,
Waited long for her to speak.
When at last she murmured sadly,
As she raised her tearful eyes
With a look so flush of anguish
That it filled him with surprise.

"I have summoned you, my darling,
That I may tell you all,

E'er our vows by angels written
Are forever past recall.
Do not turn your face away, Love,
It is best that we should part
Though the ties of love be severed
That are wound around my heart.

"For you say you love another,
And that you have never loved me.
If these cruel words be true, Dear,
I'll forever set you free."
Then she paused with eager yearning,
Gazed upon that face so fair
Till she stamped upon his memory
Dark blue eyes and raven hair.

"It is true," he answered hoarsely,
"But by yonder stars above,
To deceive I never intended
When I told you of my love."
Quickly from her blue eyes vanished
All the tender mystic love,
And her small hands clinched the poison
As her face grew stern and white.

"It's enough," she cried in anguish,
"Stain no more thy guilty soul.
May oblivious silent waters
Ever more between us roll.
I return each little missive
You have written in the past.
But the cruel words there written
E'er shall haunt me till the last.

"May your heart be always happy,
Though my own shall ache with pain.
When you meet me as a stranger
Pass me by with proud disdain.
Do not think that I'll forget three.
No, I'll love thee just as now
Till my arms in death are folded
And the dew is on my brow.

"Fare you well," she added gently
As she seized his outstretched hand,
Covering it with burning kisses
Saying, "God will understand.
He has gone," the white lips murmured;
Lower bent the golden head
And her little arms were folded
As the gentle spirit fled.

B

"Broken Engagement," sung by Mrs. Rosa Jenkins, Wetumpka, Elmore County, 1952.

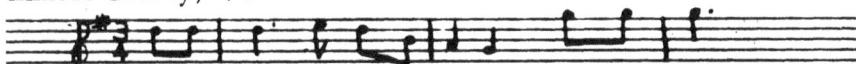

He was stand-ing by the win-dow, While the breez-

es kissed the cheeks. He had wait-ed long in. si-lence,

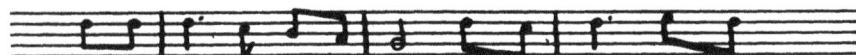

Wait-ed long for her to speak. Then she raised her voice

so gent-ly, Look-ing up with an-gry eyes, And the an-swer

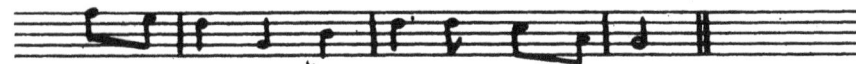

that she gave him Filled him with great sur-prise.

He was standing by the window
While the breezes kissed her cheeks.
He had waited long in silence,
Waited long for her to speak.

Then she raised her voice so gently,
Looking up with angry eyes,
And the answer that she gave him
Filled him with a great surprise.

"They tell me that you love another,
And you never have loved me.
If these words are true, my darling,
I'll forever set you free."

"They are true, my dear," he answered,
"True as the shining stars above.
When they told you my intentions,
Then they told you of my love."

He had gone the pathway trembling,
Left her standing by the gate.
"Tell, oh tell, oh tell him, sister,
That his message came too late."

God's mercy sent an angel
To relieve her dreadful pain;

As she drifted unto heaven
On a snow white angel's wings.

As he looked into her casket,
Looking down into her face,
Then he realized that he loved her
And no one could take her place.

48
Blue Belle

In the Brown Collection (III, 471) there is the chorus of this song, remembered by Newman I. White from about 1900-1913. White thought it was a Spanish-American War song. As far as I can determine that is the only occurrence of the song outside of my collection.

"Blue Belle," sung by Mrs. Nola Browne, Millport, Lamar County, 1952. She has sung it all her life. She learned it from the singing of friends.

Blue Belle, my heart is breaking.
Sweetheart, we two must part.
Blue Belle, my tears have started;
It's time to say goodbye.

Goodbye, my Blue Belle,
Farewell to you.
I will be dreaming of you.
Your eyes are so blue.
Bright lights are shining.
When we are apart
I will be dreaming of my own Blue Belle.

49
Zula

Such a name for a girl is unusual in Alabama. The sentiment, however, is common. This song is again unusual in having thirteen stanzas, more than the average folk song. I have not found it in other collections. It apparently is not widespread in Alabama, since I have only one text.

"Zula," sung by Mrs. Velma Dean, Kennedy, Lamar County, 1952. She has known it for at least forty years.

Thou lov'st an-oth-er, Zu-la. Thou lov-est him
a-lone. Thine eyes con-fess it, Zu-la, thy looks, thy

Thou lov'st another, Zula.
Thou lovest him alone.
Thine eyes confess it, Zula,
Thy looks, thy words, thy tone.

Thou art sad when he is absent.
Thou art happy by his side.
He has woo'd and won thee, Zula,
And thou shall be his bride.

But does he love thee, Zula,
As I have loved thee long,
As I will ever love thee,
Though the world may deem it wrong?

Does he love thee as I love thee?
With that pure and heavenly flame?
Would he die to serve thee, Zula,
Would he give up wealth and fame?

I will meet you at the Bridal,
They have asked me to be there.

My friends will smile and greet thee,
But tears for me will shed.

When words are past recalling,
And you are no longer free,
When your heart is pledged forever.
Then perhaps you'll think of me.

When his heart is turned to coldness,
And his heart is turned from thee,
When your home is dark and chilly,
Then you'll sigh for love like me.

Farewell, perhaps forever,
Beloved one adieu.
Will thou this token please to take,
And keep it for friendship's sake.

We meet and part, the world is wide,
We journey onward side by side.
A little while and then again,
Our paths diverge and there is pain.

Farewell, how oft the sound of sadness
Like thorns of sorrow pierce the heart,
And hush the harp tones of its gladness
And tear the bleeding chords apart.

Farewell, and if by distance parted,
We see each other's face no more.
Ah, may we with the faithful hearted
Meet beyond this parting shore.

Farewell, ah, farewell, but whenever you give
A thought to the days of yore,
Of the bright sunny things that in memory live,
Let a thought of me sweep o'er.

Be always kind hearted,
Do good deeds without end.
But never forget
Your affectionate friend.

50
Thou Hast Learned to Love Another

A song entitled "Thou Hast Learned to Love Another," was published in 1849 (Spaeth, *History of Popular Music,* p. 594). In Ditson's *Home Melodist* (1859, p. 38) the same title is credited to Charles Slade. Randolph (IV, 249), however, says this song is "evidently a derivative" of 'Now Go and Leave Me If you Wish,' for a copy of which see Spaeth *(Weep Some More, My Lady,* p. 32). Though keeping the central theme, the song has undergone wide change, as can be seen from an examination of Randolph's nine texts or my eight below. For comment on the song see Belden *(Ballads and Songs,* p. 211) in addition to Randolph. For an interesting variation see my last text.

A

"Broken Vows," sung by Mrs. J. V. Tarwater, Fayette, Fayette County, 1951. She has sung it "many years."

Thou hast learned to love an-oth-er. Thou hast

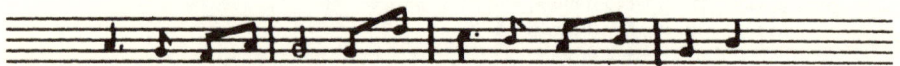

bro-ken ev-ery vow. We have part-ed from each oth-er

And my heart is hea-vy now. I have loved you, dear-ly

loved you More than all this world could know. But you

proved to me false heart-ed And I say, "For-ev-er go."

Thou hast learned to love another.
Thou has broken every vow.
We have parted from each other
And my heart is heavy now.

Chorus:
    I have loved you, dearly loved you

More than all this world could know.
But you proved to me false hearted
And I say, "Forever go."

Go, and when you're with another
Try and take her for your bride.
This poor aching heart can struggle.
Love can never conquer pride.

Go, and when you are with another
Cast one single thought on me;
Think of the one who loves you dearly,
One who would have died for thee.

B

"Thou Hast Learned to Love Another," sung by Mrs. Velma Blakeney, Newtonville, Fayette County, 1952. Five stanzas. The first four are practically identical with the one quoted above. The fifth is needed for illustration of further development.

I will send you back your letters
And the ring I love so well,
And from now we will be as strangers.
I can never say, "Farewell."

C

"Broken Vow," sung by Miss Drucilla Hall, Millport, Lamar County, 1952. Five stanzas identical with version B.

D

"Thou Hast Learned to Love," sung by Mrs. Flora Phillips, Cullman, Cullman County, 1953, from a manuscript she had made, dated 1938. This version is a wide variant from those above.

Thou hast learned to love another;
    Thou hast broken every vow;
We have parted from each other,
    And my heart is lonely now;
I have taught my looks to shun thee,
    When coldly we have met;
For another's smile hath won thee,

And thy voice I must forget.
O, is it well to sever
    This heart from thine forever?
Can I ere forget thee? Never!
Farewell! Farewell! Farewell!

We have met in scenes of pleasure,
    We have met in halls of pride;
I have seen thy new-found pleasure,
    I have gazed upon thy bride;
I have marked the timid lustre
    Of thy downcast, happy eye;
I have seen thee gaze upon her,
    Forgetting I was by;
I grieve that e'er I met thee;
    Fain, fain would I forget thee;
'Twere folly to regret thee;
Farewell! Farewell! Farewell!

We have met and we have parted,
    But I uttered scarce a word;
Like a guilty thing I started,
    When they well-known voice I heard,
Thy looks were stern and altered,
    And thy words were cold and high;
How my traitor courage faltered,
    When I dared to meet thine eye!
O, woman's love will grieve her,
    And woman's pride will leave her;
Life has fled when love deceives her;
Farewell! Farewell! Farewell!

E

"Thou Hast Learned to Love," contributed by Miss Florence Bailey, Crane Hill, Cullman County, 1953. Miss Bailey is Mrs. Phillip's sister. Her version is identical with D.

F

"Broken Vows," sung by Mrs. Maggie Lee Hays, Vernon, Lamar County, 1953. Six stanzas. The first five parallel closely B but the sixth takes a firmer stand.

For I loved you, dearly loved you
More than all this world could know.

You have proved to be false hearted.
Now I say, "Forever go."

G

"Thou Hast Learned to Love Another," a two-stanza fragment sung by Mrs. Nola Browne, Millport, Lamar County, 1952.

H

"My Last Gold Dollar is Gone," from the Alabama Archives, collected by Mrs. Emory P. Morrow.

My last gold dollar is gone,
My last gold dollar is gone.
My board bill is due
And my whiskey bill too,
And my last gold dollar is gone,
And my last old rowdy is dead.

Chorus:
    We have met and we have parted.
    We have said one last farewell.
    My poor heart is almost broken,
    There is not but one can tell.

51

You Are False But I Forgive You

Spaeth *(History Of Popular Music In America,* p. 612) lists this song as being popular after its probable composition around 1899. Actually it was listed as "Words and Music by Ned Straight, Copyright 1880 by Pauline Lieder, N.Y." in *Burnett's Pacific Pearl Songster* (N.Y. 1881, p. 23). It was "Sung with great success by Miss Georgie Melnotte, the Queen of Serio-Comique" *(Birth & Barton's Songs Of The San Francisco Minstrels* (N.Y. c. 1881, p. 137), from which songster I give the first two of three stanzas for comparison with the folk version:

> Fare thee well, for once I loved you
> Even more than tongue can tell.
> Little did I think you'd leave me.
> Now I bid you a farewell.
> You have wrecked the heart I cherished.
> You have doomed me day by day.
> You are false but I forgive you,
> But forget you I never may.
> You are false but I forgive you,
> But forget you I never may.
>
> When I saw your eyes in virtue
> I could scarce believe my own.
> When I heard your voice in anger
> It was death to every tone.
> They have told you some false stories
> And you believed them all they say.
> You are false but I forgive you,
> But forget you I never may.

The song appeared in numerous other songsters. For example: *Coleman & McCarthy's Champion Song & Dance Book* (N.Y. 1882); *Cronin & Sullivan's Jack O'Hare Songster* (N.Y. 1880, p. 26); *Fairfield & Irwin's America & Ireland Songster* (N.Y. 1884, n.p.); *Ferguson & Mack's Tony Pastor Songster* (N.Y. c. 1881, p. 28); *Chas. Glidden's Banjo Songster* (N.Y. 1881, p. 53); *Hogan Bros' Nigs Of The Mozambique Songster* (N.Y. 1881, p. 13); *Jac. Aberle's Tivoli Theatre Songster* (N.Y. 1882, p. 22); *The Jerome's Burlesqueing Songster* (N.Y. 1880, p. 57); *Leavitt & Allen's God Bless Our Boy Songster* (N.Y. 1882, p. 48); *Miss Lizzie Derious Pretty Rosy Lips*

Songster (N.Y. 1882, p. 43); *Bonnie Runnell's Der Brave Huzzars Songster* (N.Y. 1881, p. 39); *William Carroll's Regan's Party Songster* (N.Y. 1881, p. 46); *Wm. C. Cameron's Volks Theatre Songster* (N. Y. 1882, p. 31).

Despite the wide dissemination of this song through the songsters, it seems not to have been popular among the folk. The Brown Collection (II, 408) reports three texts. Randolph (IV, 214) gives one. Davis (*Folksongs Of Virginia*, p. 88) gives the title. I have recovered it only once in Alabama, in a fragment.

"You Are False But I'll Forgive You," sung by Mrs. Nola Browne, Millport, Lamar County, 1952. She has sung it for at least forty years.

When I saw your eyes in virtue,
I scarce could believe my own.
When I heard your voice in anger,
It was death in every tone.

You have wrecked the heart I cherish.
You have doomed me day by day.
You are false but I'll forgive you,
But forget you I never may.

D
ANTI-MARRIAGE SONGS

52
Don't Like Your Family

Comic songs about real or potential trouble with in-laws are common with the folk. This one seems to develop the old proverb that the best kind of woman, or man, to marry is an orphan. I have not seen this song in any other collection. I have only one Alabama text.

"Don't Like Your Family," sung by Mrs. W. L. Tuggles, Newtonville, Fayette County, 1952.

I don't like your family.
They don't make a hit with me.
I don't like to bother
Lending money to your father,
While your mother would live on me.
I don't think your Uncle Joe
Ever had a collar on,
Though you're a perfect lady.
But when I get hitched for life,
I want an orphan.

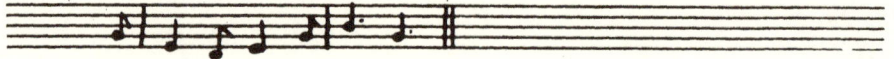

53
Twenty Long Years Since I Married

Numerous are the songs depicting the trials of married life. This particular song, however, seems not to have been sung widely. The Brown Collection (III, 56) has two texts, and a few references to others. I have only one Alabama text, and it is a fragment.

"Twenty Long Years Since I Married," sung by Mrs. Monroe Perkins, Crossville, Lamar County, 1952.

It's twenty long years since I married, I married.
I wish I had lived an old maid,
For I see nothing but trouble, but trouble.
My husband won't work at his trade.

Chorus:
    And off to the barroom, the barroom,
    And bring him back if you can.
    Now, girls, you'll never know trouble, know trouble
    Until you are tied to a man.

Sometimes I live in the country, the country,
Sometimes I live in the town.
Sometimes I take a fool notion, fool notion,
To jump in the river and drown.

54
A Single Life

The female point of view in the "I wouldn't marry" theme is not so common as is the man's. This song is not common. Brown (III, 36) reports a version which consists of my second stanza and a close parallel to my chorus. The rest of my song I have not found elsewhere.

"A Single Life," sung by Miss Drucilla Hall, Millport, Lamar County, 1953. She has sung this "silly song" for at least thirty years. Probably learned it from her father.

Some go court-ing on Sat-ur-day night, Some go court-ing on Sun-day. And if you give them a chance to talk,

Chorus

They won't go home till Mon-day. A sin-gle life is a hap-py life, A sin-gle life is love-ly. I'll live sin-gle and no man's wife, And no man can con-trol me.

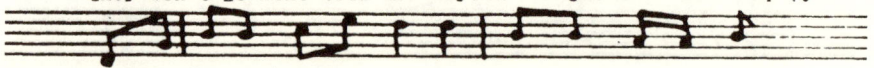

Some go courting on Saturday night,
Some go courting on Sunday.
And if you give them a chance to talk,
They won't go home till Monday.

Chorus:
    A single life is a happy life,
    A single life is lovely.
    I'll live single and no man's wife,
    And no man can control me.

Some say there are nice young men.
Girls, where will you find them?
I've traveled this wide world over,
And never been able to find them.

Some will court you for your love,
Some to deceive you.
When they find they have gained your love,
They'll run away and leave you.

I want one that's got black hair,
I want one with money.
I want one that's got blue eyes,
That'll kiss and call me honey.

55
Spinsters Gay

This piece reverses the usual theme of "Poor Old Maids" (in this volume). Instead of lamenting living alone, the women of this song are glad to escape the nuisance of husbands. I have not found this song in other collections.

"We Are a Set of Spinsters Gay," contributed by Mrs. Velma Blakeney, Newtonville, Fayette County, 1952, from a manuscript copy. She probably copied this song from another manuscript copy belonging to a girl friend about thirty-five years ago. Tune: "Yankee Doodle."

We are a set of spinsters gay,
As you can plainly see.
And we can prove it's all from choice
And not necessity.

Leap Year comes once in four years.
We then could change our station.
So chance we do not lack, you see,
But just the inclination.

We want no man to drive us round,
And find fault with our cooking.
Our pussy cats less trouble are,
And just as pretty looking.

We're spinsters all, and happy are
That Fate has so decreed it.
So keep your pity to yourselves.
We surely do not need it.

56
The Old Maid's Song

Stanzas of this song are likely to be found in other songs. Thomas (*Devil's Ditties*, p. 160), for instance, includes several in her "Paper of Pins." For a short list of references to this song see Randolph (III, 63). It is not widespread in Alabama. I have only two texts.

A

"Take My Knitting and Go to the Shade," sung by Miss Drucilla Hall, Millport, Lamar County, 1952.

Take my knit-ting and go to the shade, I won't

mar-ry at all. All my life I'll be an old maid, I

won't mar-ry at all. I won't mar-ry at all, at all.

I won't mar-ry at all. I'll not mar-ry a...... boy,

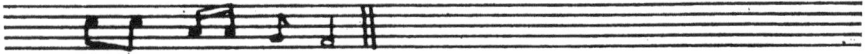

I won't mar-ry at all.

Take my knitting and go to the shade;
I won't marry at all.
All my life I'll be an old maid;
I won't marry at all.

I won't marry at all, at all;
I won't marry at all.

I'll not marry a . . . . . . .boy;
I won't marry at all.

I'll not marry a rich man;
He'll get drunk and fall in a ditch.
I will not marry at all, at all.
I would not marry at all.

I would not marry a poor boy.
No, he goes begging from door to door.
Would not marry at all, at all.
Would not marry at all.

There's the old doctor, I forgot,
He's the first one in the lot.
Would not marry at all, at all.
Would not marry at all.

B

"I'm Bound to be an Old Maid," sung by Mrs. Nola Browne, Millport, Lamar County, 1951. She has sung it for at least forty years.

I'm bound to be an old maid,
I'm bound to be an old maid,
I'm bound to be an old maid,
And I'll not marry at all.

I'll not marry a man that gets drunk,
I'll not marry at all,
For fear he'll hit me with a chair or chunk,
So I'll not marry at all.

I'll not marry a man that chews,
I'll not marry at all,
For the ambrew'll run from his head to his shoes,
So I'll not marry at all.

57
Poor Old Maids

This traditional English song must be well over a hundred years old. That it was popular so long ago is indicated by the fact that it was included in the *Universal Songster, or Museum of Mirth* (London, 1846, p. 308), in a four-stanza version. It is also found in Christie's *Traditional Ballad Airs* (I, 140). It was published in *The American Songster* (N.Y. c, 1847, pp. 166-167); *The Nightingale Or Jenny Lind Songster* (N.Y. 18--, p. 13); and *Singers Companion* (N.Y. 1857, p. 13) with the following note: "We have never seen this song in print and give it from recollection in childhood. Anyone who can make rhymes can run up words to suit himself. It is an old English air, at least as early as the days of George III, to whom these highly respectable ladies proposed, in the original song, to petition for redress of grievances." It was widely reprinted in other songsters: *The Grigg's Western Songster* (N.Y. 1827, p. 87); *The Little American Songster* (N.Y. 1875, p. 166); *Tony Pastor's Carte de Visite Album Songster* (N.Y. c. 1865, p. 47); *Trifit's Multum Im Parvo* (N.Y. 1890, p. 13); *United States Songster* (Cincinnati, 186—, p. 174); *Gus Williams, Latest & Best 250 Songster* (N.Y. 1875, p. 163).

American texts are in Sharp (II, 337), Davis *(Folk-Songs of Virginia,* pp. 224-225, by title), and Morris *(Folksongs of Florida,* p. 384). It appeared in *Beadle's Dime Song Book,* No. 4 (N.Y., 1859, p. 45). I have three Alabama texts, indicating rather wide popularity. One is the longest text I have seen; the other two are fragments.

A

"Poor Old Maids," sung by Mr. Isaac Rollins, Wedowee, Randolph County, 1953.

Three score and ten of us Poor old maids. Three
score and ten of us, Not a pen-ny in our purse. Some-thing
must be done for us Poor old maids.

Three score and ten of us
Pore old maids.
Three score and ten of us,
Not a penny in our purse.
Something must be done for us
Pore old maids.

Some of these days we'll fade and die,
Pore old maids.
Some of these days we'll fade and die,
And then be lifted to the sky.
Something must be done for us
Pore old maids.

Then the boys will holler good,
Pore old maids.
Then the boys will holler good,
"You ought to married when you could,"
Something must be done for us
Pore old maids.

We feed the pigs, the chickens, and the hen,
Pore old maids.
We feed the pigs, the chickens, and the hen,
And spend our whole life dreaming of the men.
Something must be done for us
Pore old maids.

We wear yeller, pink and blue,
Pore old maids.
We wear yeller, pink and blue.
Kiss the cats is all we do.
Something must be done for us
Pore old maids.

We love the men, you bet we do,
Pore old maids.
We love the men, you bet we do,
The bald headed men and the bachelors too.
Something must be done for us
Pore old maids.

B

"Pore Old Maids," sung by Mrs. Eli Thornton, Fayette, Fayette County, 1952. She has known it for some seventy years. She does not remember when or how she learned it, but probably from friends' singing.

Four score and ten of us Pore old maids; Four score

and ten of us Pore old maids; Four score and ten of us.

Not a pen-ny in our purse. Some-thing must be done for us

Pore old maids.

Four score and ten of us
Pore old maids;
Four score and ten of us
Pore old maids;
Four score and ten of us,
Not a penny in our purse.
Something must be done for us
Pore old maids.

We're all of a willing mind,
Pore old maids.
We're all of a willing mind,
Pore old maids.
We're all of a willing mind.
Hope some young man will be so kind
To take us pore old womankind,
Pore old maids.

C

"Pore Old Maids," sung by Miss Malissa Richardson, Kennedy, Lamar County, 1952. A fragment, like B.

E
COMICAL LOVE SONGS

58
The Waterfall

A "waterfall" is a mass of hair worn at the back of the neck. Webster's *New International* defines the word also as "a neck scarf with long pendant ends." Colloquially it means "a chignon likened to a waterfall." Professor Kittredge wrote Randolph that the waterfall was still used in New England when he was a boy. The *Dictionary of American English* gives its last quote for 1901. Several different songs mentioning the waterfall have been reported. Tally *(Negro Folk Rhymes,* p. 80) has a game song with the lines, "If I lives to see next fall, I's gwinter buy my wife a waterfall." Scarborough *(On the Trail of Negro Folk-Songs,* p. 239) quotes from a Negro song: "Hold your bonnet, hold your shawl, don't let go that waterfall." Henry *(Folk-Songs from the Southern Highlands,* p. 307) has a full version of what seems the Alabama song. Compare also "The Dark Girl Dressed in Blue" (Spaeth, *Read 'Em and Weep,* p. 86), Roe and Schwenk *(The Home Bartender's Guide and Song Book,* p. 67), and "The Charming Young Widow I Met on the Train" (Pound, *Syllabus,* p. 59). Randolph (III, 111) has a four-stanza version and a good headnote. The song seems not to have been popular in Alabama.

This idea was rather popular in the songsters, at least in title, for several songs appeared under this title that were not the one included here: *Just Down the Lane; Or Under the Old Oak Tree Songster* (N. Y. 18--, p. 45); *The Greenback Songster* (Phila., c. 1867, p. 113), "Sung by Carncross & Dixie Minstrels." One version obviously was the original of my song *(John Foster's Favorite Clown's Songster,* (N.Y. 1872, p. 10). I quote it here for comparison:

All you that have ever been in love can sympathize with me.
For I have loved the fairest girl
That ever you did see.
Her age is scarcely seventeen.
She is a figure straight and tall.
She dressed so near, she looked so sweet,
She wore a *waterfall.*

The first time that I met her,
I never can forget,
I went into a dry good store,
Some handkerchiefs to get.

She stood behind the counter
Dressed up like a Doll.
I never saw a face so fair
Or such a *waterfall.*

It was at a pic-nic party
I met her after that.
I quickly introduced myself
And had a pleasant chat.
Losts of pretty girls were there
But none among them all
Could dance with me except the girl
That wore the *waterfall.*

"The Waterfall," sung by Mrs. Ercelle Hand, Sargossa, Walker County, 1953. She has sung it some thirty years.

The ver-y first time I saw my girl, I nev-er
will for-get. I went in-to a dry-goods store, A hand-
ker-chief to get. She stood up by the count-er, She
was so fair and tall. She was a hand-some maid-en.
She wore a wa-ter-fall.

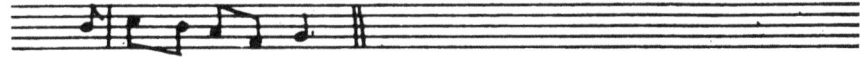

The very first time I saw my girl,
I never will forget,
I went into a drygoods store,
A handkerchief to get.
She stood up by the counter,
She was so fair and tall.
She was a handsome maiden,
She wore a waterfall.

The very next time I saw my girl,
A picnic we were at,
And when I introduced myself,
We had a little chat.

59

Kissing

Songs about the girl who kisses against her will are rather numerous in folk tradition. The treatments are more often humorous than serious. This volume contains several of this kind. This piece I have not found reported from elsewhere, and I have only one text.

"Kissing," sung by Mrs. J.V. Tarwater, Fayette, Fayette County, 1952. She sang what appears to be the chorus, later she sent me a ballad of the whole song.

For I'm go-ing to be a bet-ter girl, I'm nev-er
gon-na kiss a-gain. I'm a-fraid my moth-er will find it
out, And it will give her pain. You may walk and talk and
hold my hand, But kiss-ing is a crime. I'll nev-er kiss
you an-y more Un-til the next time.

I know a pretty little girl,
I want her for my wife.
She's neat and sweet with her pretty little feet,
And never been kissed in her life.

I asked her for a kiss.
She said, "Oh what a boy.
I'll kiss you just this one time,
But will never do so any more."

Chorus:
　　"For I'm going to be a better girl,
　　I'm never going to kiss again.
　　I'm afraid my mother will find it out,
　　And it will give her pain.
　　You may walk and talk and hold my hand,
　　But kissing is a crime.

I'll never kiss you any more
Until the next time."

Come all of you young boys,
A lesson learn from this.
If she thinks you will not tell,
She's sure to give you a kiss.

60
James and A

This humorous courting song is typical of several in this volume which treat courtship in a light vein. The title as it stands now is nonsense. What it was originally I do not know, possibly something like "Jameson A." I have two texts, from people who associated together several years ago and possibly learned the title one from the other. I have not seen the song in any other collection.

A

"James and A," sung by Mrs. Della Collins, Vernon, Lamar County, 1952.

James and A, it can-not be al-though you know so

well, I love you as I've of-ten said, yes, more than

ton-gues can tell.

James and A, it cannot be,
Although you know so well,
I love you as I've often said,
Yes, more than tongues can tell.

James, do not tease me any more.
I cannot kiss you you know
Because it's very wrong indeed;
Grandmother told me so.

James, do not look so sad,
Just take your arms away.
It will not be so very long
Until our wedding day.

But when we are dressed and ready for church,
And just before we go,
It won't be wrong to kiss you then;
Grandmother told me so.

But if you cannot wait till then,
I do not like to see you
Look so downcast and sad,
Suppose you just kiss me.

B

"James and A," sung by Miss Drucilla Hall, Millport, Lamar County, 1952.

James and A, it cannot be
Although you know so well,
I love you as I've often said,
Yes, more than tongue can tell.

I cannot kiss you I know
Because it's very wrong.
Indeed. . . . .
Grandmother told me so.

When we're dressed and ready for church,
And just before we go,
It won't be wrong to kiss you then,
Grandmother told me so.

Do not look so sad, my love,
Just take your arms away.
It will not be so very long
Before our wedding day.

But if you cannot wait till then,
I do not like to see
You look so downcast and so sad,
So suppose you just kiss me.

61
I Don't Know Why I Feel So Shy

Forthright declarations of need for love are usually given in funny songs, as in this case. I have not found this song in any collection, and have only one text. Similar songs appear elsewhere in this volume.

"I Don't Know Why I Feel So Shy," sung by Mrs. A.J. Shea, Sheffield, Colbert County, 1953. She might have learned it in Mississippi forty years ago.

I don't know why that I feel so shy Ev-'ry time I

look in-to my hon-ey's eye. He's quite po-lite, and he

treats me right, Yet when he's a-round I al-ways shake

with fright. I've been told that he thinks me cold,

Though my lov-ing heart is worth its weight in gold. So

yes-ter-day in a ner-vous way I sim-ply had to go to him

Chorus

and say: "I'd like a lit-tle lov-ing now and then, If the

lov-ing one were you. I've been miss-ing all the kiss-ing

that all oth-er men give their sweet-hearts true. So put

your arms a-round me and don't let go Un-til I tell you

when. Though I'm shy I of-ten sigh for some lov-ing now

and then.

I don't know why I feel so shy
Ev'ry time I look into my honey's eye.
He's quite polite, and he treats me right.
Yet when he's around I always shake with fright.
I've been told that he thinks me cold,
Though my loving heart is worth its weight in gold.
So yesterday in a nervous way
I simply had to go to him and say:

Chorus:
    "I'd like a little loving now and then,
    If the loving one were you.
    I been missing all the kissing
    That all other men give their sweethearts true.
    So put your arms around me and don't let go
    Until I tell you when.
    Though I'm shy I often sigh
    For some loving now and then."

When I said this, joy oh bliss,
Honey gave me a tender loving kiss.
Then as we strolled and love tales told,
I couldn't help but think that I'd been over bold.
My cheeks turned red, but Honey said,
"Don't you think it's time that you and I were wed?"
I answered, "Yes," and I really guess
The secret that he was glad to know that I confessed.

62
Once I Was Single, Boo Hoo Hoo Hoo

The crying laments about being married are not so common as are the simple regrets. This song is different, too, in being a dialogue between husband and wife. I have not found it in any collection.

"Once I Was Single," sung by Mrs. Nancy Ann Bates, Crane Hill, Cullman County, 1953. She has known it for around seventy years.

Once I was sin-gle, boo hoo hoo hoo. Oh, once I was

sin-gle, boo hoo hoo hoo. I saw noth-ing but peace and

plea-sure, Fa la did-dle did-dle, fa la lay. I saw noth-ing

but peace and plea-sure, fa la da day.

Once I was single, boo hoo hoo hoo.
Oh, once I was single, boo hoo hoo hoo.
I saw nothing but peace and pleasure,
Fa la diddle diddle, fa la lay.
I saw nothing but peace and pleasure,
Fa la da day.

Oh, now I've got married, boo hoo hoo hoo.
Oh, now I've got married, boo hoo hoo hoo.
Now I see nothing but a pack of trouble,
Fa la diddle diddle, fa la lay.
I see nothing but a pack of trouble,
Fa la da day.

You told me you loved me, boo hoo hoo hoo.
You told me you loved me, boo hoo hoo hoo.
If I did I told you a story,
Fa la diddle diddle, fa la lay.
If I did I told you a story,
Fa la da day.

My heart is almost broken, boo hoo hoo hoo.
My heart is almost broken, boo hoo hoo hoo.

If it's broke it's mighty easy broken,
Fa la diddle diddle, fa la lay.
If it's broke it's mighty easy broken,
Fa la da day.

I'll go away and leave you, boo hoo hoo hoo.
I'll go away and leave you, boo hoo hoo hoo.
If you go you can just keep a-going,
Fa la diddle diddle, fa la lay.
If you go you can just keep a-going,
Fa la da day.

63
Early In The Spring When I Was Young

This song, according to Barry *(The New Green Mountain Songster,* pp. 233-4), "was first printed, without music, by H. De Marsan, on a broadside, at some time between 1860 and 1878." Brown (II, 344) gives a short bibliography and two full texts. The one Alabama text is hardly more than a fragment.

"Early In The Spring When I Was Young," sung by Mrs. Nancy Ann Bates, Crane Hill, Cullman County, 1953.

So ear-ly in the spring when I was young, The flowers they bloomed and the lit-tle birds sung. Nev-er was a bo-dy as hap-py as I When my sol-dier boy came nigh.

Chorus

Sol la do, la do sol, la do me meme's she la do re. Soul to God, the bo-dy and the sea. The dark blue waves came a-roll-ing o-ver me.

So early in the spring when I was young
The flowers they bloomed and the little birds sung.
Never was a body as happy as I,
When my soldier boy came nigh.

Chorus:
    Sol la do la do sol la do me meme's she la do re.
    Soul to God the body and the sea,
    The dark blue waves came rolling over me.
    Sol la do la do sol lad do me mem's she la do re.
    Soul to God the body and the sea,
    The dark blue waves came a-rolling over me.

Adieu, my loving girl, adieu,
It grieves my heart to part with you.
The hour has come that I must go.
So read your mind, I'd like to know.

64

Boys, Keep Away From the Girls

This humorous song is probably American. Gilbert *(Lost Chords,* pp. 103-105) says this song was sung very successfully by Matt O'Reardon, a successful entertainer in the "hard-schooled free and easies" of the 70's. It was a follow up to the song "Marriage Bells," and was succeeded by "the comic highspot of the evening," when the audience asked for "Her Age It Was Red." As a folk song "Boys, Keep Away From The Girls" has not been widely reported. In Brown (II, 485) there is a two-stanza and chorus text and a reference to Henry *(Songs Sung in the Southern Appalachians,* p. 34). Randolph (III, 105) has two texts and a reference to Marchant's *Gargling Oil Songster* (n.p., c. 1885). The L.C. Checklist (pp. 15; 36; 283) reports texts from Ohio, North Carolina, Kentucky, and Texas. In Alabama the song is relatively popular; perhaps more popular than my two texts would seem to indicate. My informants would shudder to think of the earlier popular use of the song.

A

"Boys, Keep Away From The Girls," contributed by Mrs. Guy B. Johnson, Oneonta, Blount County, 1953, from a manuscript ballad book written down some thirty years ago.

O love is just such a very funny thing
It catches the young and the old.
It serves you like a plate of boarding house hash,
And many a man it's sold.
It makes you feel like a fresh water eel,
And causes your head for to swim.
You'll lose your mind, for love is blind,
And empties your pocketbook as well.

Chorus:
Boys, keep away from the girls, I say,
And give them plenty of room.
You'll find when you wed
They'll bang you on the head
With the bald headed end of the broom.

When a man has gone with a pretty little girl,
He talks as gentle as a dove.
He calls her his honey and spends all his money

For to show her he's solid on his love.
When his money is all gone and his clothes are in rags,
He finds the old saying is true:
That a bird in hand is worth two in the bush;
But what is he going to do?

When married folks have a lots of cash,
Their love is firm and strong.
But when they have to live on hash,
Their love don't last so long.
With a wife and seventeen half starved kids,
I tell you it's no fun,
When the butcher comes around to collect his bill
With a dog and a double barreled gun.

Young fellows, just take my advice I say,
And don't be in a hurry for to wed.
You'll think you're in clover till the honeymoon is over,
And then you'll wish you was dead.
With a cross eyed baby on each knee
And a wife with a plaster on her nose,
You'll think true love don't run so smooth
When you have to wear second handed clothes.

When the rent is high and the kids all cry
Cause they got no grub for to chaw,
You'll holler for your son to load up his gun
While you vaccinate your mother-in-law.

B

"Boys, Keep Away From The Gals, I Say," sung by Mrs. Nola Browne, Millport, Lamar County, 1951. She says it must be a hundred years old.

Young fel-lows, just take my ad-vice And don't be in a hur-ry for to wed. You'll find when you wed she'll bang you till you're dead With the bald-head-ed end of the broom. Boys, keep a-way from the gals, I say, And give them lots of room. You will find when you're wed, she'll bang you till you're dead With a bald-head-ed end of the broom.

Young fellows, just take my advice,
And don't be in a hurry for to wed.
You'll find when you're wed
She'll bang you till you are dead
With a bald-headed end of the broom.

Boys, keep away from the gals, I say,
And give them lots of room.
You'll find when you're wed
She'll bang you till you are dead
With a bald-headed end of the broom.

With a cross-eyed baby on each knee
And a wife with a plaster on her nose,
I'll tell you, boys, it's no fun
When the butcher comes around to collect his bill
With a dog and a double-barreled gun.

With a wife and seventeen housefull kids
I'll tell you it's no fun,
When the butcher comes around to collect his bill
With a dog and a double-barreled gun.

65
Old Straw Bonnet

This piece might well have been originally a play-party song. All such associations, however, have now disappeared, at least in the mind of my informant, and it has become only a "silly song" sung only for fun. I have not found it elsewhere.

"Old Straw Bonnet," sung by Miss Drucilla Hall, Millport, Lamar County, 1952. She has known it at least forty years.

Come a-long, boys, and let's go to meet-ing; Come
a-long, boys, and let's go to meet-ing; Come a-long, boys,
and let's go to meet-ing. And wear our old straw bon-nets.

Come along, boys, and let's go to meeting,
Come along, boys, and let's go to meeting,
Come along, boys, and let's go to meeting,
And wear our old straw bonnets.

Come along, girls, and let's go with them,
Come along, girls, and let's go with them,
Come along, girls, and let's go with them,
And wear our old straw bonnets.

Mama, oh, Mama, I won't go to meeting,
Mama, oh, Mama, I won't go to meeting,
Mama, oh, Mama, I won't go to meeting,
And wear my old straw bonnet.

No, no, Johnny, you can't go to meeting,
No, no, Johnny, you can't go to meeting,
No, no, Johnny, you can't go to meeting,
And wear your old straw bonnet.

Never mind, Johnny, I'll tell your papa,
Never mind, Johnny, I'll tell your papa,
Never mind, Johnny, I'll tell your papa,
Where you go a-courting.

66
Shoemaker's Song

This funny song, like so many, does not have only one theme. It starts out talking about the shoemaker and changes to any kind of nonsense stanza that presents itself. Such songs are popular, though often individual songs are limited in dissemination. I have not found this piece in other collections. I have only one text.

"Shoemaker's Song," sung by Mr. Andrew Aldrich, Hubbertville, Fayette County, 1953. He has known it some forty years.

Mar-ried me a wife and I set-tled here for life.

She had no shoes; I had no time to make them, Tom a link,

ta link, tom a link ta lar-ry. Oh, she is my dear.

Married me a wife and I settled here for life.
She had no shoes, I had no time to make them,
Tom a link, ta link, tom a link ta larry.
Oh, she is my dear.

You furnish the awl and I'll furnish the leather,
And we'll try sticking together,
Tom a link, ta link, tom a link ta larry.
Oh, she is my dear.

I didn't have but one old hen, I sot her in the kitchen,
She sot for a week on a dozen eggs, and didn't hatch but one little chicken,
Tom a link, ta link, tom a link ta larry.
Oh, she is my dear.

I didn't have but one old steer, I always drove to meeting.
They always knowed it was me when they heard my wagon squeaking,
Tom a link, ta link, tom a link ta larry.
Oh, she is my dear.

I didn't have but one old cow, she didn't have but one old horn.
She give me plenty of milk and I fed her well on corn,
Tom a link, ta link, tom a link ta larry.
Oh, she is my dear.

67
Dumma Locy Locy

This piece is the nonsense song carried to an extreme. Like words in the "holler" (see my article "Some Notes on the Southern 'Holler'," JAFL, LXVII, 75-77) the expressions in this kind of song are used only as a means of singing, the vehicle of sound. They are literally nonsense. I have not seen this piece in any other collection. As a person would expect, I have found only one informant to sing it.

"Dumma Locy Locy," sung by Mr. Ulysses Faught, Saragossa, Walker County, 1953.

Dum-ma rum-ma lo-cy, dum doe doe, 'um-ma rum-ma lo-cy, doe doe. Dum-ma rum-ma lo-cy, doe doe doe. And I nev-er saw a new sweet 'thout I sang a love song.

Dumma rumma locy, dum doe doe,
Dumma rumma locy, doe doe,
Dumma rumma locy, doe doe doe,
Never saw a new sweet 'thout I sang a love song.

Dumma rumma locy, dum doe doe,
Dumma rumma locy, doe doe,
Dumma rumma locy, doe doe doe,
Never saw a new babe but told her that I loved some.

Dumma rumma locy, dum doe doe,
Dumma rumma locy, doe doe,
Dumma rumma locy, doe doe doe,
Never saw a pretty girl but what I loved her so.

68
Rolling River

There are several songs — and fragments — which echo the words "rolling river," but this Alabama text bears no further resemblance to them. For a brief bibliography of such songs see Randolph (III, 170). These stanzas recorded in Alabama — they do not constitute a song — perhaps are the remains of a banjo or fiddle song. Their lack of continuity implies interrupted singing — as in the case of a banjo or fiddle song.

"Rolling River," sung by Miss Drucilla Hall, Millport, Lamar County, 1952. She probably learned it from her father.

Pass-ing sheep and rock-ing po-ny, My wife

died and no ba-lo-ney. Ha ha ha roll-ing riv-er,

My wife died and left me a wid-der.

Passing sheep and rocking pony,
My wife died and no baloney.
Ha ha ha rolling river,
My wife died and left me a widder.

All night long I want your daughter
To milk my cow and tote me water.
Ha ha ha rolling river,
My wife died and left me a widder.

Rolling river and falling water,
Some old man's gonna lose his daughter,
Ha ha ha rolling river,
My wife died and left me a widder.

69
Little Black Mustache

The Brown Collection (II, 479) says this song is "clearly a music hall production." perhaps that is why it is especially popular with the folk in the South, and in Alabama. See Brown and Randolp (III, 128) for references. I have eight texts. All are practically identical with the one printed here except that all others telescope the story into six or seven stanzas.

A

"Little Black Mustache," sung by Miss Drucilla Hall, Millport, Lamar County, 1952.

I used to have a charm-ing beau; I loved him dear

as life. I thought the time would sure-ly come when I

would be his wife.

I used to have a charming beau;
I loved him dear as life.
I thought the time would really come
When I would be his wife.

His pockets they were lined with gold;
He really cut a dash:
A diamond ring, a watch and chain;
He wore a black mustache.

He came to see me one Sunday night.
He stayed till almost three.
He said he never loved a girl
As well as he loved me.

He said we'd live in grandest style,
For he had lots of cash,
And then he pressed upon my lips
Those little black mustache.

One day there came a sour old maid;
She owned her weight in gold.
She wore false hair; she wore false teeth.
She was forty-five years old.

He carelessly deserted me
Just for this old maid's cash.
And now I lost my charming beau
Who wore the black mustache.

And now they're living just across the street
In a little mansion bold.
She married him for his black mustache;
He married her for her gold.

Now, girls, beware of my sad fate
And do not be so rash.
Just leave along those gents who wear
Those little black mustache.

B

"Little Black Mustache," sung by Mrs. Leila Robertson, Millport, Lamar County, Alabama, 1952. Mrs. Robertson, who died in 1953, was Miss Hall's sister. Though they had had close association all through their lives, Mrs. Robertson's version is different from her sister's. It has only seven stanzas and a slightly different tune.

I oncet did have a charm-ing beau; I loved him

dear as life. I thought the time would sure-ly come

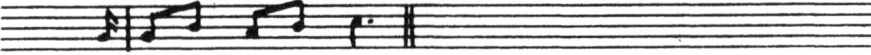

Then I would be his wife.

C

"Little Black Mustache," sung by Mrs. Velma Blakeney, Newtonville, Fayette County, 1952, from a manuscript dated 1902. Six stanzas.

D

"Charming Black Mustache," sung by Mrs. Guy J. Johnson, Oneonta, Blount County, 1953. Six stanzas.

E

"Little Black Mustache," sung by Mrs. Mary Crowder, Sulligent, Lamar County, 1952. Six stanzas.

On, I once had a hand-some beau; I loved as dear

as life. I thought the time would sure-ly come when I

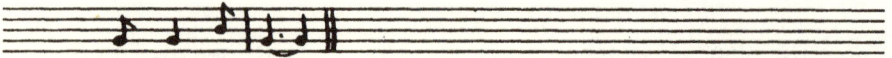

would be his wife.

F

"Little Black Mustache," sung by Mrs. Mary Todd, Sulligent, Lamar County, 1952. Five stanzas.

G

"My Charming Beau," sung by Mrs. Roma Hankins, Vernon, Lamar County, 1952. Six stanzas.

Once I had a charm-ing beau. I loved him dear-er

than life. I thought the time would sure-ly come when I

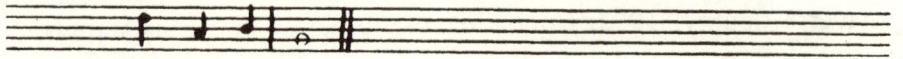

would be his wife.

70
Devilish Mary

This old English song has not been widely recovered in America. Some American versions retain English references; others are thoroughly Americanized. The song has been reported from Kentucky (Sharp, *English Folk-Songs from the Southern Appalachians*, II, 200), Virginia Davis, *Folk-Songs from Virginia*, p. 66) and the Ozarks (Randolph, III, 186-190). The L.C. Checklist (pp. 75-6) lists five entries. My three texts indicate a continued popularity in Alabama.

A

"Dev'lish Mary," sung by Mrs. Monroe Perkins, Crossville, Lamar County, 1952.

Once I was young and fool-ish, Thought I nev-er could mar-ry. Fell in love with a pret-ty lit-tle girl, And sure e-nough we did mar-ry. Ro-sum a dink tum a dur-ly, The pret-ti-est lit-tle girl I ev-er did see. Her name was Dev-'lish Mar-y.

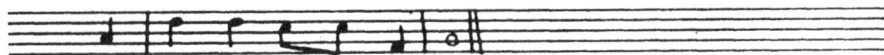

Once I was young and foolish,
Thought I never could marry.
Fell in love with a pretty little girl,
And sure enough we did marry.

Chorus:
 Ro-sum a dink tum a dur-ly,
 The prettiest little girl I ever did see.
 Her name was Dev'lish Mary.

We hadn't been married but about three weeks,
She got as mean as the devil.
Ever' time I looked cross-eyed at her
She knocked me down with the shovel.

She washed my clothes in the old soap suds.
She filled my back with switches.
She let me know right at the start
She aimed to wear the britches.

We hadn't been married but about six weeks,
Decided we better be parted.
She packed up her little duds
And down the road she started.

If I ever marry again or a-tall,
It won't be for love or riches.
I'll marry a girl about two feet tall
Where she can't wear my britches.

B

"Dev'lish Mary," sung by Mrs. Crosley, Vernon, Lamar County, 1952. Two stanzas and chorus.

C

"Dev'lish Mary," sung by Mr. J.H. McKenzie, Sulligent, Lamar County, 1952. A fragment, but different. Tune is Yankee Doodle.

As I walked out to London Street,
From there to Londonderry,
There I met a pretty little Miss,
And I called her Dev'lish Mary.

We made it up one night
That we should marry next Thursday.
. . . .
. . . .

Next time I marry,
I'll marry for love not for riches.
I'll tell you, boys, it's hard on a man,
When the woman wears the britches.

71
Fare You Well, Sister Phoebe

This comic piece undoubtedly used to be a play-party song. But it is sung now only as a comic item, as much of the play-party element has disappeared. The tune is kindred to but the text different from "Old Sister Phoebe" in Wolford *(The Play-Party in Indiana,* p. 80). The L.C. Checklist reports a similar title from Indiana, Arkansas and Virginia.

"Fare You Well, Sister Phoebe," sung by Miss Drucilla Hall, Millport, Lamar County, 1952.

Fare you well, sis-ter Phoe-be, fare you well,

For I hate to leave you, I love you so well. Oak grows

tall, pine grows slim. Buy you up a true love, true love.

Buy you up a true love, and bring it home to him.

Fare you well, sister Phoebe, fare you well,
For I hate to leave you, I love you so well.
Oak grows tall,
Pine grows slim.
Buy you a true love, true love,
Buy you a true love, and bring it home to him.

Fare you well, brother Longnose, fare you well,
For I hate to leave you, I love you so well.

72
A Farmer's Life For Me

This song has been reported only once before, in the Brown Collection (III, 177), as a fragment. There it is only a series of animal sounds. In this one Alabama text the song is fuller and has more motivation, though it seems a mixture of at least two songs. The tune is good, especially for a baritone. The song allows a great virtuosity in phrasing, a fact which probably implies greater popularity for the song than my one text would seem to indicate.

"A Farmer's Life For Me," sung by Mr. W.A. "Lawyer" Davis, Aliceville, Pickens County, 1952.

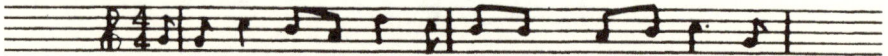

A farm-er, a farm-er, a farm-er's life for me. If
ev-er I get mar-ried, a farm-er's girl 'twill be. The
cows in the mea-dow, they go moo, moo, moo. The dogs in
the back-yard, they go bow, bow bow. The cats on the
back fence, they go meow, meow, meow. And the roost-er
he says cock-a-doo-dle do. Doo-dle dum, doo-dle dum do,
that's what he played on his harp. Doo-dle dum, doo-dle dum

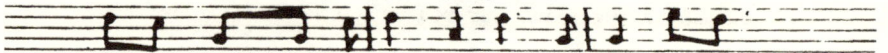

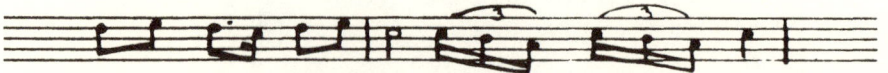

do, he played it from mid-night to dawn. Doo-dle dum,

doo-dle dum do, I tell it all to you. He won the heart of

his sweet Mar-y Jane, As he played on his doo-dle dum do.

A farmer's, a farmer's, a farmer's life for me.
If ever I get married, a farmer's girl 'twill be.
The cows in the meadow, they go moo, moo, moo.
The dogs in the backyard, they go bow, bow woo.
The cats on the back fence, they go meow, meow, meow.
And the rooster, he says cocka-doodle-do.
Doodle dum doodle dum do — that's what he played on his harp.
Doodle dum doodle dum do — he played it from midnight to dawn.
Doodle dum doodle dum do — I tell it all to you.
He won the heart of his sweet Mary Jane
As he played on his doodle dum do.

73
Little Automobile Song

Songs about the newfangled automobile, usually the malfunctioning of it, are not unusual in folk tradition. This piece I have not found any where else.

"Little Automobile Song," sung by Mrs. Ernest Phillips, Tuscaloosa, Tuscaloosa County, 1953.

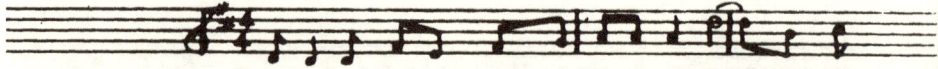

John-ny Mc-Con-ny bought an au-to-mo-bile. He took

his girl-ie for a ride one Sun-day. John-ny was dressed

up in his best Sun-day coat. She nest-led close to his

side. Ev-'ry thing was love-ly till they got down the

road, Then some-thing hap-pened to the old ma-chine-ry.

That en-gine got his goat. Off came his hat and coat.

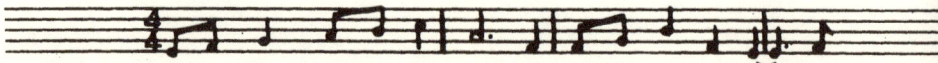

Ev-'ry thing need-ed re-pair. He had to get un-der, get

out and get un-der. Then get back at the wheel. On the way

to town she started to hug and kiss, And this darned old

en-gine it would miss. He'd have to get un-der, get out

and get un-der, Fix up his au-to-mo-bile.

Johnny McConny bought an automobile.
He took his girlie for a ride on Sunday.
Johnny was dressed up in his best Sunday coat.
She nestled close to his side.
Ev'rything was lovely till they got down the road,
Then something happened to the old machinery.
That engine got his goat,
Off came his hat and coat.
Ev'rything needed repair.
He had to get under, get out and get under,
Then get back at the wheel.
On the way to town she starts to hug and kiss,
And this darned old engine it would miss.
He'd have to get under, get out and get under,
To fix up his automobile.

74
The Burglar Man

The Brown Collection (II, 465) has one text. The editors call it a "piece of music-hall humor," as it doubtless is. Hudson *(Folksongs of Mississippi,* pp. 249-250) prints it, and there is a copy from Kentucky in the Archieve of American Folk Song. Davis *(Folk-Songs of Virginia,* pp. 178-179) lists the title. The L.C. Checklist (p. 42) reports a text from Kentucky. I have only one text.

"Burglar Man," sung by Miss Drucilla Hall, Millport, Lamar County, 1952. She has known it thirty-five years.

Sto-ry I will tell you of a burg-lar man Start-ed to rob a house. Climbed in the win-dow, crawled un-der the bed As qui-et as a mouse.

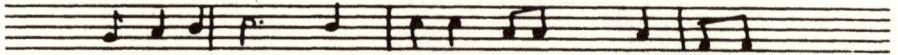

Story I will tell you of a burglar man
Started to rob a house.
Climbed in the window, crawled under the bed,
As quiet as a mouse.

Eleven o'clock till the maid came in.
"It is so dark," she said.
She was thinking forever of the pain in her heart.
She forgot to look under the bed.

Well, under the bed the burglar man
Quietly he lay.
He certainly saw a sight that night
That made his hair turn gray.

She taken out her teeth and her big glass eye,
And the hair came off her head.
That burglar man had nigh unto a fit,
When he crawled from under the bed.

Well, from under the bed the burglar came.
He was a total wreck.

That old maid never hollered at all,
Just grabbed him around the neck.

And from her drawer a revolver she drew
And to that burglar she said:
"Young man, you've got to marry me
Or I'll shoot off the top of your head."

He looked at her teeth and her big glass eye,
And he had no place to scoot.
So he just hollered to the gods above,
Saying, "Woman, for the lord's sake, shoot!"

75
Pretty Fanny O

This adaptation of the English song "Pretty Girl of Derby O" has been reported by Belden *(Ballads and Songs,* p. 169), with bibliography, and Brown (III, 456). Sharp *(English Folksongs from the Southern Appalachians,* II, 59-61) gives four texts and shows that the song is found in Grieg *(Folk-Song of the Northeast of Scotland),* Christie *(Traditional Ballad Airs)* and in a Pitts broadside entitled "Pretty Peggy of Derby." The one text I have recovered differs more or less from the reported pieces.

"Pretty Fanny O," sung by Miss Drucilla Hall, Millport, Lamar County, 1952. She does not remember when or how she learned it, but probably some thirty-five years ago from the singing of neighborhood girls.

Come skipping down the stairs, pretty Fanny O.
Come skipping down the stairs, pretty Fanny O.
Come skipping down the stairs, combing back your hair,
And bid farewell to your mammy o,
And bid farewell to your mammy o.

What would your mammy think, pretty Fanny O?
What would your mammy think, pretty Fanny O?
What would your mammy think to hear the guineas chink,
And the sovereigns to clink so plainly o,
And the sovereigns to clink so plainly o?

Will you marry me, pretty Fanny O?
Will you marry me, pretty Fanny O?
Will you marry me, a lady you will be
As fine as any in the country o,
As fine as any in the country o.

In the buggy you shall ride, pretty Fanny O.
In the buggy you shall ride, pretty Fanny O.
In the buggy you shall ride. Your true love by your side.
And the soldiers marching before you o,
And the soldiers marching before you o.

76
Man Without a Woman

This comic battle of the sexes is undoubtedly a fragment of a music-hall, minstrel or songster piece. It is an excellent piece for harmonizing, as I learned by my informant's fine rendition. I have not found it elsewhere.

"Man Without a Woman," sung by Mr. W.A. "Lawyer" Davis, Aliceville, Pickens County, 1952. He might have learned it while a student at the University of Alabama.

A man without a woman is like an arm without a hand,
Like a boat without a rudder, like a fish without a tail.
A man without a woman is like a ship without a sail.
But the saddest thing in this old world to me
Is a woman without a man.

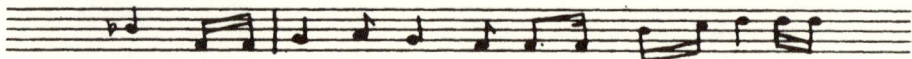

77
How Sad

This comic lamentation of the married man is one of several in this volume representing the type. This one has a lighter and less satiric tone than the usual. I have not see it reported in any other collection. I have only one text.

"How Sad," sung by Miss Drucilla Hall, Millport, Lamar County, 1952. She has known it about thirty years, and probably learned it from her father.

Be-hold in me a mar-ried man whose life is full of

gloom. How sad, oh, how sad. My eyes have lost their

bright-ness, my cheeks their ros-y bloom. How sad, oh,

how sad. Your face has taught a les-son that I nev-er can

for-get. All the trou-bles and the tri-als, poor dear

soul you must have met. Oh, yes, but I have trou-bles

that I have-n't told you yet. How sad, oh, how sad.

Behold in me a married man whose life is full of gloom.
How sad, oh, how sad.
My eyes have lost their brightness, my cheeks their rosy bloom.
How sad, oh, how sad.
Your face has taught a lesson I never can forget,
All the troubles and the trials, poor soul, you must have met.
Oh, yes, but I have troubles that I haven't told you yet.
How sad, oh, how sad.

I've walked the floor at midnight with a child upon my chest,
How sad, oh, how sad,
While my darling little wife snores away in peaceful rest.
How sad, oh, how sad.
I have to wash the dishes, all the clothes, and mop the floor,
How sad, oh, how sad,
While my wifey talks of suffrage with Mike Clooney's wife next door.
How sad, oh, how sad.

78
The Boys Won't Do To Trust

The Brown Collection (II, 486) gives a scant list of reportings of this song — from Kentucky and Virginia. Randolph (III, 216) gives three texts. The L.C. Checklist (pp. 36; 116) reports texts from Kentucky and Arkansas. In Alabama it is a popular song. I have four rather complete texts.

A

"The Boys Won't Do To Trust," sung by Mrs. Mary Crowder, Sulligent, Lamar County, 1952.

The boys, I know, are hand-some and sweet as sweet can be. I know I love them dear-ly; say aren't you just like me? They make us charm-ing sweet-hearts but they not.........To pin them down to busi-ness;

Chorus

The boys won't do to trust. The boys won't do to trust, girls; The boys won't do to trust. They'll do to love and look at. Put the boys won't do to trust.

The boys I know are handsome
And sweet as sweet can be.
I know I love them dearly;
Say, aren't you just like me?
They make us charming sweethearts
But they not . . . .
To pin them down to business:
The boys won't do to trust.
Chorus:
    The boys won't do to trust, girls,

The boys won't do to trust.
They'll do to love and look at,
But the boys won't do to trust.

Your sweetheart says he loves you,
And swears that he adores.
He writes you charming letters
And signs that he adores.
But you compare with others
As diamond rings with myrrh.
Just as I told you rather,
The boys won't do to trust.

I know you'll sit and wonder
At me in deep surprise,
How one so young as I am
Could be so wonderfully wise.
Well, well, I hate to tell you,
But I suppose I must.
I found out by experience
The boys won't do to trust.

B

"The Boys Won't Do To Trust," sung by Mrs. Flora Phillips, Cullman, Cullman County, 1953, from a manuscript in her possession. Three stanzas. Identical with A.

C

"Boys Won't Do To Trust," sung by Miss Drucilla Hall, Millport, Lamar County, 1953. Two stanzas. Similar to A.

D

"The Boys Won't Do To Trust," sung by Mrs. Monroe Perkins, Crossville, Lamar County, 1952. Two stanzas. Last is similar to second of A. The first is different:

The boys, I know, are hand-some, and sweet as sweet

can be. I own I love them dear-ly; say aren't you just

like me? I own that they're much brav-er than we poor

tim-id girls. I know they chew to-bac-co and smoke and

swear and curse. I know they drink cheap liq-uor and

will get on a burst. I know you've got to watch them,

For the boys won't do to trust. The boys won't do to

trust, girls, The boys won't do to trust. They'll do to

love and look at, But the boys won't do to trust.

The boys, I know, are handsome
And sweet as sweet can be.
I own I love them dearly;
Say, aren't you just like me?
I own that they're much braver
Than we poor timid girls.
I know they chew tobacco
And smoke and swear and curse.
I know they drink cheap liquor
And will go on a burst.
I know you've got to watch them,
For the boys won't do to trust.

79
Sorghum Molasses

This Georgia-Alabama mixture was reported in the Brown Collection (III, 460), in one version. The L.C. Checklist (p. 162) reports a similar title from North Carolina. I have one Alabama text, which has been sung in one family for the past sixty years.

"By and By, or Sorghum Molasses," sung by Miss Malissa Richardson, Kennedy, Lamar County, 1952.

A sol-dier sat by the road one day, And he was look-ing ver-y gay. He had a quart of corn and meal, Which he had stole from an old Tar Heel. By and by, by and by. I'm gon-na mar-ry be-fore I die. By and by, by and by, Mar-ry a boy with a dark brown eye. No such boys, there's none sur-pass-es Good corn bread and sor-ghum mo-las-ses. By and by.

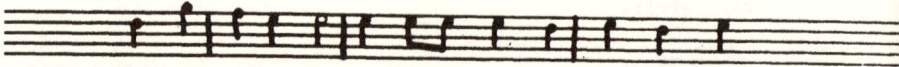

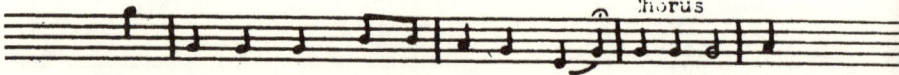

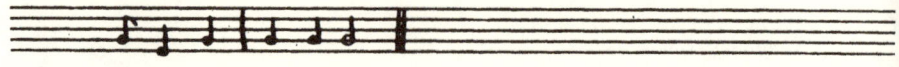

A soldier sat by the road one day
And he was feeling very gay.
He had a quart of corn and meal
Which he had stole from an old Tar Heel.
Chorus:
    By and by, by and by,
    I'm going to marry before I die.
    By and by, by and by,
    Marry a boy with a dark brown eye.
    No such boy, there's none surpasses
    Good corn break and sorghum molasses.
    By and by.

He made a fire to bake his bread,
And when 'twas done he left and said,
"There's nothing in this world surpasses
Good corn bread and sorghum molasses."

In Alabama a dish of peas,
In Tennessee just what you please,
In North Carolina tar and rosin,
But old Georgia goobers and sorghum.

As I went walking down the street,
A pretty Tar Heel I chanced to meet.
Says she, "Young man, are you a traveller?"
"No, my dear, I'm a goober grabbler."

Oh, by and by, by and by,
I'm bound to marry before I die.
And if ever you become a traveller,
Just call on this goober grabbler.

80
Common Bill

Probably of English origin, this humorous song is known and sung with enjoyment all over Alabama, as it is over much of the United States. For references to this country and England see Brown (II, 469) and Randolph (I, 427). For a note on its occurrence in songbooks see Kittredge (JAFL, XXXV, 364). I have not found it in the songsters I examined. All five of my Alabama informants sang this song as a "silly song," but all obviously enjoyed singing it.

A

"A Strange Fellow," sung by Mrs. Monroe Perkins, Crossville, Lamar County, 1952.

Let me tell you of a fel-ler, of a fel-ler I have seen. He's nei-ther white nor yel-ler, but he's al-to-geth-er green. His name is not hand-some, but it's on-ly com-mon Bill. He wants me to wed him, but I hard-ly think I will. Oh, I hard-ly think I will, oh, I hard-ly think I will. He wants me to wed him, but I hard-ly think I will.

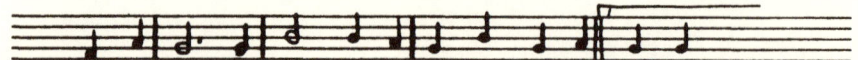

Let me tell you of a fellow, of a fellow I have seen.
He's neither white nor yellow, but he's altogether green.
His name is not handsome but it's only common Bill.
He wants me to wed him but I hardly think I will

Chorus:
    Oh, I hardly think I will, oh I hardly think I will.

He wants me to wed him, but I hardly think I will.

Oh, he came the other day and he made so long a stay,
Oh, I really thought the fellow never meant to go away.
Oh, I hardly think I will, oh I hardly think I will.
He wants me to wed him, but I hardly think I will.

He told me if I did not wed him he could not live another while.
You know the blessed Bible says you shall not kill.
So I thought the matter over, so I thought the matter over,
So I thought the matter over, and I rather guess I will.

Chorus:

B

"Common Bill," sung by Mrs. Mary Todd, Sulligent, Lamar County, 1952. Three stanzas and chorus. First stanza and chorus as A, but stanzas two and three are somewhat different and much clearer than in A:

Last night he came to see me and he made so long a stay
I began to think that fellow never meant to go away.
He said that we would travel, we would travel down life's hill,
We had better go together, but I hardly think I will.

He wrote me a letter; I will tell you what was in it.
He said if I didn't wed him be couldn't live another minute.
And you know the blessed Bible plainly says you must not kill.
So I've thought the matter over, and I rather think I will.

C

"I Rather Think I Will," sung by Miss Drucilla Hall, Millport, Lamar County, 1952. Two stanzas and chorus. First stanza as A. The second stanza begins, "I'm sure I would not choose him but the very deuce is in him."

D

"Common Bill," sung by Mrs. Susie Bell Hankins, Lamar County, 1952. Essentially same as A, but second stanza has second line, "I began to think the block head never meant to go away."

E

"Common Bill," sung by Mrs. Nettie Coleman, Tucson, Arizona, 1952. She learned it in Greene County, Alabama, forty years ago. A one-stanza fragment.

81
Want To Go A-Courting

The Brown Collection (III, 393) includes one text of this song, and it is discussed as a "widely known satire on frontier manners and condition." For a discussion of this aspect see Belden *(Ballads and Songs,* p. 426). For full references see also Randolph (III, 222). The two rather full Alabama texts indicate a certain popularity in the state.

A

"Want to Go A-Courting," sung by Miss Drucilla Hall, Millport, Lamar County, 1952. She sang of the bad conditions as though they might be in the same county with her.

Want to go a-court-ing, then I'll tell you where to go; Down at the old man's way down be-low, Down at the old man's way down be-low.

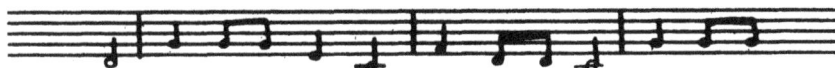

Want to go a-courting and I'll tell you where to go,
Down at the old man's way down below,
Down at the old man's way down below.

Floor's not swept cause they have no broom,
Children all squalling and the old folks gone,
Children all squalling and the old folks gone.

Heads not combed for they had no comb,
Old dirty clothes are hanging on the line,
Old dirty clothes are hanging on the line.

Old dirty dishes sitting on the shelf,
If you got one washed then you washed it yourself,
If you got one washed then you washed it yourself.

Got dinner ready and all sat to eat,
Called on me for to carve up the meat,
Called on me for to carve up the meat.

Had no knife, had no fork,
I sawed and I sawed but I couldn't make a mark,
I sawed and I sawed but I couldn't make a mark.

Carved it on the table, carved it on the floor,
Gave it a kick and sent it through the door,
Gave it a kick and sent it through the door.

Up stepped the old man and he had a gun,
One of them girls said, "Run, mister, run,"
One of them girls said, "Run, mister, run."

"Run, mister, run as hard as you can tear,
While I tangle my fingers in the old man's hair,
While I tangle my fingers in the old man's hair."

When they go to meeting I'll tell you how they dress,
Old black calico that's the very best,
Old black calico that's the very best.

Old black sack hemmed all around,
Old leather bonnet with a hole in the crown,
Old leather bonnet with a hole in the crown.

B

"Started Out Courting," sung by Mrs. Nettie Coleman, Tucson, Arizona, 1952. She learned it in Greene County, Alabama, forty years ago.

I start-ed out court-ing, didn't know where to go.

I went to a man's house a-way down be-low. The child-ren

were all cry-ing, and the old folks gone. The gals all

mad and their hair not combed. Gals all mad and their

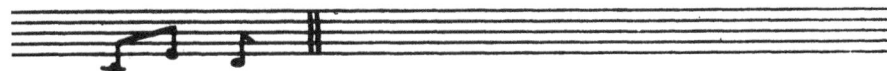

hair not combed.

I started out courting and didn't know where to go.
I went to a man's house away down below.
The children were all crying, and the old folks gone.
The gals all mad and their hair not combed.
The gals all mad and their hair not combed.

The old dirty dishes were sitting on the shelf.
If you got a clean plate you washed it yourself.
Trash was scattered in every room.
The house all littered and they had no broom.
The house all littered and they had no broom.

When they go to meeting, I'll tell you how they dress.
A dirty black dress and that is the best.
An old soiled apron greased all around.
An old leather bonnet with a hole in the crown.
An old leather bonnet with a hole in the crown.

They asked me to supper and I thought I'd go and see.
The first thing I seen was a piece o' tough beef.
They gave me an old knife, they gave me an old fork.
I sawed and I sawed, but I couldn't make a mark.
I gave it a kick and sent it out in the dark.

Out came the old man with a double-barrel gun.
One of the gals said, "Run, mister, run."
I stood and fought as brave as a bear
Till I got my hands tangled in the old man's hair.
Till I got my hands tangled in the old man's hair.

82

When I Was a Little Boy

This fragment of comic love song is hardly long enough to give any hint of the direction the song took. I have not found it in other collections, and I have only the one text.

"When I Was a Little Boy," sung by Mrs. Della Collins, Vernon, Lamar County, 1952. She has been singing it for at least thirty years.

When I was a ba-by boy in my cra-dle bough, The girls

would hug and kiss me then. They won't do it now.

When I was a baby boy
In my cradle bough,
The girls would hug and kiss me.
They won't do it now.

83
Don't Stay After Ten

This half-serious courting song has not been widely reported. The Brown Collection (III, 28) has two rather full versions. Randolph (III, 86) has one. Pound (*Syllabus*, 60) lists the title. I have not found it elsewhere. As my four texts would indicate, the song is more popular in Alabama than elsewhere.

A

"Oh Don't Stay After Ten," sung by Mrs. Nola Browne, Millport, Lamar County, 1951.

Oh don't stay after ten, my love,
Oh don't stay after ten.
But come again, my darling,
But don't stay after ten.

Oh don't stay after ten, my love,
Oh don't stay after ten.
For after ten the moments fly,
And I tremble again and again.

When down to breakfast next morning I go,
Papa will frown on me.
Says he: "My child, that beau of yours
Is going to hear from me.

"This sort of thing I will not have,
And when he comes again,
I'll walk right in and invite him out,
If he stays till after ten."

Oh don't stay after ten, my love,
Oh don't stay after ten.
But come again, my darling,
But don't stay after ten.

B

"Don't Stay After Ten," sung by Mrs. O.C. Powell, Titus, Elmore County, 1953.

I've one request to make of you
When next you come again

To see me in the evening,
Oh don't stay after ten.

Chorus:
  Oh don't stay after ten, my love,
  Oh don't stay after ten.
  But come again, my darling,
  And don't stay after ten.

For after ten the moments fly;
I tremble o'er and o'er,
Lest Mother's visage I should spy
Come peeping at the door.

You know you're welcome, darling,
The best beloved of men,
But many scoldings you have had
For staying after ten.

C

"Don't Stay After Ten," sung by the Richardson Sisters, Kennedy, Lamar County, 1952. Five stanzas same as A.

D

"Don't Stay After Ten," sung by Mrs. Mary Todd, Sulligent, Lamar County, 1952. Three stanzas, one, three and five of A.

Don't stay af-ter ten, my love, Oh, don't stay

af-ter ten. But come a-gain, my dar-ling And don't

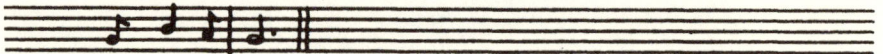

stay af-ter ten.

84
I'm Sighing To Catch A Nice Beau

This piece is a half-comic half-serious treatment of the plight of the unmarried girl, typical of several in this volume. My informant was aware of the comic aspects and sang the song with a broad smile. I have not found it elsewhere.

"I'm Sighing To Catch A Nice Beau," sung by Mrs. Nola Browne, Millport, Lamar County, 1952. She has known it around fifty-five years.

I'm sighing, I'm sighing,
I'm sighing to catch a nice beau.
And if I don't catch the right fellow,
My heart will be sad I know.
I'm sighing, I'm sighing,
I'm sighing to catch a nice beau.
And if I get the wrong fellow,
My heart will be sad I know.

85
My Wife's Gone Off And Left Me

The impossible-task motif is old but apparently not widespread. "The Elfin Knight" is perhaps one of the oldest songs to make use of the motif. For songs that impose impossible tasks as prerequisites to true love see Ashton *(A Century of Ballads,* pp. 315-318), *The Rosburghe Ballads* (VII, 295-296), JAFL, (XXX, 352-353), Wyman and Brockway *(Twenty Kentucky Mountain Songs,* p. 106), Logan *(A Pedlar's Pack of Ballads and Songs,* pp. 360-361), Gardner and Chickering *(Ballads and Songs of Southern Michigan,* pp. 385-386), and Morris *(Folksongs of Florida,* p. 152).

A

"My Wife's Gone Off and Left Me," mailed in to me anonymously, without music, 1953.

My wife she's gone off and she's left
Alone in this wide world to roam,
Of happiness and joy she bereft me.
She has gone off and left a good home.

I wrote her a letter last Tuesday.
I wrote it way out to Cawkee.
The answer came back this morning,
And this is what she said to me:

When the grocer don't put sand in sugar,
And the milkman don't make milk of chalk,
When Texas goes for Prohibition,
And women forget how to talk.

When the boys of this glorious Republic
Don't go out at night on a spree.
But stay right at home with their mammy
Then, my darling, I'll come back to thee.

Oh, wait till the gang on the corner
Refuses to drink from a bowl.
Wait till cashiers in Canada
Will bring back the boodle they've stole.

Wait till the girls quit flirting
And railroads run over the sea.

Wait till the baseball is snowed under,
Then, my darling, I'll come back to thee.

Wait till the flowers in springtime
Don't open their petals till fall,
The oyster, the clam and the codfish
Will dance a can can at the ball.

When all the old maids will have sweethearts,
And married people all agree.
When the man in the moon comes in a balloon,
Then, my darling, I'll come back to thee.

B

"Song," contributed by Mrs. Mattie Dewberry, Wedowee, Randolph County, 1953, from a manuscript in her possession. Four stanzas, the first four of A.

86
Good-Bye, Susan Jane

The satiric treatment of a girl who rejects a boy in love is not unusual in songs of the folk, as several pieces in this volume show.
This particular song is undoubtedly a minstrel piece. Owens *(Texas
Folk Songs,* p. 242) gives a text with three stanzas and chorus;
stanzas one and three are similar to my one and two, and the choruses are similar. Owens lists texts found in *Texas and Southwestern
Lore* ("Publications of the Texas Folk-Lore Society," VI, 134)
and in *Minstrel Songs Old and New* (1882; where the sheet music
is published).

"Good-Bye, Susan Jane," sung by Miss Drucilla Hall, Millport, Lamar
County, 1952. She has known it for at least thirty years but does
not remember how she learned it.

I went to see my Susan;
She met me at the door.
She told me that I needn't come
To see her any more.
She'd fell in love with Rufus Andrew Jackson Paine.
I looked her in the face and said:
"Good-Bye, Susan Jane.

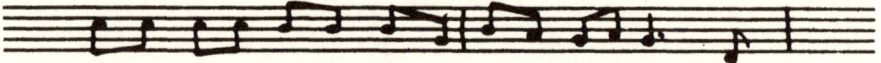

Chorus:
   Oh, Susan, quit your fooling
   And give your love to me.
   Oh give me back my heart again,
   And I will let you be.
   I once did love you dearly;
   I cannot love again.

I'm going away to leave you;
So good-bye, Susan Jane.

Her mouth was like a cellar;
Her foot was like a ham.
Her eyes were like an owl's at night;
Her voice was never calm.
Her hair was long and curly;
She looked just like a crane.
I bid good-bye to all my love;
So good-bye, Susan Jane.

Oh Susan so deceiving,
She'll never do to trust.
I threatened once to leave her,
And leave her now I must.
I ne'er will trust another
To cause me any pain.
I trusted her, and all the girls
Are just like Susan Jane.

87
Coochie Coo

Humorous treatments of love, courtship and mothers-in-law are numerous in folk songs, and in this volume. This piece might be the creation of Monroe H. Rosenfeld. In 1888 he published a "Kutchy, Kutchy, Coo!" (Spaeth, *History of Popular Music*, p. 232). Such nonsense songs have always been popular with the folk. I have not found this piece reported in any other collection. I have two texts.

A

"She's My Cootsie Coo," sung by Mrs. Mona Johnson, Vernon, Lamar County, 1952. She does not remember when she learned it.

Want to tell you a-bout my love. She's my dar-ling

tur-tle dove. Ma-ry Lize is her name, but she gets there

all the same.

Want to tell you about my love.
She's my darling turtle dove.
Mary Lize is her name,
But she gets there all the same.

Chorus:
    Oh, coochie, coochie, coochie coo,
    'Ou love 'e, and I love 'ou.
    Cheeks so red and eyes so blue.
    She's my darling cootsie coo.

I met her at the ten cent show,
Where so many darlings go.
Cheeks so red and eyes so blue,
She's my darling cootsie coo.

First time I went out to ride,
Took my darling by my side.

Asked her to be my little Lize,
Took my darling by surprise.

Said she'd always be my love
If she always found me true,
Cheeks so red and eyes so blue,
She's my darling cootsie coo.

B

"Coochie Coo," contributed by Mrs. Velma Blakeney, Newtonville, Fayette County, 1952, from a manuscript dated 1907.

I'll tell you about my love,
She's my darling turtle dove.
Mary Lize is her name,
But she gets there just the same.
I met her at a ten cent show,
Where so many darlings go.
Cheeks of red and eyes of blue,
She's my darling coochie coo.

Chorus:
    Oh, coochie, coochie, coochie coo,
    'Ou love I and I love 'ou.
    Cheeks of red and eyes of blue,
    She's my darling coochie coo.

One day as I went out to ride,
I took my darling by my side.
Sez I, "Be mine, my sweetest Lize,"
And it seemed to take her by surprise.
She said, "My love, I'll be your rue,
If I always find you true."
Cheeks of red and eyes of blue,
She's my darling coochie coo.

I hired a preacher with no sense.
I paid him cash of fifteen cents.
The knot was tied before I saw
My terrible, terrible mother-in-law.
She waded right in and at me flew.
She kissed me till I was black and blue.
She squeezed me till my bones came through,
And called me a darling coochie coo.

My mother-in-law is rough, 'tis true,
But you bet your life she gets there too.
And when she gets in one of her spats,
She's worse in the house than rough on rats.

She quarrels all day and snores all night.
Up the next morning and works to fight.
She pulls my hair and bumps my head,
Till I wish my mother-in-law was dead.

88
You Say You Love Me

Suspicion of lack of fidelity in love is the theme of many songs — both love and comic — among the folk. The following song is rather unusual in treatment, since it is both serious and comic at the same time. I have not found it reported from elsewhere, and I have only one version.

"You Say You Love Me," sung by Miss Drucilla Hall, Millport, Lamar County, 1952. She has known it for at least thirty years.

Ev-'ry time.................It seems there's

on-ly a doubt that you are fool-ing me, yes sir-ree. And

that feel-ing comes a-steal-ing, says you're not true.

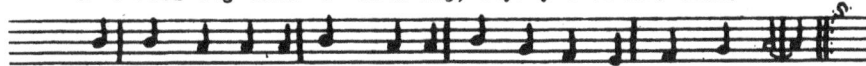

And that is why I sigh, why I cry, and why I think of you.

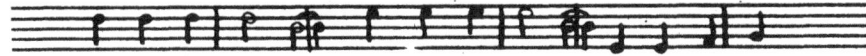

You say you love me, think o-eeans of me, But I'm a-fraid

you'll sing this song to some-bod-y else.

Ev'ry time. . . . .
It seems there's only a doubt that you are fooling me,
Yes, sirree.
And that feeling comes a-stealing, says you're not true,
And that is why I sigh, why I cry, and why I think of you.

Chorus:
    You say you love me, think oceans of me,
    But I'm afraid you'll sing this song to somebody else.
    You say you'll thrill me, with love you'll kill me,
    But I'm afraid you'll sing this song to somebody else.

Ev'ry time I come around to make a social call,
It seems I always find a strange hat in the hall.
I'm not suspicious, just superstitious,
But I'm afraid you'll sing this song to somebody else.

89
Oh, Where Is My Sweetheart?

This song has not been widely reported. The Brown Collection (III, 357) has three texts, but I have not found it elsewhere. The Brown headnote points out that the song is "of the same general temper" as "Adieu to Cold Weather," which is in Belden *(Ballads and Songs,* pp. 491-2). My one Alabama text is a localized version. Columbus (Mississippi), the town mentioned in the text, is some twenty-three miles from Millport and is the nearest town of any size. Beer is legal in Mississippi, whereas Lamar County has long since been dry. Columbus, therefore, has long been the place where Lamar County people go to let their hair down. As far as I know there has never been a "Famous Hotel" there. Probably the word means "notorious," and as such might refer to a house of ill-repute, although my informant would certainly be unconscious of any such overtones.

"Oh, Where Is My Sweetheart?" sung by Miss Drucilla Hall, Millport, Lamar County, 1952.

Oh, where is my sweetheart, can anyone tell,
Can anyone tell, can anyone tell?
Oh, where is my sweetheart, can anyone tell,
Can any, can anyone tell?

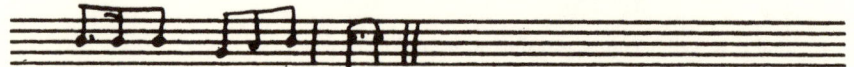

He's down in Columbus at the famous hotel,
At the famous hotel, at the famous hotel.

He's down in Columbus at the famous hotel,
At the famous, at the famous hotel.

He's courting another, I know just as well,
I know just as well, I know just as well.
He's courting another, I know just as well,
I know, I know just as well.

But there is another I love just as well,
I love just as well, I love just as well.
But there is another I love just as well,
I love, I love just as well.

And if you will listen his name I will tell,
His name I will tell, his name I will tell.
And if you will listen his name I will tell,
His own dear name I will tell.

It begins with a W and ends with an E,
And ends with an E, and ends with an E.
It begins with a W and ends with an E,
For his name is Willie, you see.

90
Lula Walls

Randolph (III, 101) reports one text and cites a text by C.V. Wheat (Aurora, Missouri, *Advertiser,* August 1, 1941) entitled "A Maiden Young and Fair." The L.C. Checklist (pp. 226; 247; 293) reports texts from New York City, Kentucky, North Carolina, Arkansas, and California. This piece is one of the most popular in Alabama. The texts are quite different, as are the tunes.

A

"Lula Walls," sung by Miss Drucilla Hall, Millport, Lamar County, 1952.

One eve-ning it was dark; I was stroll-ing through the park. She was sit-ting by the foun-tain all a-lone. I neat-ly tipped my hat and we be-gan to chat. She asked me to es-cort her to her home. Ev-'ry once and a while she would greet me with a smile; She asked me to her home a-lone to call. Oh, it must be jeal-ous-y that I know no one but me with that ag-gra-vat-ing beau-ty Lu-la Walls.

One evening it was dark;
I was strolling through the park.
She was sitting by the fountain all alone.
I neatly tipped my hat
And we began to chat.
She asked me to escort her to her home.

Every once and a while
She would greet me with a smile.
She asked me to her home alone to call.
Oh, it must be jealousy
For I know no one but me
With that aggravating beauty, Lula Walls.

One evening getting late
I met her at the gate.
I asked her if she'd wed me in the fall.
She only turned away
And nothing would she say,
That aggravating beauty, Lula Walls.

B

"Lula Walts," sung by Mrs. Mary Crowder, Sulligent, Lamar County, 1952. She believed she has sung it for the last forty years.

I know a maid-en ev-er so fair. She has ev-er

gold-en hair. She's as pure as an an-gel from a-bove.

She has stole my heart a-way and I live in mis-e-ry.

I fear there's some-one else she's in love.

I know a maiden ever so fair.
She has ever golden hair.
She's as pure as an angel from above.
She has stole my heart away
And I live in misery.
I fear there's someone else that she's in love.

It was ever little while
She would greet me with a smile.
And ask me at her happy home to call.
If she'd only be my wife
I'd live happy all my life.
She's that aggravating beauty, Lula Walts.

She was there in the park
When I met her just at dark.
She was standing by the fountain all alone.
As I passed I tipped my hat
And we both began to chat.
She allowed me to escort her to her home.

If she only would be mine,
I would build a house so fine.
All around it I'd erect a fence so tall.
But it's only jealousy
For there's no one else but me
That can gaze upon that beauty, Lula Walls.

C

"Lula Walls," sung by Mrs. Mittie Aldrich, Fayette, Fayette County, 1952. Practically same as B.

II
SENTIMENTAL SONGS

91
She Was Bred In Old Kentucky

Folk singers often take a song which appears ridiculous to more sophisticated people and sing it seriously. Often, it should be added, they will treat as absurd a song treated seriously by the sophisticate. The present song is a case in point of the former kind. Spaeth *(History of Popular Music,* p. 293) has an interesting note on it. The song was written by Harry Braisted and Stanley Carter (real names Harry B. Berdan and Frederick J. Redcliffe). "Supposedly the title of their greatest hit was suggested when Redcliffe, buying a horse, was told by the trainer, 'She was bred in old Kentucky.' The parodists refused to take the ballad seriously, adding, 'She was cake in New Orleans, She was pie in Louisiana, and in Boston she was beans.' " The melody of the verse "seems to have been the basis of A. Baldwin Sloane's later tune for the chorus of his satirical *Heaven Will Protect the Working Girl.*" Pound *(Syllabus,* p. 48) reports the song from Nebraska. It is still one of the most popular love songs in Alabama, as the four full texts show.

A

"Bred In Old Kentucky," sung by Mrs. Mary Crowder, Sulligent, Lamar County, 1952. She has known it at least forty years.

As a lad I sat one day in a cot-tage far a-way.

And to me that day all na-ture seemed so grand. For my

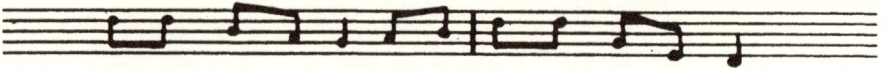

Sue with blush-es red had just prom-ised we would wed,

And I'd come to ask her moth-er for her hand. As I told

the old, old tale of a love that ne'er would fail, The

gray-haired moth-er stroked her daugh-ter's hair, And I

fan-cied I could trace just a tear on her kind face, As

Chorus

she placed my sweet-heart's hand in mine and said: She

was bred in old Ken-tuck-y, where the mea-dow grass is

blue. There's the sun-shine of the coun-try in her face

and man-ner too. She was bred in old Ken-tuck-y; take her,

boy, you're might-y luck-y, When you mar-ry a girl like

Sue.

As a lad I sat one day in a cottage far away,
And to me that day all nature seemed so grand,
For my Sue with blushes red had just promised we would wed,

And I'd come to ask her mother fro her hand.
As I told the old, old tale of a love that ne'er would fail,
The gray haired mother stroked her daughter's hair,
And I fancied I could trace just a tear on her kind face,
As she placed my sweetheart's hand in mine and said:

Chorus:
    She was bred in old Kentucky, where the meadow grass is blue.
    There's the sunshine of the country in her face and manner too.
    She was bred in old Kentucky; take her, boy, you're mighty lucky,
    When you marry a girl like Sue.

Many years have passed since that well remembered day,
When to the dear old Kentucky home I came.
All my happiness through life was my sweetheart, friend, and wife,
For the sunshine in her heart remained the same.
I'm sitting all alone in the place I long called home,
For yesterday my darling passed away.
But through tears I think with joy of that day as just a boy,
When I took her hand and heard her mother say:

B

"She Was Bred in Old Kentucky," sung by Mrs. C. L. Kennedy, Vernon, Lamar County, 1952. She learned it from her mother, who was a great singer, some fifty years ago. Words practically identical to A. Tune somewhat different.

As a boy I stood one day by a cot-tage far a-way,

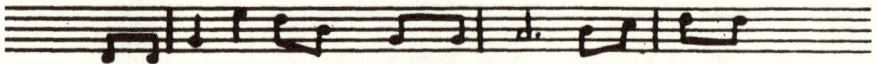

And to me all nat-ure seemed so grand. For my Sue with

blush-es red had just prom-ised we would wed, And I'd

come to ask her moth-er for her hand. As I told the old,

old tale of a love that ne'er would fail, The gray haired

moth-er stroked her daugh-ter's hand. And I fan-cied I

could trace just a tear on her kind face As she laid my

Chorus

sweet-heart's hand in mine and said: She was bred in old

Ken-tuck-y, where the mea-dow grass is blue. There's the

sun-shine of her coun-try in her face and man-ner too.

She was bred in old Ken-tuck-y; take her, boy, you're

might-y luck-y When you mar-ry a girl like Sue.

C

"She Was Bred in Old Kentucky," sung by Mrs. O.C. Powell, Titus, Elmore County, 1952. She has sung it for fifty or sixty years. Practically identical with A.

D

"Song," sung by Mrs. Eva Collins, Vernon, Lamar County, 1953. She has sung it for about thirty-five years. Text practically same as A.

92
The Hills of Tennessee

Tennessee was a favorite place in Alabama folk songs. There are three songs in this volume about the state. This pleasant piece reflects a nostalgia which is pleasing to the folk. I have not found it reported in other collections. It is likely a music hall piece.

"The Hills of Tennessee," sung by Mrs. Nola Browne, Millport, Lamar County, 1952. She has sung it for at least forty years.

How we jol-ly boys did play in the month of mer-ry

May, As we gath-ered flow-ers grow-ing by the stream.

All we boys were young and gay in the mer-ry month of

May, When we played a-mong the hills of Ten-nes-see.

Oh, how I love those grand old hills, How my heart with

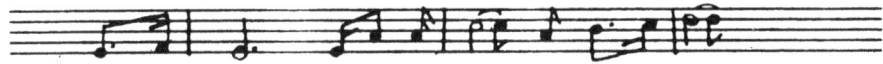

rap-ture thrills. Man-y the charms of life for me,

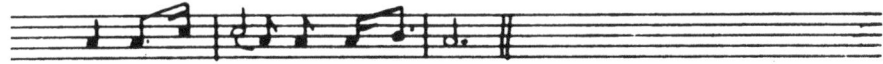

A-mong the hills of Ten-nes-see.

How we jolly boys did play,
In the month of merry May,
As we gathered flowers growing by the stream.
All we boys were young and gay,
In the merry month of May,
When we played among the hills of Tennessee.

Chorus:
  Oh, how I love those grand old hills,
  How my heart with rapture thrills.
  Many the charms of life for me,
  Among the hills of Tennessee.

Those days are past and gone,
But their memory lingers still,
When we boys were happy,
Young and so gay.

93
Two Sweethearts

Randolph (IV, 390) reports a three-stanza version of this song. He says it appears in *Morley's Wonderful Eight Songster* (St. Louis, n.d.) with the note: "Copyright 1897 by J.C. Groen & Co., words by E.P. Moran, music by J. Fred Holf." I have not found it reported elsewhere. The song seems not so firmly rooted in tradition in Alabama. I have two versions, one incomplete from an elderly man, a complete version from two young men around thirty.

A

"Two Sweethearts," sung by Dalton and Murray Hubbert, Fayette, Fayette County, 1952.

A crowd of young fel-lers one night at a ball was tell-ing of sweet-hearts they'd had. All of them jol-ly ex-cept one lad, who seemed down-heart-ed and sad.

"Come join us, Ned," some fel-ler said. "Sure-ly some

girl has loved you." Then rais-ing his head he proud-ly

said: "I am in love with two. One has hair of sil-ver-y

gray, the oth-er is just like gold. One is young and

youth-ful too, the oth-er is aged and old. Dearer than

life are they both to me, From nei-ther would I part.

One is my moth-er, God bless her I love her, The oth-er

one is my sweet-heart."

A crowd of young fellows one night at a ball
Was telling of sweethearts they'd had.
All seemed jolly except one lad,
Who seemed downhearted and sad.
"Come join us, Ned," some feller said,
"Surely some girl has loved you."
Then raising his head he proudly said:
"I am in love with two."

"One has hair of silvery gray,
The other is just like gold.

One is young and youthful too,
The other is aged and old.
Dearer than life are they both to me,
From neither would I part.
One is my mother, God bless her I love her.
The other is my sweetheart.

"My sweetheart is a poor working girl,
Whom I am determined to wed.
Father said No, it will never be so;
You must marry a niece instead.
But Mother was young and knows how it is;
When Father met her she was poor."
"Ned, don't fret, she'll be your wife yet;
He'll consent I am sure."

"One has hair of silvery gray,
The other is just like gold.
One is young and youthful too,
The other is aged and old.
Dearer than life are they both to me,
From neither would I part.
One is my mother, God bless her I love her.
The other is my sweetheart."

B

"Telling of Sweethearts We Had," sung by Mr. J.B. Estes, Millport, Lamar County, 1952. Two stanzas, one and two of A. He has sung the song for forty years at least.

94
The Little Old Log Cabin in the Lane

This song was written in 1871, by Will Hays, and was a popular success (Spaeth, *History of Popular Music,* p. 159). Called "A sentimental Plantation Sketch," it was performed by "the celebrated Winnetts" *(The Daytons' Songster,* N.Y. 18–, p. 43), in a version somewhat different from the one regularly heard. In a 6 stanza version rather close to the regularly heard one, it was sung by Billy and Maggie Ray *(Alice Harrison's Olympic Songster,* N.Y. 1875). For comparison I give the first of the six stanzas:

> I am getting old and feeble now, I cannot work no more,
> I have laid the rusty-bladed hoe to rest,
> Old Massa and old Missus they're sleeping side by side,
> And their spirits are now roaming with the blest;
> Things are changed about the place, the darkies are all gone,
> And I cannot hear them singing in the cane,
> And the only friend that's left me is that little boy of mine,
> In my little log cabin in the land.

The song was circulated by numerous other songsters: *Bryant & Williams' Slender Nigs Songster* (N.Y. 1877, p. 37); *Cool Burgess's Don't Get Weary Children Songster* (N.Y. 1877, p. 30); *Daly Bros. South Carolina Cloe Songster* (N.Y. 1878, p. 17); *Han-Town Students Songster* (N.Y. c. 1875, p. 41); *Harris & Carroll's Song & Sketch Book* (N.Y. 1878, p. 53); *Harrigan & Hart's Slavery Days Songster* ("Sung by Ike in 'Baffled'," N.Y., 1877, p. 54); *Wm. A. Huntley's Take Me Back To Home And Mother Songster* (N.Y. c. 1879, p. 49); *Haverly's Genuine Colored Minstrel's Songster* N.Y. c. 1879, p. 48); *I Want To See The Old Home Songster* ("Written by Grace Carleton, Copyright 1875," N.Y. c. 1877, p. 45); *The Jerome's Burlesqueing Songster* (N.Y. 1883, p. 42); *Johnson & Bruno's Mania, Mania Nigs Songster* ("Sung by *Ike* in Roland Howards great play 'Baffled.' " Published by Edward Hopkins, N.Y., c. 1875); *Alicia Jourdan's Will You Love Me When I'm Old Songster* (N.Y. 1876, p. 44); *King Of Clowns Songster* (N.Y. 1881, p. 32); *Frank Lewis Hurrah For The Minstrel Band Songster* (N.Y. 1876, p. 46); *Lowell & Drew's Carnival Novelty Company's Songster* ("Will Hays," N.Y. 1881, p. 55); *Lowell & Drews "Dat Golden Chariot" Songster* ("Will S. Hays," N.Y. 1880, p. 23); *Lowell & Drews "Sassy Nigger" Song-*

ster (N.Y. c. 1880); *Willie E. Lyle's Balm Of Gilead Song Book* (N.Y. 1877, p. 38); *Willie E. Lyle's Great Georgia Minstrels Songster* (N.Y. 1875, p. 6).

This song has not been widely reported as a folk song, despite its popularity among a popular audience. Shoemaker *(North Pennsylvania Minstrelsy, p. 162)* reports a full text, with the notation that the informant got it from the Toledo *Blade* but that he learned it about 1870. Ford *(Traditional Music In America, p. 281)* reports it. The L.C. Checklist (p. 232) gives it from New York City, Florida and California. I have only one Alabama text.

"Little Old Log Cabin in the Lane," sung by Mrs. Martha Jane Snyder, Tucson, Arizona, 1952. She learned it in Greene County, Alabama, in the 1890s.

I'm get-ting old and fee-ble und I can-not work no more. I have laid the rust-y blad-ed hoe to rest. And the on-ly friend they left me now is this good old dog of mine And the lit-tle old log cab-in in the lane.

I'm getting old and feeble
And I cannot work no more.
I have laid the rusty bladed hoe to rest.
And the only friend they left me now
Is this good old dog of mine
And the little old log cabin in the lane.

I ain't got long to stay here.
What little time I got
I'll try to be contented to remain.
For the angels they watch over me
When I lay me down to sleep
In the little old log cabin in the lane.

95
Widow in The Cottage by the Sea

Dichter and Shapiro *(Early American Sheet Music,* p. 154) say that this song was written by C.A. White and published in Boston in 1868. It was immensely popular in the songsters, in almost exactly my B version. For example: *Andy Collum's Get Thee Gone, Jane, Songster* (N.Y. 1878, p. 30); *Erin-Go-Brach Songster* (N.Y. 1890, p. 165); *Jennie Hughes; Dolly Varden Songster* (N.Y. 1872, p. 34); *Jennie Hughes' Vocal Gems* (N.Y. 1874, p. 167); *The Little Maggie May Songster* (N.Y. 1869, p. 29); *Sheffer & Slavin's "Kick Me Again" Songster* (N.Y. n.d., p. 57); *Trifet's Multum im Parvo* (N.Y. c. 1890, p. 25); *Virginia Trio Dutch Niggers Songster* (N.Y. 1883, p. 42).

Randolph (IV, 160) reports two texts. Brown (II, 347) says that it is popular both in the mountains and on the coast of North Carolina. Davis *(Folksongs of Virginia,* P. 130) gives the title, and Shay *(Pious Friends and Drunken Companions).* Possessing three qualities that endear songs to the folk — unhappiness, widowhood, and the sea — this piece is popular in Alabama, as my five texts indicate.

A

"All Alone by the Seaside," sung by Mrs. Nola Browne, Millport, Lamar County, 1951. She has sung it for the last fifty years.

All a-lone by the sea-side he has left me, And

no oth-er's bride I'll be, For to-night I am a wid-ow

In our cot-tage by the sea.

All alone by the seaside he has left me
And no other's bride I'll be,
For tonight I am a widow
In our cottage by the sea.

He told me I'd be happy,
But no happiness I see,
For tonight I am a widow
In the cottage by the sea.

He told me he would always love me,
And how happy we would be.
But tonight I am a widow
In the cottage by the sea.

All alone by the seaside I am watching,
Waiting for his return.
But tonight I am a widow
In our cottage by the sea.

B

"Widow In the Cottage By The Sea," contributed by Mrs. R. Van Iderstine, Daphne, Baldwin County, 1953, from a manuscript copy.

Just one year ago today, love,
I became your happy bride,
Changed a mansion for a cottage,
To dwell by the riverside.
You told me I'd be happy
But no happiness I see —
For tonight I am a widow
In the cottage by the sea.

Chorus:
Alone, all alone by the seaside he left me,
And no other's bride I'll be,
For in bridal flowers he decked me,
In the cottage by the sea.

From my cottage by the seaside
I can see my mansion home.
I can see those hills and valleys
Where with pleasure I have roamed.
The last time that I saw him,
Oh how happy then were we,
But tonight I am a widow
In the collage by the sea.

C

"In a Cottage By The Sea," contributed by Mrs. Ada Vail, Millport, Lamar County, 1952. A newspaper clipping in her possession. Three stanzas and chorus. Same as B, except third stanza is different:

Oh! my poor and aged father,
How in sorrow he would fail,
And my poor and aged mother,
How in tears her eyes would swell;
And my poor and only brother,
O how he would weep for me,
If he only knew his sister,
Was a widow by the sea.

D

"All Alone," from the Alabama Archives. Similar to B. First four lines from B, then Chorus, then first four lines of second stanza. Note: "This song was popular in Shelby County about 1875-1885."

E

"The Cottage By The Sea," sung by Mrs. Nettie Coleman, Tucson, Arizona, 1952. She learned it in Greene County, Alabama, thirty years ago. A fragment.

All a-lone, all a-lone he left me, And no oth-er's bride I'll be. But for to-night I am a wid-ow In the cot-tage by the sea.

96
Mabel Clare

This piece is not the same as Foster's "Gentle Lena Clare," which was written in 1862, but seems to have been written by R. Hunt, with the music by A.J. Higgins (see Sears' *Index*, Sup., p. 189). It obviously is not of folk origin, although it contains the figures of speech, allusions,and sentiment of songs that some folk singers like. A song called "Mable Clare" was published in *The Dime Song Book*, No. 2 (Beadle, 1859, p. 64) which was different from my texts but possibly the original. Another was published in Charley Konallman's *New York Variety Songster* (N.Y. c. 1877, p. 9) "written by R.J. Pigott, for Callahan & Flynn." My two Alabama texts indicate a certain popularity. I have not found the song reported elsewhere as a folk song.

A

"Beautiful Mabel Clare," sung by Mrs. Nola Browne, Millport, Lamar County, 1952. She has sung it for around fifty years.

All alone by the stream in the May time, "e are

gath-er-ing vi-o-lets blue, To clasp in her dain-ty

fin-gers or to braid in her shin-y hair. "e will gath-er

them for sweet Mab-le, beau-ti-ful Mab-le Clare, To clasp

in her dain-ty fin-gers or to braid in her shin-y hair.

Yes we'll gath-er them for sweet Mab-le, beau-ti-ful

Mab-le Clare, To clasp in her dain-ty fin-ger or to braid

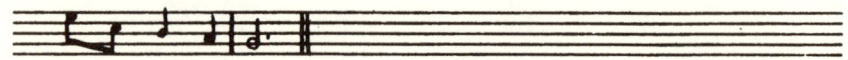

in her shin-y hair.

All alone by the stream in the May time,
We are gathering violets blue,
To clasp in her dainty fingers
Or to braid in her shiny hair.

Chorus:
    We will gather them for sweet Mable,
    Beautiful Mable Clare,
    To clasp in her dainty fingers,
    Or to braid in her shiny hair.
    Yes we'll gather them for sweet Mable,
    Beautiful Mable Clare,
    To clasp in her dainty fingers,
    Or to braid in her shiny hair.

B

"Mable Dear," contributed by Mrs. J.R. Phares, Moundville, Hale County, 1953.

In the spring as I walked in the garden,
My thoughts were of Mable dear,
And how I would gather the roses
To braid in her golden hair.

Gather them for sweet Mable,
Beautiful Mable dear,
To clasp in her dainty fingers
To braid in her golden hair.

But comes now the dreary November,
Making us to mourn and to weep,
For, closing her brown eyes gently,
Mable has gone to sleep.

Closing her brown eyes gently,
Beautiful Mable dear.
No more will I gather the roses
To braid in her shining hair.

97
After The Ball

This song was written in 1892 by Charles K. Harris. Ordered for an amateur minstrel show in Milwaukee, the song failed because Sam Doctor, the singer, forgot the lines. J. Aldrich Libby, a baritone, sang it later in the farce *A Trip To Chinatown,* and in this extravaganza it was carried all over the country by May Irwin and other singers. The song perhaps received its greatest boost from John Philip Sousa, who played it daily at the World's Columbian Exposition in Chicago in 1893. Over 5 million copies of the sheet music were sold.

It was distributed partially by the songsters, by at least one: *Harrigan & Braham's Daniel's Tribulations Songster* (N.Y. c, 1892, p. 7); and was parodied in many others, thus attesting to the song's popularity: *Wehman's Collection of Songs,* No. 42 (N.Y. c. 1890, p. 14); "After the Fair," *Edison Phonograph Songster* (N.P. 18--, p. 7) presents an interesting chorus about the Chicago World's Fair:

> After the Fair is over,
> Just watch the rents come down.
> When all the rubes and hayseeds
> Have skipped away from town.
> Many a man will be busted,
> People will tear their hair.
> Hyde Park will be dead and buried,
> After the Fair.

"After the Scare" *(W. Clark's Lyceum Songster,* N.Y. c. 1893, p. 1) has an interesting chorus that tries to reassure the public about the "panic" of that year:

> After the scare is over,
> Good times will then return.
> After a few more days, love,
> We all will have money to burn.
> Many a heart will stop aching,
> Both here and everywhere.
> Many a bank will stop breaking,
> After the scare.

It is not widely reported as a folk song. Pound *(Poetic Origins and the Ballad,* p. 92) said it was still popular in villages and on western ranches. Shearin *(Syllabus,* p. 29) gives the title for Kentucky. Cambiaire *(East Tennessee and Western Virginia Ballads,* p. 105) gives it, as does Stout *(Folklore from Iowa,* p. 62). It is still one of the most popular folk love songs in Alabama, though rapidly fading out.

A

"After The Ball," sung by Mrs. Nettie Coleman, Tucson, Arizona, 1952. She learned it in Greene County, Alabama, forty years ago.

A lit-tle maid-en climbed an old man's knees,

Begged for a sto-ry, "Do, Un-cle, please. Why have

you no ba-bies, why have you no home? Why are you sin-gle,

why live a-lone?" "I had a sweet-heart, years, years

a-go. Where she is now, Pet, you will soon know. Lis-

ten to the sto-ry, I will tell it all. I broke her

heart, Pet, af-ter the ball." Af-ter the ball is ov-er

af-ter the break of day. Af-ter the dan-cers are

leav-ing, af-ter the stars are gray. Man-y a heart

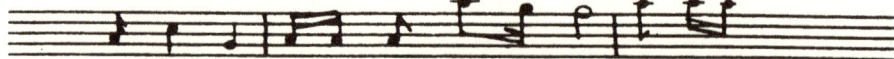

is break-ing, if you could read them all. Man-y a

hope has van-ished, af-ter the ball.

A little maiden climbed an old man's knees,
Begged for a story, "Do, Uncle, please.
Why have you no babies, why have you no home?
Why are you single, why live alone?"
"I had a sweetheart, years, years ago.
Where she is now, Pet, you will soon know.
Listen to the story, I will tell it all.
I broke her heart, Pet, after the ball."

Chorus:
    After the ball is over, after the break of day,
    After the dancers are leaving, after the stars are gray.
    Many a heart is breaking, if you could read them all.
    Many a hope has vanished, after the ball.

B

"After The Ball," sung by Mrs. J.V. Tarwater, Fayette, Fayette
County, 1952, who learned it more than sixty years ago. Three
stanzas and chorus. First stanza and chorus are identical with A.
Second stanza continues:

    "Bright lights were flashing in the proud ballroom.
    Softly the music was playing sweet tunes.
    There came my sweetheart, my love, my own.
    'I wish some water, Dear, my own.'
    When I returned, Dear, there stood a man
    Kissing my sweetheart as lovers can.
    Down fell the glass, Pet, broken and all.
    I believed her faithless after the ball.

    She tried to tell, tried to explain.
    I would not listen, pleadings were vain.
    One day a letter came from that man.
    He was her brother, the letter ran.
    Long years have passed, child, I never wed.
    True to my lost love though she is dead.
    That's why I'm lonely, no home at all.
    I broke her heart, Pet, after the ball."

C

"After The Ball," sung by Mrs. O.C. Powell, Titus, Elmore County, 1952. Three stanzas and chorus. First two stanzas and chorus very similar to B. Final stanza somewhat different:

"Years, years have passed, child, I've never wed.
True to my lost love, though she is dead.
She tried to tell me, tried to explain.
I would not listen, pleadings were vain.
Long came a letter, 'twas from that man.
He was her brother, the letter ran.
That's why I'm lonely, no home at all.
I broke her heart, Pet, after the ball."

D

"After The Ball," sung by Mrs. Nola Browne, Millport, Lamar County, 1952. She has sung it all her life. First two stanzas and chorus of B.

E

"After The Ball," from a newspaper clipping sent in by Mrs. Lenora Williams, McKenzie, Butler County, 1953, who says she has known the song for the last fifty years. Three stanzas and chorus. Very similar to B.

98
The Girl I Loved in Sunny Tennessee

Probably of music-hall origin, this song has not been widely reported as a folk song. Randolph (IV, 332) gives one text of two
stanzas and a chorus. Davis *(Folk-Songs of Virginia,* p. 101) lists
the title. The L.C. Checklist (pp. 184; 384) reports texts from
Kentucky, New York City and Arkansas. The song is rather popular
in Alabama. My four texts are complete.

A

"Sunny Tennessee," sung by Mrs. Della Collins, Vernon, Lamar
County, 1952.

On one morning bright and clear
To my old home I drew near,
Just a village down in sunny Tennessee.
I was speeding on a train
That would bring me back again
To my sweetheart who was waiting there for me.

Chorus:
    I could hear those darkies singing,
    As she bade farewell to me.
    Far across the fields of cotton
    My old homestead I could see.
    As the moon rose in the glory,
    And I told my saddest story
    To that girl I love in sunny Tennessee.

As the train drew in at last,
Familiar scenes I passed,
And I kissed my mother at the station door.
But as crowds gathered round,
Tears on every face I found.
Then I missed the one that I'd been waiting for.

And I whispered, "Mother dear,
Where is Mary, she's not here?"
All the world seemed lone,
And sadness changed to me,
For she pointed to a spot
In our little churchyard lot
Where my sweetheart sleeps in sunny Tennessee.

It had been but quite a few years,
Since I kissed away her tears,
And lift her by my dear old mother's side.
But each year that we'd been apart
She grew dearer to my heart
Than the day I asked her for to be my bride.

B

"Sweetheart Down In Tennessee," sung by Miss Drucilla Hall, Millport, Lamar County, 1952. Three stanzas and chorus.

On a morn-ing bright and fair to my old home I drew

near, Just a vil-lage down in sun-ny Ten-nes-see. I was

speed-ing on the train that would bring me back a-gain

To my sweet-heart who was wait-ing there for me. You

could hear those dar-kies sing-ing As she bade fare-

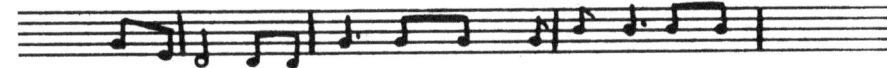

well to me. Far a-cross the fields of cot-ton my old

home-stead I could see. As the moon rose in her glo-ry,

there I told love's sweet-est sto-ry To the girl I loved

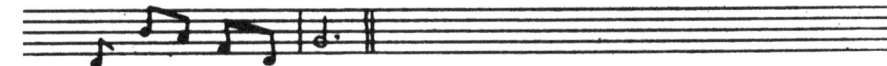

in sun-ny Ten-nes-see.

On a morning bright and fair to my old home I drew near,
Just a village down in sunny Tennessee.
I was speeding on the train that would bring me back again
To my sweetheart who was waiting there for me.
You could hear those darkies singing as she bade farewell to me.
Far across the fields of cotton my old homestead I could see.
As the moon rose in her glory, there I told love's sweetest story
To the girl I loved in sunny Tennessee.

As the train drew up at last, old familiar scenes I passed,
And I kissed my mother at the station door.
As the crowd gathered round, tears on every face I found.
And I missed the one that I'd been waiting for.
Then I whispered, "Mother dear, where's Mary; she's not here?"
All the world seemed lost and sadness come to me.
For she pointed to a spot in the little churchyard lot,
Where my sweetheart sleeps in sunny Tennessee.

C

"In Sunny Tennessee," sung by Mrs. C. L. Kennedy, Vernon, Lamar County, 1952. She learned it from her mother, Mrs. Priscilla Finch, who was a great singer. The order of stanzas seems most logical in this version. It begins with stanza one of A and then continues with stanza five. The rest of the stanzas then develop like those in A.

D

"Sunny Tennessee," sung by Mrs. Nettie Coleman, Tucson, Arizona, 1952. She learned it as a child in Greene County. Three stanzas and chorus.

On a morning bright and clear to my old home I drew near,
Just a village down in sunny Tennessee.
I was speeding on a train that would bring me back again
To my sweetheart who was waiting there for me.

Chorus:
    We could hear the darkies singing as she bade farewell to me.
    Far across the fields of cotton my old homestead I could see.
    When the moon rose in its glory, I told my sweetest story
    To the girl I loved in sunny Tennessee.

The train drew up at last. Old familiar scenes I passed.
Then I kissed my mother at the station door.
And as old friends gathered round, tears on every face I found.
I missed the one that I'd been longing for.

I whispered, "Mother dear, where is Mary; she's not here?"
All the world seemed lost and sadness came to me.
For she pointed to a spot in that little churchyard lot,
Where my sweetheart sleeps in sunny Tennessee.

99
In The Shadow of The Pines

This sentimental love song was written by Hattie Lummis and
G.O. Lang in 1895 (Spaeth, *History of Popular Music,* p. 608).
It has not been widely reported as a folk song. Wheeler *(Kentucky
Mountain Folksongs,* p. 56) gives it, saying it "is sung in many New
England states as well as in Kentucky." Shearin *(Syllabus,* p. 29)
reports the title from Kentucky. The L.C. Checklist (pp. 185; 358)
lists it from New York City and California. The song is one of the
most popular love songs in Alabama.

A

"In the Shadow of The Pines," sung by an anonymous informant
in the Women's State Prison, Wetumpka, Elmore County, 1952. She
probably learned it in Alabama or Mississippi, but might have picked
it up anywhere in her traveling through much of the United States.

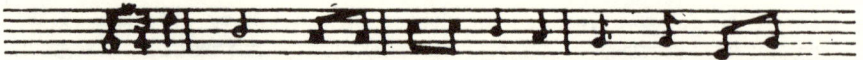

We strolled in the sha-dow of the pines, my love and
I, As the wind was blow-ing gent-ly from the sea. Then a
sud-den fit-ful dark-ness stole a-cross the sum-mer sky,
And the sha-dow stole be-tween my love and I. Come back to

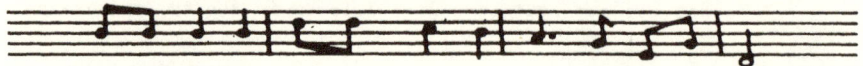

me, Sweet-heart, And love me ev-er-more. Come back to me,

Sweet-heart, And leave me nev-er-more. In life's dark path-

ways The sun no lon-ger shines. Come, Love, and meet me

In the sha-dow of the pines.

We strolled in the shadow of the pines, my love and I,
As the wind was blowing gently from the sea.
Then a sudden fitful darkness stole across the summer sky,
And the shadow stole between my love and I.

Chorus:
Come back to me, Sweetheart, and love me evermore.
Come back to me, Sweetheart, and leave me nevermore.
In life's dark pathways the sun no longer shines.
Come, Love, and meet me in the shadow of the pines.

B

"In The Shadow of The Pines," sung by Mr. Claude Springfield, Vernon, Lamar County, 1952. He has been signing it fifty-five years, at least.

We had wandered in the shadow of the pine, my love and I,
And the wind was blowing gently from the sea.

And a sudden fitful darkness stole across the peaceful sky,
And a shadow fell between my love and me.
Some hasty words were spoken and then almost unawares,
Hasty answers to unthinking anger led.
And our heartsick, bitter longing and our weeping in our prayers
Ne'er can make those false and cruel words unsaid.

Chorus:
    Come back to me, Sweetheart, and love me as before.
    Come back to me, Sweetheart, and leave me nevermore.
    In life's dark pathway the sun no longer shines.
    Come, Love, and meet me in the shadow of the pines.

You took the ring I gave you and cast one glance at me
As you took the jeweled trinket in your hand,
And then you turned and tossed it in the waters of the sea,
When the waves were speaking idly on the sand.

You went your way unheeding the tears I could not hide,
You went your way and not a word was said,
But my anger was breaking underneath its load of pride,
As the pine tree sobbed in pity overhead.

I awoke from bitter dreaming just to call aloud your name.
I slept again to dream of you once more.
My stubborn pride has left me; I'll admit I was to blame.
Forgive me, Dear, and love me as before.
My pathway is overshadowed with the darkness of despair.
In the sky of life the sun no longer shines.
I would give this whole world gladly once again to meet you there,
Reunited in the shadow of the pines.

C

"In The Shadow Of The Pines," from a newspaper clipping in the possession of Mrs. R. Van Iderstine, Daphne, Baldwin County, 1953. Practically identical with B.

D

"Shadow of the Pine," sung by Mrs. A.J. Shea, Sheffield, Colbert County, 1953. She probably learned it in Mississippi, forty years ago. First stanza and chorus of B.

E

"In the Shadow of the Pine," sung by Mrs. Nola Browne, Millport,

Lamar County, 1952. She learned it fifty years ago around Kennedy, Lamar County. A fragment consisting of stanza two and chorus of B.

F

"Shadow of the Pines," sung by Mrs. Susy Bell Hankins, Vernon, Lamar County, 1953. A full version similar to B.

100
I'll Wear The Violets, Sweetheart

This sentimental love song has all the necessary ingredients for popularity with the folk — a broken heart, a letter, "violets from the dell" and pathos — yet it apparently was not a widely sung piece. I have not found it in any other collection, and I have only one text.

"I'll Wear The Violets, Sweetheart," sung by Mrs. A.J. Shea, Sheffield, Colbert County, 1953. She does not know how long she has known it.

A lad was one day read-ing while the tears ran down

his cheeks a blot-ted let-ter from his old sweet-heart.

With-in the tear-stained let-ter were vi'-lets from the

dell. "You'll wear them if you love me, thus it read.

I'll wear the vi'-lets, sweet-heart, be-cause I love you

so, Though we may meet as strang-ers as in the long a-go.

We're part-ed now for-ev-er; Though it may cause a sigh,

I'll wear the vi'-lets, sweet-heart, and think of days

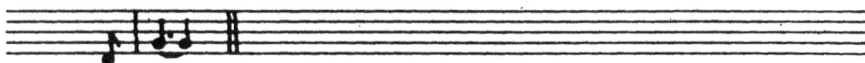

gone by.

A lad was one day reading,
While the tears ran down his cheeks,
A blotted letter from his old sweetheart.
Within the tear-stained letter were violets from the dell.
"You'll wear them if you love me,"
Thus it read.

I'll wear the violets, Sweetheart,
Because I love you so.
Though we may meet as strangers,
As in the long ago.
We're parted now forever.
Though it may cause a sigh,
I'll wear the violets, Sweetheart,
And think of days gone by.

101
I'll Remember You, Love, In My Prayers

This song was written by Will Hays in 1869. A great hit, it sold around three hundred thousand copies of sheet music (Spaeth, *History of Popular Music*, p. 159). Dichter and Shapiro *(Early American Sheet Music,* p. 145) say it is popularly classed as a cowboy song. It apparently, however, is more widely considered a love song. It is not widely reported as a folk song. Sandburg gives it in *The American Songbag* (p. 259) and in *The New American Songbag* (p. 95), where he says: "The cowboys of Colorado took a garrulous popular song of the 1870's and kept a fragment, the heart's essence of it." Shearin *(Syllabus,* p. 28) reports it from Kentucky, and Davis *(Folk-Songs of Virginia,* p. 104) cites it. The songsters helped popularize it. *Beadle's Half Dime Singer's Library, No. 7* (N.Y. 1878, p. 13) gives it, as do *Leavitt's Gargantuan Minstrels Songster* (N.Y. 18--, p. 6); *Wehman's Good Old Time Songs, No. 1* (N. Y. 1910, p. 35); *Wehman's Good Old Time Songs No. 28* (N.Y. 18--, p. 24); and *Wm. J. Scanlan's Bye, Bye, Baby, Bye, Bye Songster* (N.Y. 1884, p. 6).

The L.C. Checklist (p. 176) reports one version from New York City. The piece, which has some poetic merit, is one of the most popular love songs in Alabama, I have eight texts.

A

"I'll Remember you, Love, in my Prayers," sung by Miss Drucilla Hall, Millport, Lamar County, 1952.

The cur-tains of night are pinned back by the stars,

And the glo-ri-ous sun meets the sky. When the dew-drops

of hea-ven are kiss-ing the rose, It is there that my

mem-o-ry flies.

The curtains of night are pinned back by the stars,
And the glorious sun meets the sky.
When the dewdrops of heaven are kissing the rose,
It is there that my memory flies.

As if on the wings of some beautiful dove
To hasten the message it bears,
And bring you a kiss of affection and faith,
I'll remember you, Love, in my prayers.

I've loved you too fondly to ever forget
The love you have spoken to me,
And the kiss of affection was borne on my lips,
When you told me how true you would be.

I know not if Fortune be fickle or friend,
Or if time your memory wears.
I know that I'll love you wherever you go.
I'll remember you love in my prayers.

If the angels of heaven are guarding the good,
As God has ordained them to do,
In answer to prayers I've offered to Him,
I know there is one watching you.

And may His bright spirit be with you through life,
To guide you up heaven's bright path,
To meet with the one who has loved you so true,
And remember you, Love, in her prayers.

Go where you will, on land or on sea,
I share all your trouble and care.
At night when I kneel by my bedside to pray,
I'll remember you, Love, in my prayer.

B

"I'll Remember You, Love, In My Prayers," from a manuscript in the possession of Miss Florence Bailey, Crane Hill, Cullman County, 1953. She wrote it some thirty years ago. Essentially same as A, but has a chorus consisting of stanza seven of A. Different tune.

When the cur-tains of night are pinned back by the

stars, And the beau-ti-ful moon lights the skies, And

the dew-drops of Hea-ven are kiss-ing the rose, It is

then that the mem-o-ry flies. As if on the wings of some

beau-ti-ful dove, In haste with the mes-sage it bears, To

bring you a kiss of af-fec-tion and say, "I'll re-mem-ber

you, love, in my pray-ers. Then go where you will, ov-er

land or sea, I'll share all your sor-row and cares. And

when by my bed-side I kneel down to pray, I'll re-mem-ber

you, love, in my prayers.

C

"I'll Remember You, Love, In My Prayers," sung by Mrs. A.J. Shea, Sheffield, Colbert County, 1953. She might have learned it in Mississippi as a child. Four stanzas, similar to one, two, seven and four of A.

D

"I'll Remember You, Love, In My Prayers," sung by Mrs. J.V. Tarwater, Fayette, Fayette County, 1952. She has sung it probably fifty years. A full version, similar to A.

E

"I'll Remember You, Love, In My Prayers," contributed by Mrs. Johnnie Gregory, Millport, Lamar County, 1952. She has known it perhaps sixty-five years. A full version, similar to A.

F

"When the Curtains of Night," contributed by Mrs. O.C. Powell, Titus, Elmore County, 1952. Two stanzas, similar to one and four of A. She does not remember when and how she learned it. Probably from neighborhood girls.

G

"The Curtain of Night," sung by Mrs. Nola Browne, Millport, Lamar County, 1952. A one-stanza fragment, the first stanza of A.

H

"I'll Remember you, Love," sung by "Mama" Daisy Key, Florence, Colbert County, 1953. She has known it over fifty years. A fragment consisting of several lines from various stanzas of A.

102
Come, Birdie, Come

This sentimental song was written by C.A. White and published in Boston in 1870 (Dichter and Shapiro, *Early American Sheet Music*, p. 141). It quickly went into the songsters. I quote one version in order to demonstrate how the popular song was cut and telescoped, for one reason or another, in the folk version *(Erin-Go-Brach Songster* N.Y. 1890, p. 171):

Beautiful Bird of spring has come
Seeking a place to build his home,
Warbling his song so light and free,
Beautiful bird, come life with me.
Come life with me, you shall be free
If you will come and live with me.
Come life with me, come live with me.
I'm all alone,
Come live with me.
Come live with me.

Chorus:
    Come, birdie, come live with me.
    We will by happy, light and free;
    You shall be all the world to me.
    Come, birdie, come and live with me.

It was published also in *Beadle's Dime Song Book, No. 28* (N.Y. 1871, p. 12); *Girls, Don't Fool with Cupid Songster* (N.Y. n.d. p. 13); *Jennie Hughes' Vocal Gems* (N.Y. 1874, p. 30); *Kirk and Drew's Mischievous Offspring Songster* (N.Y. 1876, p. 44); *Miss Clara Moore's Character & Descriptive Songster* (N.Y. 1877, p. 58); *Wehman Bros' Good Old Time Songs*, No. 2 (N.Y. 1910, p. 80).

As a folk song this piece has not been widely reported. Pound *(Syllabus,* p. 70) gives a fragment. I have not found it elsewhere.

"Come, Birdie, Come," sung by Mrs. Nola Browne, Millport, Lamar County, 1952. She learned it forty-five years ago in Lamar County.

Come, birdie, come. Spring has come,
You are seeking a place to build your home.
Come live with me, you shall be free.
Beautiful bird, come live with me.

Come live with me, you shall be free,
Beautiful bird, come live with me.

Come live with me, you shall be free,
Bring your sweet mate and live with me.

103
The Chickadee Song

This song, as do several others in this volume, represents the folk singer's liking of animal and bird songs. The song was credited to Rev. F. C. Woodworth in the *Franklin Square Song Collection* (edited by J.P. McCoskey, 1881, p. 124), where eight stanzas are published. But my Alabama informant more likely got it from one of her school books. McGuffey's *New Third Eclectic Reader* (first published 1857, then in 1865, and copyrighted in 1885), for instance, has eight stanzas (called "The Snow-Bird's Song," p. 240). The chorus is likely a folk addition. Davis *(Folk-Songs of Virginia,* p. 203) reports the title. The L.C. Checklist reports a text from Texas. I have not found it elsewhere. My Alabama text is greatly abbreviated.

"The Chickadee Song," sung by Mrs. Maggie Lee Hayes, Vernon, Lamar County, 1953. She does not remember how long she has sung it, but probably fifty years.

The ground was all cov-ered in snow one day, and two lit-tle sis-ters were bus-y at play, when a snow-bird was sit-ting close by on a tree, And mer-ri-ly sing-ing his chick-a-dee-dee. Chick-a-dee-dee, chick-a-dee-dee, and mer-ri-ly sing-ing his chick-a-dee-dee.

The ground was all covered in snow one day,
And two little sisters were busy at play,
When a snowbird was sitting close by on a tree,
And merrily singing his chickadee-dee.

Chorus:
> Chickadee-dee, chickadee-dee
> And merrily singing his chickadee-dee.

Oh, Mother, do get him some stockings and shoes,
And a nice little hat and a frock, if you choose.
I wish he'd come into the parlor and sing,
How warm we would make him, poor chickadee-dee.

Chorus:
> Checkadee-dee, chickadee-dee.
> How warm we would make him, poor chickadee-dee.

104
Erin's Green Shore

This song is also known as "The Irishman's Dream." According to Randolph (I, 324) it is "common in cheap English songbooks." Cox *(Folk-Songs of the South,* p. 442) has a brief note on the English literature. The song has been found in Kentucky (Thomas, *Devil's Ditties,* p. 176). Newfoundland (Greenleaf, *Ballads and Sea Songs of Newfoundland,* pp. 142-143) and Missouri (Belden, *Ballads and Songs,* pp. 282-283). The L.C. Checklist (p. 95) reports a text from Kentucky. My one text is a fragment, indicating that the song is no longer popular in the state.

"One Evening While Strolling Down River," sung by Mrs. Gilbert Davis, Montgomery, Montgomery County, 1952. He learned it in Fayette County some forty years ago.

One eve-ning while stroll-ing down the riv-er, I

laid my-self down on a bed of prim-ros-es And quick-ly

I fell in a dream. I dreamed that I saw a fair dam-sel,

Her e-qual I'd ne'er seen be-fore. Her cheeks were like

two bloom-ing ros-es, Her teeth were the i-v'ry so

white. She had come to a-wak-en her breth-ern Who

slum-bered a-long Er-in's green shore.

One evening while strolling down the river
I laid myself down on a bed of primroses,
And quickly I fell in a dream.
I dreamed that I saw a fair damsel.
Her equal I'd never seen before.
Her cheeks were like two blooming roses,
Her teeth were the ivory so white.
She had come to awaken her brethren
Who slumbered along Erin's green shore.

105
Mandelin

This piece seems to be "Mandy Lee," written by John Thurland Chattaway in 1899, a barber-shop favorite. Spaeth *(History of Popular Music,* p. 299) says "its natural harmonies are a constant urge to improvisation as well as to a variety of arrangements." If "Mandelin" is not a version of "Mandy Lee," it is obviously not a folk composition. The subject is not a folk subject; the treatment is too "arty." It has not been reported as a folk song in other collections.

"Mandelin," sung by Mrs. Ernest Phillips, Tuscaloosa, Tuscaloosa County, 1953. She has sung it around thirty years but does not remember how she learned it.

There's a lit-tle old cab-in on the Swan-nee shore far

a-way. That's where my heart is long-ing, night and day.

Pret-ty lit-tle maid-en wait-ing there for me, by the

shore. When the steam-boat floats a-long the Swan-nee,

I will say to the shore: "Man-de-lin, Man-de-lin, moon

is shin-ing on the fields of sug-ar cane. Come to me,

Dear, for I love you. I'm your hon-ey boy, and you're

my la-dy lou. Man-dy, my pret-ty Man-de-lin, I love you.

There's a little old cabin on the Swannee shore far away.
That's where my heart is longing night and day.

Pretty little maiden waiting there for me by the shore.

Mandelin, Mandelin, moon is shining on the fields of sugar cane.
Come to me, Dear, for I love you.
I'm your honey boy, and you're my lady-lou.
Mandy, my pretty Mandelin, I love you.

106
My Little Home In Tennessee

This song is another example of the Alabama folk singer's liking to sing about Tennessee. This one, too, reflects nostalgia for the old homeplace and the old girl friend left behind, typical subjects in folk songs. The song has not been reported from elsewhere, and I have only one Alabama text. Though I am sure this song is authentic, it is rough enough to suggest that faulty memory has had to be assisted.

"My Little Home in Tennessee," sung by Miss Drucilla Hall, Millport, Lamar County, 1952.

Ev-'ry night I'm dream-ing of that lit-tle home

down a-mong the hills of Ten-nes-see. I am al-ways

lone-ly un-til I re-turn to the place that means so

much to me. Just a lit-tle shack, roof is turn-ing

black; Still it is as fair to me. Birds are al-ways

sing-ing a-round the cab-in door In my lit-tle home

in Ten-nes-see.

Ev'ry night I'm dreaming of that little home
Down among the hills of Tennessee.
I am always lonely until I return
To that place that means so much to me.
Just a little shack, roof is turning black;
Still it is as fair to me.
Birds are always singing around the cabin door,
In my little home in Tenneseee.

I can see my mother waiting by the gate.
When I drove the old horse up the lane,
She would never scold me when I got home late.
Oh, I wish I'd never caused her pain,
With her tender smile guided me all the while.
No one could be dearer far than she.
Now she's gone to heaven and she'll never return
To my little home in Tennessee.

I can still remember many years ago,
When I wandered by my sweetheart's side,
Down among the mountains where wild flowers grow,
And she promised she would be my bride.
Then another man won her heart and hand,
And I knew hoe much she meant to me.
I was broken hearted and I went away
From my little home in Tennessee.

107
Ben Bolt

This piece was written by Thomas Dunn English. Nelson Kneass, a young actor, needing a song, set the words to an old German air. The resulting song seems to have been an immediate success, though it has been reported only once as a folk song (in Carl Carmer, *Songs of the Rivers of America,* p. 10, where he gives a two-stanza version — my first two — and an interesting note). But there is no question of the wide dissemination of the song in the songsters: *American Vocalist* (N.Y. 1853, p. 248); *Banner Songster* (N.Y. 1865, p. 30); *Book of American Songs,* (N.Y. c. 1865, p. 16); *Beadle's Dime Song Book, No. 1* (N.Y. 1859, p. 25); *Beadle's Dime Song Book, No. 10* (N.Y. 1860, p. 53); *The "Blonde" of The Period Songster* (N.Y. 1869, p. 21); *Chattanooga 20th Century Songster* (Chattanooga, c. 1869, p. 12); *Erin-Go-Brach Songster* (N.Y. 1890, p. 18); *The Love And Sentimental Songster* (N.Y. 1862, p. 42); *The Love And Sentimental Songster* (N.Y. 1864, p. 43); *Metropolitan Songster* (N.Y. c. 1862, p. 94); *Songs of The Hutchinsons* (N.Y. c, 1860, p. 9). It was also widely parodied. For example: "John Jones," in *Ben Cotton's Own Songster, No. 2* (S.F. 1864), a portion running —

> Oh, don't you remember Lame Sally, John Jones,
> Lame Sally, whose nose was so brown,
> Who looked like a clam if you gave her a smile,
> And went into fits at your frown?

And sentimentally as "Ben Bolt's Reply," Sung by Marry Richmond, in *Richmond's My Young Wife Songster* (N.Y. n.d. p. 71):

> Ah yes I remember that name with delight
> Sweet Alice, so cherished and dear,
> I seek her lone grave in the pale hour of night
> And moisten the turf with a tear.

See Carmer *(Songs of the Rivers of America,* p. 10) for a two-stanza version (my first two) and an interesting headnote.

"Ben Bolt," contributed by Mrs. R. Van Iderstine, Daphne, Baldwin County, 1953, from a manuscript copy.

Oh, don't you remember sweet Alice, Ben Bolt?
Sweet Alice with hair so brown;
She wept with delight when you gave her a smile,
And trembled with fear at your frown.
In the old churchyard in the valley, Ben Bolt,
In a corner obscure and alone,
They have fitted a slab of granite so gray,
And sweet Alice lies under the stone.
They have fitted a slab of granite so gray,
And sweet Alice lies under the stone.

Oh, don't you remember the wood, Ben Bolt,
Near the green, sunny slope of the hill
Where oft we have sung, 'neath its wide spreading shade,
And kept time to the click of the mill?
The mill has gone to decay, Ben Bolt,
And a quiet now reigns all around;
See, the old rustic porch, with its roses so sweet,
Lies scattered and fallen to the ground.

Oh, don't you remember the school, Ben Bolt,
And the master so kind and so true,
And the little nook by the clear running brook,
Where we gathered the flowers as they grew?
In the master's grave grows the grass, Ben Bolt,
And the running little brook is now dry,
And of all the friends who were schoolmates then,
There remain, Ben, but you and I.
And of all the friends who were schoolmates then,
There remain, Ben, but you and I.

108
The Fisherman's Girl

This song, and its companion piece "The Fisherman's Boy," has not been widely reported despite the fact that it apparently was popular in the latter half of the nineteenth century. It seemingly is an Irish song. Shoemaker *(North Pennsylvania Minstrelsy,* p. 209) has one stanza. Eddy *(Ballads and Songs from Ohio,* p. 177) reports both songs from a manuscript dated 1852. Jackson *(Early Songs of Uncle Sam,* pp. 149-150) gives it. It is reported from Newfoundland (Greenleaf, *Ballads and Sea Songs of Newfoundland,* p. 200), and Kentucky *(Ballads of the Kentucky Highlands,* p. 186). The song was rather popular in the songsters. It was in *Beadle's Dime Song Book, No. 5* (N.Y., 1860, p. 41), *The Patriotic Songster* (N.Y., 1863, p. 25), and *Beadle's Half-Dime Singer's Library, No. 20* (N.Y., 1878, p. 4). "The Fisherman's Boy," the companion piece, was also rather popular in the songsters. It was in *The Patriotic Songster* (N.Y., c. 1863, p. 21), *The American Singer's Own Book* (N.Y., 18--, p. 368), and *The Patriotic Songster* (N.Y., n.d., p. 23). Neither song apparently was popular in Alabama. I have only one copy of "The Fisherman's Girl."

"The Fisherman's Girl," sung by Mrs. Nola Browne, Millport, Lamar County, 1953. She has sung it for fifty years.

A-round my hat I will wear a green wil-ler, A-round

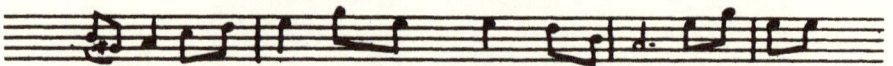

my hat I will wear it twelve months and a day. And if an-y-

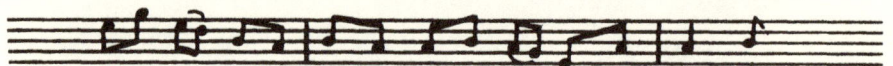

bod-y asks me the rea-son why I wear it, I'll tell them

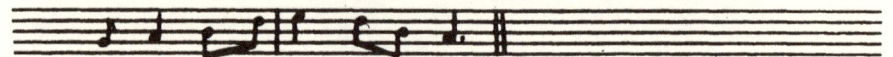

my true love is far, far a-way.

Around my hat I will wear a green willer,
Around my hat I will wear it twelve months and a day.
And if anybody asks me the reason why I wear it,
I'll tell them my true love is far, far away.

Away in the low lands a poor girl she wandered,
Away in the low lands she wandered away.
She wandered through some nation and lost her bright relation,
Just a poor little fisherman's girl, whose friends are all dead and gone.

I gave my love a ring the same day he started,
I gave my love a ring, that he might remember me.
And if he ever returns then we surely will get married.
We surely will get married; forever it will be.

And then I'll have a friend, and surely a true one.
And then I'll have a friend that is nigh unto me.
And when united hearted, we never shall be parted,
Cried a poor little fisherman's girl, whose friends are all dead and gone.

109
Marionene

This piece probably originated in one of the many sentimental songsters of the latter half of the nineteenth century. Its ingredients are such as would make it appealing to the folk. Yet I have not found it in any other collection of folk songs, and I have only one copy.

"Marionene," from a manuscript copy in the possession of Mrs. R. Van Iderstine, Daphne, Baldwin County, 1953.

Marionene, when you said to me
That your love would never fade away,
Maidens some times break their vows, they say,
Did you know what love might do?
'Tis a mystery so rare,
Bringing nought but grief and care.
Marionene, I adore thee.
Heart and soul are only thine.
Marionene, hear my prayer.
Heart and soul are only thine.

Marionene, I will love no more,
Yet, alas, I cannot sever,
I must love and love forever.
Stay then, Darling, I implore.
Yes, I yield to move's decree.
Without thee to death I'd pine.
Marionene, hear my prayer.
Heart and soul are only thine.
Marionene, hear my prayer.
Heart and soul are only thine.

110
I'm Wearing My Heart Away For You

This piece was written by Charles K. Harris in 1902 (Spaeth, *History of Popular Music,* p. 615). Despite its having the right sentiment and language, the song seems not to have been taken up by the folk. I have one text.

"I'm Wearing My Heart Away For You," sung by Mrs. Nola Browne, Millport, Lamar County, 1951. She has sung it for the past forty years at least.

The bees are hum-ming in the wild woods, Love. The

flo-wers their ti-ny heads bow low. The birds are

sing-ing in the wild woods, Love. They miss your kind

sweet face, I know. I'm wear-ing my heart a-way for you.

It cries a-loud, "My love, be true." I dream of you by

night; I long for you by day. I'm wear-ing my heart a-way

for you.

The bees are humming in the wild woods, Love.
The flowers their tiny heads bow low.
The birds are singing in the wild wood, Love.
They miss your kind, sweet face, I know.

Chorus:
   I'm wearing my heart away for you.
   It cries aloud, "My love be true."
   I dream of you by night; I long for you by day.
   I'm wearing my heart away for you.

I wonder where you are tonight, my love,
As all alone I sit and dream.
I wonder if your heart's with me tonight,
And if the same stars for you gleam.

Some time I think there is another, Dear.
Some fairer face has won your heart.
I hope the day will never come,
The day we two must part.

111
Where Is My Darling Tonight?

This piece is one of the popular sentimental love songs in Alabama. Undoubtedly it is from an origin outside of folk tradition. The L.C. Checklist (p. 4) reports it from Kentucky. Other collections of folk songs do not include it. It appears, however, four times in my collection. It has the right sentiment, the right language to make it popular among the folk.

A

"Where Is My Darling Tonight?" sung by Mrs. Nola Browne, Millport, Lamar County, 1952. She learned it from neighborhood girls about fifty years ago.

Sit-ting a-lone by the door, Look-ing far out on
the sea, Think-ing of one that I love, Dear-er than life
is to me. All a-lone, all a-lone, Tell me why don't he
write? When sad-ly I look up and say: "Where is my darling to-night?"

Sitting alone by the door,
Looking far out on the sea,
Thinking of one that I love,
Dearer than life is to me.
All alone, all alone,
Tell me why don't he write?
When sadly I look up and say:
"Where is my darling tonight?"

B

"Sitting Alone," contributed by Mrs. J.V. Tarwater, Fayette, Fayette County, 1952, from a manuscript.

> Sitting alone by the door,
> Looking far out on the sea,
> Thinking of one that I love,
> Dearer than life is to me.
> Softly the pale beaming stars
> Shed their sweet lights on me,
> And all my poor heart longs to know,
> Where is my darling tonight?
>
> Chorus:
>> Sitting alone, all alone.
>> Tell me why don't he write?
>> All my poor heart longs to know:
>> Where is my darling tonight?
>
> Looking far out on the sea,
> Silver beyond the pale moon,
> Wavelets come back to the shore,
> Bringing to me the sad tune.
> Birds of the sea and the shore
> Sport on the deep in the night,
> And all my poor heart doth ask:
> Where is my darling tonight?

C

"Where Is My Darling Tonight?" sung by Mrs. Nettie Coleman, Tucson, Arizona, 1952. She learned it in Greene County, Alabama, around forty years ago. A fragment very similar to A.

D

"Where Is My Darling Tonight?" sung by Mrs. Ruth Clements, Holt, Tuscaloosa County, 1952. A fragment similar to A.

112
Only A Rosebud

Rosebuds, as well as other flowers, are common in folk love songs. I have not found this fragment of song in any other collection.

"Only A Rosebud," sung by Miss Drucilla Hall, Millport, Lamar County, 1952.

Oft-times I fan-cy at the close of day That she is

wait-ing for me far a-way. Still in my mem-'ry her sweet

face I see Smil-ing as when she gave this rose to me. On-ly

a rose-bud that she wore in her hair; On-ly a rose-bud,

noth-ing more. Sweet fad-ed flow-er that she left in my care.

Ofttimes I fancy at the close of day
That she is waiting for me far away.
Still in my mem'ry her sweet face I see
Smiling as when she gave this rose to me.

Chorus:
    Only a rosebud that she wore in her hair,
    Only a rosebud, nothing more,
    Sweet faded flower that she left in my care.

Chorus:
    "You're as welcome as flowers in May,
    And I love you in the same old way.
    I've been waiting for you day by day.
    You're as welcome as the flowers in May.

I dreamed I saw my sweetheart, Bess,
And once again we pledged our love.
I heard her answer her sweet "Yes,"
As in happy days gone by.
I awoke and found it was a dream.
My sweetheart is here no more.
I always wish she was nigh to say,
"I love you in the same old way."

113
Welcome As The Flowers In May

This song was probably a music-hall production. I have not found it reported in any other collection of folk songs. I have only one Alabama text.

"You're As Welcome As The Flowers In May," sung by Mrs. Nola Browne, Millport, Lamar County, 1951. She has sung it for at least forty-five years.

Last night I dreamed a sweet, sweet dream. I thought I saw my sweet-heart Bess. And oh how hap-py was I. I made a vow no more to roam. We were hap-py as in days gone by When we used to sit and pledge our love, And she would al-ways to me say: "I love you now and al-ways will. You're as wel-come as flowers in May, And I love you in the same old way. I've been wait-ing for you day by day. You're as wel-come as the flow-ers in May.

Last night I dreamed a sweet, sweet dream.
I thought I saw my sweetheart, Bess.
And, oh, how happy was I.
I made a vow no more to roam.
We were happy as in days gone by
When we used to sit and pledge our love,
And she would always say:
"I love you and always will."

114
Little White Rose

As the Brown Collection (II, 640) points out, this song parallels the theme of "They Say It Is Sinful To Flirt." Outside of Brown I have not found this song reported. I have two Alabama versions, one a fragment. Brown has three stanzas and a chorus — my stanzas 2, 3, 4, with 3 sung as a chorus.

A

"Little White Rose," sung by Mrs. Sam O'Brient, Reform, Pickens County, 1952. She does not remember where or when she learned it.

I'll sing you a song of a little white rose.
This song is sad but, ah, sweet,
About a cruel hearted woman whose heart was cold as a stone,
And, oh, how she flirted with the lads.

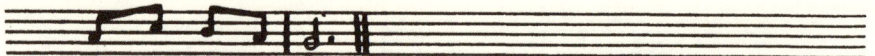

He gave me the rose, the little white rose;
He asked me to wear it for him.
I have that little rose yet and I never shall forget
To wear it just as long as he is true.

It was on the old stump where we sat side by side
And watched the beautiful stream beneath our feet.
We would whisper words of love while the little birds sang above,
Those words they were tender, low and sweet.

He was found one day in a cold, cold stream;
There he had thrown himself to drown

With the rose between his teeth, just as if he wished to speak.
I'd like to wear the white rose in my crown.

It was in the month of May, all in the mild of May,
When I sat on the . . . . . river bank.
We would whisper words of love while the little birds sang above,
Those words they were tender, low and sweet.

B

"It Was On An Old Stump," sung by Mrs. A.J. Shea, Sheffield, Colbert County, 1953.

It was on an old stump where we sat side by side
And watched the beau-ti-ful stream be-neath our feet.
They whis-pered words of love as the lit-tle bird sang
a-bove; Those words were ten-der, low and sweet. One
day he was found in the cold, cold stream, where he had
thrown him-self to drown, with a rose be-tween his teeth
as he whis-pered to say: "I want to wear this rose in
my crown."

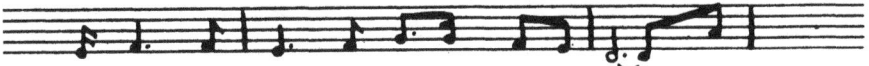

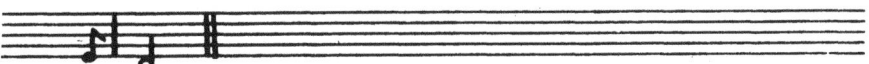

It was on an old stump where we sat side by side
And watched the beautiful stream beneath our feet.
They whispered words of love as the little bird sang above;
Those words were tender, low and sweet.

One day he was found in the cold, cold stream,
Where he had thrown himself to drown,
With a rose between his teeth as he whispered to say:
"I want to wear this rose in my crown."

115
Two Little Girls In Blue

This song, which, says Spaeth *(History of Popular Music,* p. 269), imitated "the technique, language and even the melody of 'After The Ball,' but without duplicating the naive charm of Charles K. Harris," earned for its author the payment of $10. (Gilbert, *Lost Chords,* p. 275). Charles Graham wrote it in 1893, and it was one of the most popular songs of its time. There was a broadside printed of it by H.J. Wehman, New York (sold for $.40 or 3 for a dollar). The piece has not been widely reported as a folk song. Randolph (IV, 338) gives one text but no tune. Mr. Robert T. Burns, Roanoke, Alabama, heard it on the London radio in 1951. It is still popular with the folk of Alabama.

A

"Two Little Girls In Blue," sung by Miss Drucilla Hall, Millport, Lamar County, 1952. When or how she learned it she does not remember.

An old man gazed on a pho-to-graph in a lock-et

he'd worn for years. His neph-ew then asked him the

rea-son why the pic-ture caused him tears. "Lis-ten,

my lad, and you shall hear of a sto-ry that's sad but

true. Your fath-er and I at school one day met two lit-tle

girls in blue. Two lit-tle girls in blue, lad, two lit-tle

girls in blue. They were sis-ters and we were broth-ers.

We learned to love the two. One lit-tle girl in blue, lad,

one lit-tle girl in blue, won your fath-er's heart, be-

came your moth-er. I mar-ried the oth-er, but we have

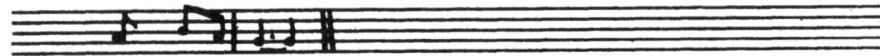

drift-ed a-part."

An old man gazed on a photograph
In a locket he'd worn for years.
His nephew then asked him the reason why
The picture caused him tears.
"Listen, my lad, and you shall hear
Of a story that's sad but true.
Your father and I at school one day
Met two little girls in blue.

Chorus:
  "Two little girls in blue, lad,

Two little girls in blue.
They were sisters and we were brothers;
We learned to love the two.
One little girl in blue, lad,
Won your father's heart,
Became your mother; I married the other,
But we have drifted apart.

"This picture is one of those girls, my lad,
And was oncet to me a wife.
I thought her unfaithful. We quarreled one night,
And, alas, we parted for life.
A fancy of jealousy wounded her heart,
A heart that was good and true.
For two better girls never lived, my lad,
Than those little girls in blue."

B

"Two Little Girls in Blue," sung by Mrs. C.L. Kennedy, Vernon, Lamar County, 1952. She has sung it for fifty years. Essentially text A, but the tune is different, and the second stanza is clearer.

An old man gazed on a pho-to-graph in a lock-et he'd worn for years. His neph-ew asked him the rea-son why this pic-ture should cause him tears. "Come lis-ten," he said, "I'll tell you, lad, of a sto-ry that's old but true: your fath-er and I at school one day met two lit-tle girls in blue. Two lit-tle girls in blue, lad,

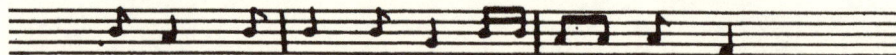

two lit-tle girls in blue. They were sis-ters, we were

broth-ers, and learned to love the two. One lit-tle

girl in blue, lad, won your fath-er's heart, Be-came

your moth-er; I mar-ried the oth-er, but we have drift-ed

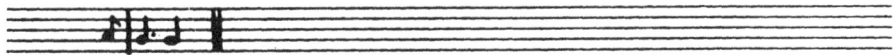

a-part.

An old man gazed on a photograph in a locket he'd worn for years.
His nephew asked him the reason why this picture should cause him tears.
"Come listen," he said, "I'll tell you, lad, of a story that's old but true:
Your father and I at school one day met two little girls in blue.
They were sisters, we were brothers, and learned to love the two.
One little girl in blue, lad, won your father's heart,
Became your mother; I married the other, but we have drifted apart."

"This picture was one of those girls," he said, "to me she was once a wife.
I thought her unfaithful, we quarreled, lad, and parted that night for life.

A fancy of jealousy wronged her heart, a heart that was good and true.
No better girls ever lived than they, those two little girls in blue."

C

"Two Little Girls In Blue," contributed by Mr. Theron Burns, Wedowee, Randolph County, 1953. He has been singing it for the last forty years at least. Essentially same as A.

D

"Two Little Girls In Blue," sung by Mrs. Nola Browne, Millport, Lamar County, 1952. A one-stanza fragment. She has sung it for the past fifty-five years. She learned it in Lamar County.

E

"Two Little Girls In Blue," sung by Mrs. O.C. Powell, Titus, Elmore County, 1952. Full version, similar to A.

F

"Two Little Girls In Blue," sung by Mrs. Nettie Coleman, Tucson, Arizona, 1952. Essentially version A. She learned it in Greene County, Alabama, forty years ago.

G

"Two Little Girls in Blue," sung by Mrs. Eva Collins, Vernon, Lamar County, 1952. Essentially version A.

116
I'll Be All Smiles Tonight

The words and music for this song were composed by T.R. Ransom; Owens *(Texas Folk Songs,* p. 138) says the music was originally published by T.B. Harms & Co., New York, 1879. According to *Fred Somers' New Collection of 250 Songs* (Chicago, 1887, p. 43), the music was also published by George Molineaux, Brooklyn. It was also published in *Wehman Bros. Good Old Time Songs No. 1* (N.Y., 1910, p. 20). Randolph (IV, 334) has two texts; Ford *(Traditional Music of America,* pp. 137, 414-415) has a text and a tune; Davis *(Folksongs of Virginia,* p. 79) lists the title; so does Pound *(Syllabus,* p. 47). Despite the few collectors reporting this song, it has been quite popular in Alabma. I collected seven texts, all similar.

A

"I'll Be All Smiles Tonight," sung by Miss Drucilla Hall, Millport, Lamar County, 1952.

I'll deck my hair with ros-es; my loved one may

be there. The gems that oth-ers gave me will shine

with-in my hair. And ev-en they who know me will think

my heart is light. Though my heart may break to-mor-row

I'll be all smiles to-night. I'll be all smiles to-night,

Love. I'll be all smiles to-night. Though my heart will

break to-mor-row I'll be all smiles to-night.

I'll deck my brow with roses, my loved one may be there.
The gems that others gave me will shine within my hair.
And even they who know me will think my heart is light.
Though my heart may break tomorrow, I'll be all smiles tonight.

Chorus:
    I'll be all smiles tonight, Love, I'll be all smiles tonight.
    Though my heart may break tomorrow, I'll be all smiles tonight.

When the room he entered, the bride upon his arm,
I stood and gazed upon them as though they were a charm.
He turned and smiled upon her as once he smiled on me.
They'll know not what I suffer, they'll find no change in me.

And when the dance commences, oh how I will rejoice.
I'll sing the songs he taught me without one faltering voice.
When flatterers come around me, they'll think my heart is light.
Though my heart may break tomorrow, I'll be all smiles tonight.

And when the dance is over and I'm at home to rest,
I'll think of him, dear Mother, the one I love the best.
He was beloved, believe me, but now is so cold and strange.
He sought not to deceive me; false friends have wrought this change.

B

"I'll Be All Smiles Tonight," sung by Mrs. Della Collins, Vernon, Lamar County, 1952. Three stanzas and chorus. First two stanzas and chorus essentially same as A. Third stanza seems obviously a mixed-up version:

And when the dance is over and all have gone to rest,
I'll think of him, dear Mother, the one I loved the best.
I once did love, believe me, but now he has grown cold.
And I sought not to deceive him; false friends have wrought his change.

C

"I'll Be All Smiles Tonight," sung by Mrs. Nola Browne, Millport, Lamar County, 1952. She has sung it for over fifty years. Two stanzas and verse. Essentially A.

D

"I'll Be All Smiles Tonight, Love," sung by Mrs. Flora Phillips,

Cullman, Cullman County, 1953, from a manuscript in her possession, dated around 1938. Four stanzas and chorus. Practically identical with A.

E

"I'll Be All Smiles Tonight," contributed by Miss Florence Bailey, Crane Hill, Cullman County, 1953. Identical with D.

F

"I'll Be All Smiles Tonight," sung by Mrs. O.C. Powell, Titus, Elmore County, 1952. Four stanzas and chorus, identical with A.

G

"I'll Be All Smiles Tonight," from the Alabama Archives, collected by John Proctor Mills, with this note: "This one seems to have been very popular at parties for grown-ups." Four stanzas and chorus. Same as A.

H

"I'll Deck My Brow With Roses," sung by the Richardson sisters, Kennedy, Lamar County, 1952. Four stanzas and chorus. Same as A.

I

"I'll Deck My Brow With Roses," from a newspaper clipping contributed by Mrs. Lenora Williams, McKenzie, Butler County, 1952. Four stanzas and chorus. Same as A.

300

III
PSEUDO-NEGRO SONGS

117
Darling Cloe

This pseudo-Negro love song is undoubtedly a minstrel or songster piece. I have not found it, however, in any of the books I have searched through. Nor have I found it reported elsewhere as a folk song. The song, as I have it here, is an interesting example of how songs are changed in the oral trandition. My informant had a manuscript copy. But she had not seen it in many years. She sang the song for me as she remembered it. Later she found the manuscript and gave it to me. I reproduce both versions below.

A

"Darling Cloe," sung by Mrs. R. Van Iderstine, Daphne, Baldwin County, 1953. She has sung it perhaps fifty years.

In the old Car-li-na state, where the sweet mag-no-

lias bloom, And the pick-a-nin-ny dar-kies learn to hoe.

There is one I long to see. She was ev-er true to me. And

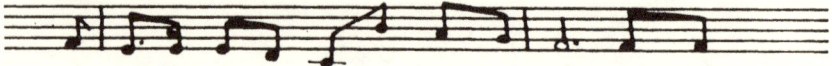

like mine I know her hair is turned to snow. But she'll

wait till I come back by the coon and the pos-sum track,

For I'm go-ing home to see my dar-ling Cloe. I'm go-ing

.... And I'm go-ing home to see

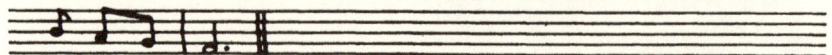

my dar-ling Cloe.

In the old Car-lina state
Where the sweet magnolias bloom,
And the pickaninny darkies learn to hoe,
There is one I long to see.
She was ever true to me,
And like mine I know her hair is turned to snow.
But she'll wait till I get back,
By the coon and the possum track,
For I'm going home to see my darling Cloe.

Chorus:
    I'm going . . . .
    . . . .
And I'm going home to see my darling Cloe.

B

"Darling Cloe," from a manuscript copy in the possession of Mrs. Van Iderstine, Daphne. She wrote it some fifty years ago, and had not seen it for at least twenty-five years before finding it, after extensive searching, for me.

In the old Car-lina state
Where the smartest flowers grow,
And the music-loving darkies all are gay,
There is one I long to see,
She was ever true to me,
But I left her many, many years ago.
But she will wait till I come back,
By de coon and possum track,
And I'm going home to see my darling Cloe.

Chorus:
    Darling Cloe, darling Cloe,
    Darling Cloe, darling Cloe,
    Your sweet face I soon shall see, I know.
    For it's twenty years or more
    Since I left her cabin door,
    And I'se gwine back to see my darling Cloe.

Where the tall palmetto trees
Fan the gentle southern breeze,
And the pickaninny darkies learn to hoe,
There is one I long to see.
She was ever true to me,
And like mine I know her hair has turned to snow.
But she'll wait till I come back,
By the coon and possum track,
For I'm going home to see my darling Cloe.

Ere they lay her 'neath the sod,
Upon which we've often trod,
When this world will hold no other charm for me.
She is waiting for her Joe,
And I'm bound to see my Cloe,
For I have not seen her since we all were free.
But she'll wait till I come back,
By de coon and possum track,
For I's going back to see my darling Cloe.

118
Old Carolina State

The Brown Collection (III, 485) reports three texts of this song. As is said there, this song is one of the early minstrel songs imitative of Stephen C. Foster. It was published in Philadelphia in 1847, the words by Francis Lynch, the music by James Power (Dichter and Shapiro, *Early American Sheet Music*, p. 142). In the *American Singer's Own Book* (18--, p. 633) the words and music are attributed to A.F. Winnemore, as they are in *The New Negro Forget-Me-Not Songster* (1848, p. 91). In the *Harmoneon's Casket of Songs and Glees* (1850, p. 51) the words are attributed to Lynch, the music to Power. The song is in *White's New Melodeon Song Book, No. 1* (18--, p. 26); *The Ethiopian Glee Book; Containing the Songs Sung by Christy's Minstrels* (1850, p. 37); *Christy's Plantation Melodies, No. 3* (C. 1851, p. 38); *Christy's Negro Songster* (1855, pp. 246-7); *Beadle's Dime Song Book, No. 6* (1860, p. 19); *Songs of Love and Liberty*, "compiled by a North Carolina Lady" (1864, p. 40); *Champagne Charlie and Coal Oil Tommy Songster* (1868, p. 33); and in *Popular Songs of All Nations* (188-, p. 154) with the words attributed to Francis Lynch, the music to L.V.H. Crosby. The popularity of the song is further attested to by its appearance as the tune for other songs in songsters — "Scott and Graham," Tune: "Dearest Mae" *(The Scott Songster,* 1852, p. 21); "Coming Around the Horn," Air: "Dearest May" *(Put's Original California Songster,* 1868, p. 37). The texts in the various songsters vary in length and treatment. My one Alabama text shows various differences and close similarities to the printed texts indicative of oral transmission.

"Old Carolina State," sung by Mrs. Jenny Weathers, Millport, Lamar County, 1951. She learned it fifty years ago.

Dar-kies, lis-ten to me, A sto-ry I'll re-late.

It hap-pened in the val-ley in the old Car-lin-a State.

Oh, Mae, my dear-est Mae, You're love-ly as the day. Your

eyes are bright, they shine at night, When the moon am

gone a-way.

Darkies, listen to me,
A story I'll relate.
It happened in the valley
In the old Carolina State.

Chorus:
    Oh, Mae, my dearest Mae,
    You're lovely as the day.
    Your eyes are bright,
    They shine at night,
    When the moon am gone away.

Way down in the valley
When they used to mow the hay,
It made me work the harder
When I thought of lovely Mae.

I love dear old Carolina.
I pray I can always stay
'Neath the trees of old Carolina,
And with you, my lovely Mae.

119
Little Old Log Cabin in Tennessee

This pseudo-Negro song shows the fondness of folk singers for songs about Tennessee. Undoubtedly it is of music-hall or songster origin, although I have not found it. Nor have I found it reported in any other collection.

"Little Old Log Cabin in Tennessee," sung by an anonymous informant in the Women's State Prison, Wetumpka, Elmore County, 1952. She has known the song for probably fifteen years. She has traveled over most of the U.S., has been to Alaska, and might have learned it anywhere.

There's a lit-tle log cab-in down in Ten-nes-see,

Where the morn-ing glo-ries go sweep-ing round the door.

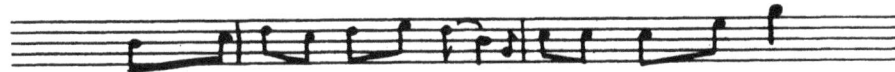

There's a lit-tle yel-ler gal a-wait-ing there for me.

She's been my la-dy friend a year or more. Hon-ey, you

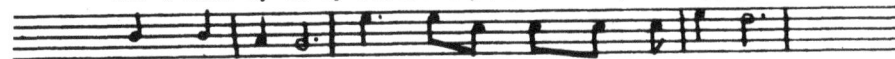

more than won me. Cast them big brown eyes up-on me.

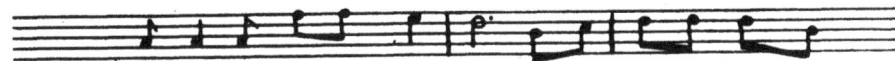

Give me your lit-tle brown hand. We will live on love and

kiss-es if you will be my miss-us. Oh, Hon-ey, does you

love your man? Now she's the col-or of a sad-dle or an

old sor-rel horse. But I would-n't love her more if she

were white.

There's a little log cabin down in Tennessee,
Where the morning glories go sweeping round the door.
There's a little yeller gal a-waiting there for me.
She has been my lady friend a year or more.
Honey, you more than won me.
Cast them big brown eyes upon me.
Give me your little brown hand.
We will live on love and kisses
If you will be my missus.
Oh, Honey, does you love your man?
Now, she's the color of a saddle or an old sorrel horse,
But I wouldn't love her more if she were white.

120
The Jawbone Song

The jawbone as a musical instrument and as humor in song has long been popular, especially with Negroes. Scarborough *(On the Trail of Negro Folk-Songs,* pp. 102-104) prints several Negro songs mentioning the jawbone as an instrument — "the jawbone of a horse or ox or mule, with the teeth left in, which made a queer sound when a key or other piece of metal was drawn across the teeth." For an interesting headnote see Randolph (II, 333). The comic value of the jawbone was recognized by the minstrels and taken up by them. White *(American Negro Folk-Songs,* pp. 305, 333) cites an old minstrel song entitled "Jawbone Walk an' Jawbone Talk." A song entitled "The Old Jawbone" was printed in *The Negro Minstrel* (Glasgow, 1850, p. 14), and "Walk Jaw Bone" was published in the *Negro Forget-Me-Not Songster* (c. 1847, p. 55), "A most popular and highly applauded Melody, as sung by Jenkins, Hallit, de great Cool White, & other celebrated Colored Saboyards." It was also published in *Christy's Negro Melodies No. 4*(Phila., c. 1854, p. 18) and in *Old Dog Tray Songster* (Balti., 18--, p. 248), in a version which deserves printing here for comparison:

De jaw bone hung agin de wall,
De gals all thought dat it would fall;
But dar it hung till de gals all gone,
Den hurra for de old jaw bone.

Chorus:
  Den walk Jawbone, ginger log
  Jaw bone gwine de whole hog.

Apparently "Jawbone" became a character in the minstrel shows. The L.C. Checklist (p. 193) gives texts from Florida, Missouri, Washington, D.C., and Ohio. My A text seems to imply a minstrel character. My B text seems a fragment of a minstrel song different from A.

A

"Old Jawbones," sung by Mrs. Maggie Lee Hayes, Vernon, Lamar County, 1953. She learned it from her father in Fayette County as a child and has sung it for fifty years.

Ev-'ry time I go from home They call on me for to

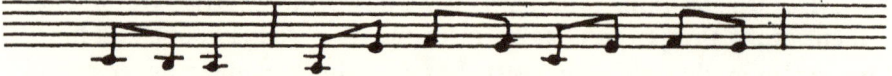

sing Jaw-bones. Jaw-bone walk, and Jaw-bone talk, and

Jaw-bone eat with a knife and fork.

Every time I go from home
They call on me for to sing Jawbones.

Chorus:
    Jawbone walk and jawbone talk.
    Jawbone eat with a knife and fork.

Jawbone's fingers long and slim.
I'se gonna run; I'm afeered of him.

Jawbone's got a crooked nose,
Got knocked knees and pigeon toes.

Jawbone's whisker's long and white,
Amber keep them out of sight.

Jawbone's belly is round as a beet,
Got flop ears and pigeon feet.

Hang old jawbone on the fence,
Young jawbone say you got no sense.

Old jawbone is dead and gone,
Young jawbone is coming on.

B

"Old Jawbones," sung by Mrs. Pennine Hayes, Vernon, Lamar County, 1952. She doesn't remember when she learned it, but probably sixty five years ago at least.

He built his house by the side of the road;
Old ladies, won't you come by?

I'll set you down with a knife and fork
And pass around the hogeye.

Jawbone walks and jawbone talks,
Jawbone eats with a knife and fork.
Walk, talk, Jawbone.

He laid his jawbone on the fence,
He hasn't seen his jawbone since.
Walk, talk, Jawbone.

121
Aunt Jemima's Plaster

This comic song dates back to the Negro minstrelsy of the 1850's, and was circulated in various versions. What may have been a later version was attributed to H. Devine and sung by Frank Moran *(Moran's Songster,* N.Y. 1871, p. 13). I quote two of six stanzas (the others are not very similar) and the chorus:

O, white folks, now I'll sing to you about my Aunt Jemima;
She used to make de best of plaster
Down in old Carolina.

  Sheep skin, bees wax
  'Gundy pitch and plaster.
  De more you try to pull it off
  De more it sticks de faster.

Uncle Tom he caught a cold,
I really don't know how, sirs,
They put the plaster on his head
And drawed him out his trousers.

One version or another appeared in numerous songsters. For example: "As sung by Harry Courtaine, copyrighted Winner & Shuster, Philadelphia (1860)" *Conner's Irish Songster,* (San Francisco, 1860, p. 12); *His Heart Was True To Poll Songster* (N.Y. c. 1871, p. 39); *Love Among The Roses Songster* (N.Y. c. 1869, p. 99); *Marching Through Georgia Songster* (San Francisco, 1867, p. 37); *Mocking Bird Songster* (Phila., 1856, p. 18); *Trifet's Multum In Parvo* (N.Y. c. 1890, p. 241); *Uncle Sam's Army Songster* (N.Y. n.d., p. 25); *Willie E. Lyle's Balm Of Gilead Songster* (N.Y. 1877, p. 50) contains an interesting variant:

The jay bird hung on the swinging limb.
Old Aunt Jemima, ah ah ah
I up with a stone and hit him on de shin
Old Aunt Jemima ah ah ah

3rd stanza

The bullfrog married the tadpole's sister
Old Aunt Jemima

He smacked his lips and then he kissed her.
Old Aunt Jemima.
She says if you love me as I love you
Old Aunt Jemima.
No knife can cut our live in two.
Old Aunt Jemima

The silly words and catchy tune invited various take-offs and parodies. One was called "Hunky Dunky Plaster" sung to the tune of "Aunt Jemima's Plaster" *(Negro Melodies and Happy Contraband, No. 1* Phila., 1865, p. 7); and another was named "The Great Sensation," sung to the air of "Aunt Jemima" by Tony Pastor *(Tony Pastor's Great Sensation Songster,* N.Y. 1864, p. 1).

The piece, surprisingly, has not been widely reported as a folk song. The Brown Collection (II, 628) includes it, with a few references. Randolph (III, 153) includes it and cites a few references. The L.C. Checklist (pp. 12, 360) lists texts from Florida, California and North Carolina. My one Alabama text indicates lack of popularity there. Versions differ sharply from place to place, but the amazing adhesiveness of the plaster is a kind of motif everywhere. My "Yankee Doodle, ha ha ha," lines are, I believe, unique.

"Aunt Jemima," sung by Mrs. Maggie Lee Hayes, Vernon, Lamar County, 1952. She learned it from her father in Fayette County, fifty years ago. The "Yankee Doodle" lines are sung to the tune of that song.

I just stepped out to sing a song a-bout old

Aunt Je-mi-ma Who used to make the blis-ter plas-ters

Way down yon-der in South Car-o-lin-a. Sheep skin and

bees-wax makes a might-y plas-ter. The more you try

to pull it off, It on-ly sticks the fast-er.

I just stepped out to sing a song about old Aunt Jemima,
Who used to make the blister plasters way down yonder in South Carolina.

Chorus:
   Sheep skin and beeswax makes a mighty plaster.
   The more you try to pull if off, it only sticks the faster.

Old Aunt Jemima had a horse and cart; they stalled upon the level.
She put a plaster on the cart and drawed it to the devil.

Old Aunt Jemima climbed a tree; she had a stick to boost her.
There she turned to throwing corn at her old bob tailed rooster.

Yankee Doodle ha ha ha, ha ha ha ha ha;
Yankee Doodle ha ha ha, ha ha ha ha ha.

Old Aunt Jemima had a box blacking, so big or little bigger.
She put a plaster on the box and drawed it to a nigger.

122
'Tater Pie

This pseudo-Negro piece might have been born in the minstrel shows or comic songsters, or it could easily have originated with some mother or father amusing a child. I have found no trace of it anywhere. My one Alabama text was known by two sisters, who have lived close to each other all their lives. To both it was a "silly song."

" 'Tater Pie." sung by Mrs. Minnie Blakeney, Millport, Lamer County, 1952. She thinks it must be at least thirty or forty years old.

For breakfast we have potato pie,
For dinner we have potato pie,
For supper we have potato pie,
And it's sliced potato pie all the time.

Chorus:
 'Tater pie, 'tater pie,
 There's a fly in the sliced potato pie.
 'Tater pie, 'tater pie,
 Choked to death on cold potato pie.

123
As I Went Down To Mas' Cornfiel'

This fragment was perhaps originally a capstan chanty, and full versions of a chanty have been reported. For references and discussion see Brown (III, 224). My two fragments have lost all sea-consciousness, and are sung as a nonsense pseudo-Negro song, with the usual inclusion or exclusion of stanzas depending on the caprice of the singer. For another version from Alabama see White *(American Negro Folk Songs,* p. 246).

A

"As I Went Down in Mas' Cornfiel'," sung by Mrs. Jennie Geer, Kennedy, Lamar County, 1952. She sang this song in the presence of her sisters, who blushingly told her that she should not sing such songs as this. She replied that it was "all right" to sing such songs because I would not mind.

As I went down in Mas' cohn-fiel' A black snake bit me on the heel. I ran, I ran, and I ran my best.

Ran my head in a hor-net's nest.

As I went down in Mas' cohnfiel'
A blacksnake bit me on the heel.
I ran, I ran, and I ran my best.
Ran my head in a hornet's nest.

B

"As I Went Up in My Cornfield," sung by Mrs. Cofield, Wedowee, Randolph County, 1953.

As I went up in my cornfield,
An old blacksnake bit me on my heel.

I looked around and I run my best.
Run my nose in a hornet's nest.

Had a little nigger
And his name was Ben.
Slit his nose to make him grin.
He opened his mouth and his nose fell in.

124
Bill Bailey

This piece, "one of the best of all rag-time 'coon' songs," was written by Hughie Cannon in 1902 (Spaeth, *History of Popular Music*, p. 317). Neely *(Tales and Songs of Southern Illinois*, p. 216) reports a full text. The L.C. Checklist (p. 23) reports a text from Florida and one from California. Without doubt the song is more popular than these examples indicate. My two Alabama texts are fragments, but they show a rather wide popularity in the state.

A

"Bill Bailey," sung by Mrs. Nola Browne, Millport, Lamar County, 1952. She has sung it around fifty years.

Won't you come home, Bill Bailey, won't you come home? I know I've done you wrong. Re-mem-ber that Sun-day eve-ning I drove you out With noth-ing but a fine tooth comb? Re-mem-ber that Sun-day eve-ning I drove you out With noth-ing but a fine tooth comb? I know I'm to blame, Ain't that a shame? Bill Bai-ley, won't you please come home?

Won't you come home, Bill Bailey, won't you come home?
I know I've done you wrong.
Remember that Sunday evening I drove you out
With nothing but a fine-tooth comb?
I know I'm to blame; ain't that a shame?
Bill Bailey, won't you please come home?

B

"Bill Bailey," sung by Mrs. Lily Turner, Crane Hill, Cullman County, 1953. She has known it thirty years.

Won't you come home, Bill Bailey, won't you come home, Be boss the whole day long? I'll do the cook-ing, dar-ling, I'll pay the rent. I know I have done you wrong. I know I'm to blame. Now ain't that a shame? Bill Bai-ley, won't you please come home?

Won't you come home, Bill Bailey, won't you come home?
Be boss the whole day long.
I'll do the cooking, darling, I'll pay the rent.
I know I have done you wrong.
I know I'm to blame; now ain't that a shame?
Bill Bailey, won't you please come home?

It was on a rainy evening that I drove you out
With nothing but a fine-tooth comb.
I know I'm to blame, and ain't that a shame?
Bill Bailey, won't you please come home?

125
Loving Henry

This pseudo-Negro comic song is likely from a minstrel show or comic songster. The L.C. Checklist (p. 246) reports nine versions of a song by the same name. I have not found it in any other printed collection. Apparently never popular in Alabama, it has come to me in only one text.

"Loving Henry," sung by Mrs. Nola Browne, Millport, Lamar County, 1951. It was sung in the 90's.

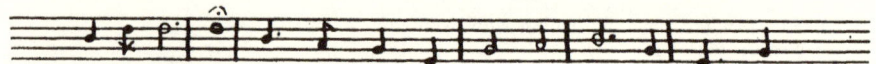

Have you seen my lovin' Henery,
Oh, have you seen dat darlin' man?
I'm jes crazy 'bout my Henery.
He's de sweetes' man in town.
Oh, have you seen my lovin' Henery,
Oh, have you see dat darlin' man?
I thought I heard a knockin'. (knocking)
"Is dat you, Henry, out dare in dat cold and chilly?"
"It's me." (deep voice)
Oh, dare's my lovin' Henery now.

126
Johnson Had an Old Gray Mule

This song undoubtedly originated with the blackface minstrel or in the comic songster. But it has undergone much change among the folk. The Brown Collection (III, 566) includes one text similar to my version B. White (*American Negro Folk Songs*, p. 288) reports the song, as do Gardner and Chickering *(Ballads and Songs of Southern Michigan*, p. 447) and Pound *(American Ballads and Songs,* pp. 213-214). The L.C. Checklist (p.399) lists it from New York City.

A

"Old Gray Mule," sung by Mrs. E. A. Savage, Newtonville, Fayette County, 1952.

Old Thomp-son had an old gray mule And he drove
him to a cart. He loved the mule and the mule loved him
With all his mul-ish heart. Old Thomp-son knew when the
roos-ter crowed The day was go-ing to break. He caught
that mule by the leg of a stool And he cur-ried him
down with a rake, rake, rake; He cur-ried him down with
a rake.

Old Thompson had an old gray mule
And he drove him to a cart.
He loved the mule, and the mule loved him
With all his mulish heart.

Old Thompson knew when the rooster crowed
The day was going to break.
He caught that mule by the leg of a stool
And he curried him down with a rake, rake, rake.
He curried him down with a rake.

B

"Sam Johnson Had a Mule," sung by Mr. Isaac Rollins, Wedowee, Randolph County, 1953. It is one of his favorite comic songs.

Sam John-son had an old gray mule. He cur-ried him
with a rake. The old mule knowed when the chick-en
crowed That it was near day-break. Hold that mule, and
hold that mule, hold that mule I say. If you can't
get your sad-dle on the blamed old fool, Then hold that
mule I say.

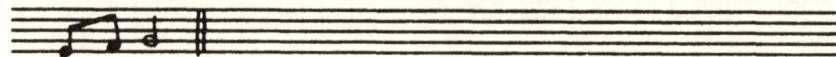

Sam Johnson had an old gray mule,
He curried him with a rake.
The old mule knowed when the rooster crowed
That it was near daybreak.

Chorus:
> Hold that mule, and hold that mule,
> Hold that mule, I say.
> If you don't get your saddle on the blamed old fool,
> Then hold that mule, I say.

That mule could pull ten thousand pounds,
That wasn't half a load.
Grab a track, both white and black,
And give that mule the road.

Sam Johnson had a great white house,
Sixteen stories high,
And every story in that house
Was filled with chicken pie.

And when I was a little man,
Just sixteen inches high,
I would climb a table leg
To get that chicken pie.

127
Old Miss Ruckett

This bit of pseudo-Negro nonsense is typical of rather a large section of humorous folk songs. The pieces are made as ridiculous and extravagant as possible, but often they show a persistence that songs that make more sense lack. I have not seen this song in any other collection. I have one text.

"Old Miss Ruckett," sung by Mrs. Maggie Lee Hayes, Vernon, Lamar County, 1952. She probably learned it from her father, in Fayette County, more than forty years ago. Her brother, Mr. Gilbert Davis, Montgomery, also knows and sings it.

Old Miss Ruck-ett she done kicked the buc-ket And

gone to hea-ven a-bove. Sit-ting up there on the top-most

bough, Sing-ing like a tur-tle dove.

Old Miss Ruckett she done kicked the bucket,
And gone to heaven above.
Sitting up there on the topmost bough
Singing like a turtle dove.

128
Old Tom Wilson

Like the piece before this one this song is a bit of pseudo-Negro nonsense that is sung simply because it is nonsense. The L.C. Checklist (p. 301) reports it from Kentucky and Tennessee.

"Old Tom Wilson," sung by Mr. Gilbert Davis, Montgomery, 1953. Mr. Davis is a brother to Mrs. Hayes. Both learned their nonsense songs in Fayette County when they were young. For more than forty years both have enjoyed singing them.

Old Tom Wilson laying in bed.
Out the window he popped his old head.
Snow ball hit him in the eyeball "Bim!"
Good Lord, nigger, don't you do that again.

129
Old Miss Wilson

This bit of pseudo-Negro nonsense, like the two pieces just above, combines "Old Dan Tucker" with other nonsense lines, and is sung because it is so ridiculous. Such songs are rather deprecated by many folk singers and many folk, and are therefore often sung for their shock effect. I have not found just this combination elsewhere.

"Old Miss Wilson," sung by Mrs. Maggie Lee Hayes, Vernon, Lamar County, 1952. See the note for "Old Tom Wilson."

Old Miss Wilson went to town Walking those streets

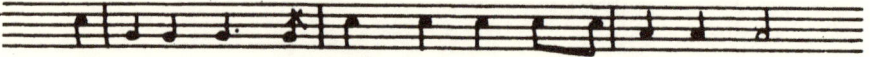

all up and down. She combed her hair with a carriage wheel

And died with the tooth-ache in her heel.

Old Miss Wilson went to town,
Walking them streets all up and down.
Combed her hair with a carriage wheel.
Died with the toothache in her heel.

IV
SOCIAL COMMENTARY SONGS

130
The High Society Girl

This criticism of the modern girl seems to have been composed as a satire. Yet my informant sang it as a funny song. Perhaps the change in time drained off the anger of the original singers. There are other pieces criticizing fashions and society, but in my opinion this one is perhaps the best. It surely is the funniest. Seemingly a local piece, it has not been reported elsewhere.

"The High Society Girl," contributed by Mrs. Maggie Lee Hayes, Vernon, Lamar County, 1953. She probably learned it from her father in Fayette County. Tune: "Shortnin' Bread."

> Granny, get your hair cut; paint your face and shine,
> Granny, get your hair cut short like mine.
> If you want to kick high and have a big time,
> Granny, get your dress cut short like mine.
>
> Chorus:
>> Then, Granny, get your hair cut, caper and shine.
>> Granny, get your dress cut short like mine.
>
> Come to the club with paint on your nose.
> Don't mind your dress so you wear your hose.
> Come to the dance like the gray mule pitches,
> Cut a big shine in granddad's britches.
>
> Stand on your head, Granny, and knock at the moon,
> Like all girls do where they want to marry soon.
> Don't be ashamed nor think you are fast,
> For modesty and virtue are things of the past.
>
> We'll go to the ball game, where the boys bat,
> And we'll go to the park, where the girls skin the cat.
> We'll ride the gray mule without skirt or saddle.
> For now the men walk and the women ride a-straddle.
>
> Come to the bathing pool, Granny, and dive like a shad,
> Like we girls do when we swim with the boys from fad.
> Come to the movies, where all silly women come,
> For that which was vulgar is now only fun.

131
Boys in This Country Trying to Advance

This comment on the manners of the day is found in several other collections. Belden *(Ballads and Songs,* p. 430) says it is doubtless from print; he gives a short bibliography. Cox *(Folksongs of the South,* p. 253) calls his text "A Comical Ditty." Lomax *(Cowboy Songs and Other Frontier Ballads,* p. 211) gives a text.

"Boys in This Country Trying to Advance," sung by Mrs. Mary Crowder, Sulligent, Lamar County, 1952.

The boys in this coun-try they are try-ing to advance by court-ing the girls and learn-ing to dance. All
in this world they want to do is get a pret-ty watch and
a spec-ial hat too. Sing down down, sing down, sing down
down, sing day.

The boys in this country they are trying to advance
By courting the girls and learning to dance.
All in this world they want to do
Is get a pretty watch and a special hat too,
Sing down down, sing down, sing down down, sing day.

They go to the ball, and whiskey they will take;
Get out in the dark and their bottles they will break.
Someone will say, "There's a jug around here.
Come on, boys, and get your share."
Sing down down, sing down, sing down down, sing day.

They go in the house with a spur on their heel;
They yelp and they bother for the next reel,
Saying, "How do I look in my brand new suit,
With my pants tucked down in my high heeled boot?"
Sing down down, sing down, sing down down, sing day.

The girls in this country they keep . . . . . .
They snigger and laugh, don't mind what at.
They snigger and laugh and they tell dirty lies,
And they can't get married to save their lives,
Sing down down, sing down, sing down down, sing day.

They go to church with their snuff in their hand.
They take a little dip to make them look grand.
They meet with a stranger and, "How do you do?"
Take a little dip or maybe take two,
Sing down down, sing down, sing down down, sing day.

132
Putting On The Style

This bit of social commentary is still quite popular in Alabama, although apparently not elsewhere. I have four texts, all rather complete. Randolph (III, 229) reports two texts, and says that one of his informants said that the song "was in all the popular songbooks in the late 90's." Pound *(Syllabus,* p. 62) gives the title, as does Davis *(Folk-Songs of Virginia,* p. 148). The piece was apparently not popular in the songsters of the 50's, 60's and 70's, or at least I have been unable to find it. *Beadle's Dime Song Book No. 16* (N.Y., 1865, p. 20) has a different song under the title "Putting on Airs." The L.C. Checklist (p. 326) reports the song from California.

A

"Putting on The Style," sung by Miss Drucilla Hall, Millport, Lamar County, 1952.

Young man in a carriage driving like he's mad
With a pair of horses borrowed from his dad.
Cracks his whip the loudest till he makes the ladies smile
For they all know he's only putting on the style.

Chorus:
    Putting on the agony, putting on the style,
    That's what the young folks are doing all the while.
    When I look around me I'm very apt to smile
    To see so many young folks putting on the style.

Young man just from college, he makes a great display
With a long jawbreaker in all he has to say;
Can't be found in Webster and won't be for a while,
But they all know he's only putting on the style.

Sweet sixteen she goes to church just to see the boys.
She turns her head and giggles at every little noise.
She flirts this way a little and then that way a while,
But they all know she's only putting on the style.

Going to a circus looking nice and clean,
Fresh as a dew drop amongst the garden green.
Gingerbread and candy eating all the while,
Going to the circus putting on the style.

B

"Putting On The Style," sung by Mrs. Ramie Hankins, Vernon, Lamar County, 1952.

> Putting on the agony, putting on the style,
> That is what the people are doing all the while.
> As I look around me something makes me smile,
> To see so many people putting on the style.
>
> Sweet sixteen, she goes to church, she goes to see the boys.
> She turns her head and giggles at every little noise.
> First it's this and then it's that, laughing all the while,
> To see so many people putting on the style.

C

"Putting On The Style," sung by Mrs. Mary Crowder, Sulligent, Lamar County, 1952. She has sung it for the past fifty years.

> Eighteen hundred and seventy six, January the first,
> Writing something excellent, something to indict (endite?)
> Looking out the window something makes me smile
> To see so many people putting on the style.
>
> A nice young man in his carriage, he drives away like mad.
> He drives a pair of horses he borrowed from his dad.
> He cracks his whip so loud to make the ladies smile.
> Now, girls, ain't he going in, putting on the style.
>
> Sweet sixteen she goes to church; she goes to see the boys.
> She turns her head and giggles at every little noise.
> First it's this and then it's that, laughing all the while.
> Now, boys, ain't she going in, putting on the style.

D

"Putting On The Style," sung by Mrs. Mary Rouse, Titus, Elmore County, 1953. Two stanzas.

Eight-een seven-ty six, Jan-u-ary the first.....

........Look-ing through the win-der some-thing made me

smile to see so man-y peo-ple put-ting on the style.

Put-ting on the ag-o-ny, put-ting on the style, That's

what the peo-ple are do-ing all the while. As I look

a-round me it of-ten makes me smile To see so man-y

peo-ple put-ting on the style.

Eighteen seventy six, January the first.
. . . .
Looking through the winder something made me smile
To see so many people putting on the style.

Putting on the agony, putting on the style,
That's what the people are doing all the while.
As I look around me it often makes me smile
To see so many people putting on the style.

133
It's The Fashion

This bitter satire against "fashion" and "fashionable people" reflects well the attitude of the folk. Such songs were popular in the songsters of the 60's. I have not found the Alabama version anywhere, though its idea parallels those of the versions in the songsters. Two Alabama texts indicate a certain popularity.

A

"It's The Fashion," sung by Mrs. Mary Crowder, Sulligent, Lamar County, 1952.

When a poor man asks for bread or a place to lay

his head, He will get a kick in-stead. That's the fash-ion.

But a poo-dle dog they'll keep, in their arms they'll let

him sleep; when he dies oh how they'll weep. That's the

Chorus

fash-ion. Oh, the fash-ion, dressed in fash-ion. To be

fash-ioned like a king, with the an-gels we will sing. Oh,

the fash-ion, dressed in fash-ion; With the white robed

hosts we'll sing. We'll be in fash-ion.

Some think I'm very queer and some others often sneer,
But I hope that I stay clear of that fashion.
If you'll only wait a while I will someday be in style.
It will be my time to smile when it's fashion.

Chorus:
    Oh, the fashion, dressed in fashion.
    To be fashioned like a king while the angels sweetly sing.
    Oh, the fashion, dressed in fashion.
    I'll be dressed in spotless white when it's fashion.

If a poor man asks for bread or some place to lay his head,
A kick he'll get instead; that's the fashion.
But a poodle dog they'll keep; in their arms they'll let him sleep.
When he dies then they'll weep, because it's fashion.

If you curse and swear and sin, ...a man and don't look in,
Let the Savior take you in from that fashion.
For I'd rather know I'm right than wear diamonds every night,
For some day I'll dress in white when it's fashion.

B

"That's The Fashion," sung by Miss Drucilla Hall, Millport, Lamar County, 1952. One stanza, two of version A, and the chorus.

134
Twenty Years Ago

The headnote in the Brown Collection (III, 390) says that this song was "perhaps newspaper verse, perhaps a music-hall piece." There are four North Carolina texts in the collection. Randolph (III, 251) reports two fragments and says that many Arkansas settlers told him that "Wilson Patent" was the trade name of the first cookstoves sold in the Ozarks. My Alabama informants told me that the "Wilson Patent" was one of the earliest stoves in Alabama. The L.C. Checklist (pp. 211; 411) reports texts from North Carolina and Virginia.

A

"Twenty Years Ago," sung by Mrs. John Hall, Millport, Lamar County, 1952. When she was singing it, Drucilla, her daughter, wanted her to bring the song up to date by substituting "cars" for "sleighs."

How well do I remember just twenty years ago,
When girls wore woolen dresses and boys wore pants of tow,
And shoes were made of cowhide and socks of homespun wool,
And children did their halfday's work before they went to school.

Chorus:
    Just twenty years ago, just twenty years ago,
    When the men and the boys and the girls and the toys
    And the work and the play and the night and the day
    And the world and its ways are all turned round
    Since twenty years ago.

How well do I remember that Wilson Patent stove
That father bought and paid for with cloth us girls had wove,
And how the people wondered when he got that thing to go
And said it would burst and kill us all some twenty years ago.

When people rode to meeting in sleds instead of sleighs,
And wagons rode as easy as wagons nowadays,
And oxen answered well for teams but now they are too slow,
For people were not half so fast just twenty years ago.

B

"Twenty Years Ago," sung by Mrs. Cornelia Franklin, Wetumpka,

Elmore County, 1953.

How won-d'rous things have changed here Since

twen-ty years a-go, When the girls wore wool-en dress-es,

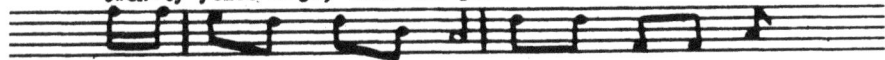

And the boys wore pants of tow. Shoes were made of cow-

hide, Socks were home-spun wool, And chil-dren did a

half day's work Be-fore they went to school. Just twen-ty

years a-go, just twen-ty years a-go. Men and boys and

girls and toys work and toil all night and day. The

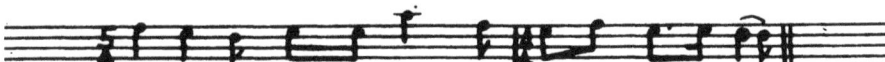

world is all turned a-round since twen-ty years a-go.

How wondrous things have changed here
Since twenty years ago,
When the girls wore woolen dresses,
And the boys wore pants of tow.
Shoes were made of cowhide,
Socks were homespun wool,
And children did a half day's work
Before they went to school.

Chorus:
    Just twenty years ago, just twenty years ago.
    Men and boys and girls and toys work and toil all night and day.
    The world is all turned around
    Since twenty years ago.

The girls they took many lessons
Upon the spinning wheel,
And practiced spinning millet
On spindles slick and real.
The boys would ride their horses
A dozen miles or so,
And boys and girls would strolling go
And hurry off before the day.

C

"Twenty Years Ago," sung by Mrs. Nola Browne, Millport, Lamar County, 1952. When Mother was singing this song my father, Garfield Browne, insisted that she sing "one hundred years ago," because the song would be "truer" that way. The text seems mixed up.

How well do I remember the Wilson Patent stove
That Father bought and paid for with the cloth us girls had wove.
We spun the thread and made the cloth and Father bought our stove.
They swore it would burst and kill us all just twenty years ago.

Chorus:
Just twenty years ago, just twenty years ago.
They swore it would burst and kill us all
Just twenty years ago.

We made the rolls and spun the thread and made the cloth at home.
We worked hard all day and some time we worked at night.
The work was hard, we did it right. The cloth we made was white,
When Father bought our stove just twenty years ago.

We spun the thread and made the cloth. We made it all at home.
Our cloth was all white. We dyed it blue and red.
We spun the thread and wove the cloth when Father bought our stove
And this I do remember, just twenty years ago.

135
Booker T. Washington

In October 1901 President Theodore Roosevelt had Booker T. Washington, the great Negro educator, to dine with him at the White House. When news of this meal got into the newspapers, Southern newsmen had a field day of vituperation, accusing the President of trying to establish Negro supremacy in the South and of making a vulgar play for Negro votes. Cartoonists were unrelenting in caricaturing Roosevelt and Washington together (see Raymond Gros, *T.R. In Cartoon*, pp. 268-269). Naturally much feeling was directed against Washington for presuming to accept the invitation. The following folk song reflects well the feeling in Alabama over the incident. It should be noticed that the effort in the song is to make Washington ridiculous. Little is said about Roosevelt except that it might not be safe for him to come South. The song probably dates from soon after the incident. I have not found it in any other collection, and I have only one text.

"Booker T. Washington," sung by Mr. Claude Springfield, Vernon, Lamar County, 1952. He does not remember how long he has sung it.

Old Book-er T. Wash-ing-ton, the big black man, To

the White House went one day. He want-ed to see the Pres-

i-dent in a qui-et sort of way. Sent in his card with a

sil-ly smile. When the Pres-i-dent met him at the door,

Old Book-er be-gin to grin. He al-most changed his col-or

when Ted-dy said: "Walk in. We'll have some din-ner in a

lit-tle while." Just be-cause he made those goo goo eyes;

When he sat down to the ta-ble there he spies Some quail

on toast, some chick-en, veal and roast, And you could-n't

blame Book-er for mak-ing those goo goo eyes.

Old Booker T. Washington, the big black man,
To the White House went one day.
He wanted to see the President in a quiet sort of way.
Sent in his card with a silly smile.
When the President met him at the door,
Old Booker begin to grin.
He almost changed his color when Teddy said, "Walk in,
We'll have some dinner in a little while."
Just because he made those goo-goo eyes.
When he sat down to the table there he spies
Some quail on toast, some chicken, veal and roast,
And you couldn't blame Booker for making those goo-goo eyes.

Old Booker felt so elated with the reception given him,
He hired a horseless carriage and took the whole town in.

Drank lots of wine, was feeling fine.
He said Teddy Roosevelt was the finest ever seen.
He said he could stump the state but never touch New Orleans,
For the South was hot and he might get shot.
Oh, then he would lose those goo-goo eyes.
This dinner here to me was a great surprise.
But you're a friend of mine; you can eat here any time.
And you can't blame Booker for making those goo-goo eyes.

136
Climbing Up The White House Stairs

This piece illustrates how a song about a temporary political situation can persist in oral tradition. The song refers to the fact that Grover Cleveland was to assume the Presidency in 1885 for the first of his two terms (1885-89, 1893-97). Cleveland was a bachelor until his marriage to Frances Folsom in 1886, and this song tells of the romantic possibilities of the White House with Cleveland there. Perhaps it was a campaign song. I have not found it reported elsewhere, and I have only one text.

"Climbing up the White House Stairs," sung by Mrs. R. Van Iderstine, Daphne, Baldwin County, 1953. She does not remember when or how she learned it.

Oh, the fourth of March is coming, And the cannons will be bumming, Climbing up the White House stairs. Cleveland will be there to occupy the chair, Oh, climbing up the White House stairs. Oh, hear those bells a-ringing, 'Tis sweet I do declare to hear those children singing, Climbing up the White House stairs.

Oh, the fourth of March is coming,
And the cannons will be bumming,
Climbing up the White House stairs.
Cleveland will be there
To occupy the chair,
Oh, climbing up the White House stairs.

Chorus:
Oh, hear those bells a-ringing.

'Tis sweet, I do declare,
To hear those girls a-singing,
Climbing up the White House stairs.

Artemisia is a great sneezer,
Takes a smart man to tease her,
Climbing up the White House stairs.
She wears such tight sleeves,
Makes the boys get on their knees,
Climbing up the White House stairs.

Beulah is a cooler,
Takes a sharper one to fool her,
Climbing up the White House stairs.
She can compose,
But she hasn't any beaus,
Climbing up the White House stairs.

Gladys is very small,
And can outdance them all,
Climbing up the White House stairs.
But mind what she's about,
Someone will cut her out,
As she climbs up the White House stairs.

Next comes Uselel,
To whom the boys will kneel,
Climbing up the White House stairs.
Her eyes are very bright.
You can see them in the night,
Climbing up the White House stairs.

Helena has been round
On the Exposition ground,
Climbing up the White House stairs.
She has a great many bangles,
But one of them don't dangle,
Climbing up the White House stairs.

Hattie Sibley's little curl
Will make the boys whirl,
Climbing up the White House stairs.
She lost her little bell,
And where she can tell,
Climbing up the White House stairs.

Florence has a beau
But thinks we don't know,
Climbing up the White House stairs.
She goes to and fro,
And she's not so very slow,
Climbing up the White House stairs.

Annie is very nice,
And as sweet as any spice,
Climbing up the White House stairs.
If she hasn't any beau,
She will get one, I know,
When she climbs up the White House stairs.

Hattie plays well
Because she has a bell,
Climbing up the White House stairs.
But it hasn't any clapper,
And that's what's the matter,
Climbing up the White House stairs.

Edna is very gay,
We meet her on the way,
Climbing up the White House stairs.
She has a little band
That just fits her hand,
Climbing up the White House stairs.

Elodia comes last
And holds them all fast,
Climbing up the White House stairs.
She is quite a poet,
I want you all to know it,
Climbing up the White House stairs.

V
SATIRIC SONGS

137
Arkansas Traveler (I)

This satire upon the state of Arkansas probably antedates 1850. Such a song was published as sheet music in New York (Firth & Pond) in 1851 (Dichter and Shapiro, *Early American Sheet Music*, pp. 139-140). An 1852 Currier and Ives lithograph gives the story in six pictures, with words and music (Spaeth, *History of Popular Music*, pp. 125-6). By 1864 the song was apparently well known. A songbook of that year was named the *Arkansas Traveler's Song Book*, in which the first song was "The Arkansas Traveler," attributed to Mose Case, and published as sheet music by Blodgett and Bradford, Buffalo. This version is a long discourse supposed to "represent an Eastern man's experience among the inhabitants of Arkansas." The song is a dialogue interrupted by the sawing out of a fiddle tune. The L.C. Checklist (pp. 9-10) lists twenty six texts. My one Alabama version is particularly full.

"Arkansas Traveler," talked and fiddled by Mr. Isaac Rollins, Wedowee, Randolph County, 1953.

"Hey, Mister, your corn looks mighty little and yellow."

"Yessir, cause I planted yeller corn."

"I know, but it doesn't look like it's going to make more than half a crop."

"That's right. We're working on the half."

"Hey, Buddy, how'd your taters turn out?"

"Heck, they didn't turn out. Me and Sal had to dig 'em."

"Not much difference 'tween you and a fool, now is there?"

"No, Sir, just a fence there."

"Hey, Buddy, looks like you'd cover your house."

"That roof is just as good as anybody's in dry weather, and it'd be a pore fool get up there and cover it in the rain."

"Hey, Sal, roll that punkin out from under the bed and give this stranger a seat."

"Hey, Son, take the stranger's horse out to the barn and feed him high. Give him three nubbins of pop corn and a bunch of broom straw and put 'em up in the hay loft so he can't reach 'em."

"Hey, Buddy, got any knives and forks?"

"No, Sir."

"Well, how in the world do you do?"

"Tolable well, thank you."

"Hey, Buddy, why'd you get my saddle on backwards?"

"Well, how in the world did I know which way you was gwine?"

"Hey, Buddy, where does this road go?"

"I don't know. We've been living here twenty year and it ain't gone no where yet."

"Well, how far is it to Little Rock?"

"I don't know, but there's a tolable big one right out there."

"Does this road fork right out here?"

"I don't know, but it splits like thunder right out there."

"Hey, Buddy, is this branch fordable down here?"

"I guess so. Mammy's ducks fords it all the time all right."

"I mean, is it very deep?"

"Water all the way to the bottom."

"Hey, head that cow there."

"She's done headed."

"Well, turn her."

"She done turned. The hair side's out."

"Well, speak to her, fool"

"Good morning, cow."

"Hey, Sal, get the churn cloth and clean this baby's nose. I do despise nastiness."

138
Arkansas Traveler (II)

There is no connection between this song and the one preceding it except that both are satires on Arkansas. This song also goes under the name of "Bill Stafford" or "Sanford Barnes." It is more popular than the other "Arkansas Traveler." For references see Brown (III, 382) and Randolph (III, 25). Not very popular in Alabama, the song has come to me in two texts, one a fragment. The L.C. Checklist (p. 23) lists a text from California.

A

"Arkansas Traveler," sung by Mrs. Christina Crowder, Vernon, Lamar County, 1952. She probably learned it from her mother, although her mother could not sing it to me.

I start-ed out one morn-ing on the twen-ty se-cond

of June, And I land-ed in that aw-ful place one Sun-day

af-ter-noon. Up stepped to me a skel-e-ton and a-hand-

ing me a paw, In-vit-ing me to a ho-tel, the best in

Ar-kan-sas.

I started out one morning
On the twenty second of June.
And I landed in that awful place
One Sunday afternoon.
Up stepped to me a skeleton
And a-handing me a paw,
Inviting me to a hotel,
The best in Arkansas.

I followed my conductor
Unto his dwelling place.

His neck was long and slender,
He had such a mountain face.
His board it was corn dodger,
As hard as any rock.
My teeth began to loosen,
My knees began to knock.

I grew so thin on sassafras tea
I could hide behind a straw,
And that's the kind of man I was
When I left Arkansas.

B

"My Trip Through Arkansas," sung by Mr. Claude Springfield, Vernon, Lamar County, 1952. He has sung it at least fifty years.

I traveled around St. Louis
About ten days or more.
I read the morning papers
Until my eyes were sore.
I read the evening papers
Until at last I saw
"Ten thousand men still wanted
In the state of Arkansas."

So I started out for Arkansas
On the twenty second of June.
I landed in that awful place
One Saturday afternoon.
Up stepped to me a fellow
And handing me his paw
Invited me to his hotel,
The best in Arkansas.

So I followed my conductor
Until his dwelling place.
His neck so long and slender,
His melancholy face.
His hair hung down in ringlets
Upon his lantern jaw.
He's the prototype of every man
That lived in Arkansas.

Well, I started out next morning
To catch an early train.
"You'd better stay and work for me.
I've got some land to drain.
I'll give you fifty cents a day,

Your washing, board and all.
And I'm sure you'll be a different man
When you leave Arkansas."

So I stayed and worked for the scoundrel beast,
Jess Harold was his name.
He was just seven feet, ten inches tall,
And as slim as any crane.
His hair hung down in ringlets
Upon his iron jaw.
He's the prototype of every man
That lived in Arkansas.

He fed me on corn dodgers
As hard as any rock.
Till my teeth begun to loosen
And my knees begun to rock.
I grew so thin on sassafras tea
I could hide behind a straw,
And that's the kind of man I was
When I left Arkansas.

Farewell to your swamp girls,
Your canebrakes and the chills.
Farewell to your sage and sassafras tea
And your corn dodger pills.
If ever I see that land again
I'll give to you my paw,
For it will be through a telescope
From here to Arkansas.

139
Tommy And Jack

This satiric treatment of marriage is similar to several others in this volume. I have not found this song reported from elsewhere. For a parallel, however, see Ford (*Traditional Music in America,* p. 285).

"Tommy And Jack," sung by Mr. Isaac Rollins, Wedowee, Randolph County, 1953. Something of a "character," he likes to shock and amuse women with this song, which he has been singing for some forty years.

Tom-my and Jack they had been friends Ev-er since child-hood days, Un-til one day they met a fair maid, Lad-en with charm-ing ways. Both fell in love; each tried to win Pret-ty lit-tle maid-en fair. Un-til one day, as peo-ple say, Two hearts were made as one.

Tommy and Jack they had been friends
Ever since childhood days,
Until one day they met a fair maid
Laden with charming ways.
Both fell in love, each tried to win
Pretty little maiden fair.
Until one day, as people say,
Two hearts were made as one,

Jack and his wife, happy were they
Until that fatal day.
Jack had been strong, sickness came on
And taken his sweet life away.
Jack in the grave, how she did grieve.
No one knowed just what to do.
Tommy come home, vigorous and strong,
Said, "Sweetheart, I'll marry you."

Many years passed, since they were wed.
Children they had four.
Ma and Pa fights, baby cries nights,
And Pa has to sleep on the floor.
Tommy looks back, thinks of poor Jack
Lying in his grave and sighs,
"Envy you, Jack, envy you, Jack;
Envy you, Jack, yes I do."

140
My Mother-In-Law

This song was disseminated to the folk by the songsters. One songster lists it as "Sung with great success by Harry McAvoy at the London Theatre, New York, in the sketch of 'Jealousy or Two can Play at that Game,' and in all the principal theatres in America" (*Harry McAvory & Emma Rogers Society Sketch Artists Songster* (N.Y. 1880, p. 3); it is so designated in *John McVeigh & Kate Montrose's Songster* (N.Y. 1881, p. 47); it is also in *McIntyre & Heath's Skedaddle Songster* (N.Y. 1880, p. 59); it is "sung by Billy Porter, air: Grandfather's days" in *Moore & Vivian's Fresh the Artist Songster* (N.Y. 1883, p. 40). Various other songsters carried a German dialect version — "Of you lisden to me I vill sing you a ditty Aboud de vorst women dot efer I saw." — for example, *J.K. Emmet's Lullaby Songster* (N.Y. 1878, p. 42).

The song has not been widely reported as a folk song. Morris (*Folksongs of Florida*, p. 147) has a seven-stanza version with no tune. Randolph (III, 120) has three stanzas and a chorus. The Archive of Amercan Folk Song reports two songs, one from Texas and one from California. Both Alabama versions are incomplete.

A

"Mother-in-law," sung by Miss Drucilla Hall, Millport, Lamar County, 1952. She has sung it for thirty years. She learned it in Alabama.

Come all you good peo-ple, a sto-ry I'll tell

you A-bout the worst wo-man that ev-er I saw. And if

you will lis-ten you'll say it's a pi-ty That ev-er I

Chorus

had a moth-er-in-law. All my life I've been care-free
and hap-py; When I o-pen my mouth she pops in her whole
jaw. I'd rath-er be be-hind pri-son bars Than spend
my days with my moth-er-in-law.

Come all you good people, a story I'll tell you
About the worst woman that ever I saw.
And if you will listen you'll say it's a pity
That ever I had a mother-in-law.

Chorus:
    All my life I've been carefree and happy.
    When I open my mouth she pops in her whole jaw.
    I'd rather be behind prison bars
    Than spend my days with my mother-in-law.

B

"My Mother-in-law," sung by Mrs. Mary Crowder, Sulligent, Lamar County, 1952. When she was singing, Mr. Crowder insisted that his wife change the line about being sent to Congress, but Mrs. Crowder would not change it because she said that was the way she had always heard the song.

Come all ye young people
A story I'll tell you
About the worst woman that ever you saw.

And when you have heard it
You'll say it's a pity
That ever I had such a mother-in-law.

She'd taken a fool notion
That she was good looking.
I'll vow she's ugly as ever you've seen.
And when she went in
To have her picture taken
The very first pop she broke down the machine.

Chorus:
    All my life seems troubled. How can I be happy?
    When I open my mouth she pops in her whole jaw.
    I'd rather be taken to jail or to Congress
    Than to live all my life with my mother-in-law.

I told her when I went
To ask for her daughter
The whole family I would not wed.
She upped with a kettle
Of very hot water
And poured it all over the top of my head.

141
I Had But Fifty Cents

This funny treatment of the perils of going out with girls dates from the songsters of the late 70s. One *(Consolidated Mammoth Minstrels Songster*, N.Y. 18--, p. 34) contains an interesting variant, of which I quote the first stanza:

> If you could only see the gal
> I took to a fancy ball,
> You could span around her little waist
> So neat and very small.
> I thought about two oysters sure
> Would fill her up complete.
> Such a dainty, delicate little thing.
> But this is what she eat.

In one version or another it appeared in at least a score of songsters. For example: *Dan Lewis, Oh She is Songster* (Boston, 1881, p. 18); *The Murphy's Don Donahue Songster* (N.Y. 18--, p. 26); *Billy Carter's Pool Songster* (N.Y. 18--, p. 18); *Pat Rooney's Star Combination Songster* (N.Y. c. 1879, p. 20); *Fred Somers New Collection of 250 Songs* (Chicago, c. 1887, p. 4).

For a full version see Gilbert *(Lost Chords*, p. 121), for another, slightly different, version see Randolph (III, 250). Shay *(Pious Friends and Drunken Companions*, p. 75) has a version sung by James E. Harris. I have only one Alabama text.

"I Took My Gal To The Ball," contributed by Mrs. R. Van Iderstine, Daphne, Baldwin County, 1953, from a manuscript in her possession.

I took my gal to the ball one night. It was a so-ci-al

hop. She stayed un-til the lights went out, The mu-sic it

did stop. Then to the res-tau-rant we went, The best one

on the street. She said she was-n't hun-gry, But this is

what she eat: A doz-en raw, a plate of slaw, a chick-en

and some toast, Some ap-ple sauce, and so-ur grass, and

soft shelled crab on toast. Then next she tried some oy-

sters fried; her ap-pe-ti te was im-mense. She called for

more, and I fell on the floor; For I had but fif-ty cents.

I took my gal to the ball one night,
It was a social hop.
She stayed until the lights went out,
The music it did stop.
Then to the restaurant we went,
The best one on the street.
She said she wasn't hungry,
But this is what she eat:
A dozen raw, a plate of slaw, a chicken and some toast,
Some apple sauce and sour grass,[1] and soft shelled crab on toast.
Then next she tried some oysters fried;
Her appetite was immense.
She called for more and I fell on the floor,
For I had but fifty cents.

She said she wasn't thirsty,
But this is what she drank:
A bottle of ale, a soda cocktail;
She made me quake with fear;
A ginger pop with rum on top
And then a bottle of beer.
She called for more and I fell on the floor,
For I had but fifty cents.

Oh, you bet I wasn't hungry,
I didn't care to eat.
I've money in my other clothes
That says she can't be beat.
She takes it in so cozy,
She's got an awful tank.
Said she'd bring her family round
Some time and we'd have some fun.
I handed the man my fifty cents,
And this is what he done:
He broke my nose, he tore my clothes,
He kicked me in the jaw.
I took the prize for a pair of black eyes,
And with me he swept the floor.
Took me by the back of my neck,
And fired me over the fence.
Take my advice and don't try it twice,
When you have but fifty cents.

[1] pate gras (?)

142
Bill Morgan

This humorous treatment of the expensiveness of women should be compared with "I Had But Fifty Cents," in this volume. The name of J.P. Morgan, the robber baron, would be a natural reference. This song was apparently less popular than "I Had But Fifty Cents." I have not found it anywhere else. I have one text.

"Bill Morgan," sung by Mrs. Lily Turner, Crane Hill, Cullman County, 1953.

Bill Mor-gan took his la-dy friend one night to see a play, And on their jour-ney home-ward they stopped in a swell ca-fe. As soon as they were seat-ed Liz-zie grabbed the bill of fare. She called the wait-er and she or-dered

Chorus

ev-'ry thing was there. My name is Mor-gan, but it ain't J.P. You must think I own some rail-road com-pan-y. You may have known me pret-ty long Though you have got my in-i-tials wrong. My name is Mor-gan, but it ain't J.P.

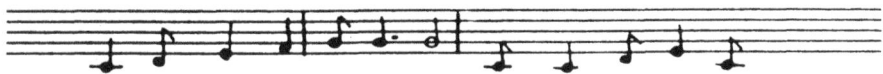

Bill Morgan took his lady friend one night to see a play,
And on their journey homeward they stopped in a swell cafe.
As soon as they were seated, Lizzie grabbed the bill of fare.
She called the waiter and she ordered everything was there.

Chorus:
    My name is Morgan, but it ain't J.P.
    You must think I own some railroad company.
    You may have known me pretty long,
    Though you have got my initials wrong.
    My name is Morgan, but it ain't J.P.

Bill said: "I know you're hungry, Gal, and I don't like to squeal,
But who do you suppose is going to pay for that big meal?
I'm satisfied to buy you two or three things that is there,
But the appetite you have tonight would break a millionaire."

Bill Morgan married Lizzie, thinking he might change her ways.
But what she did for William's purse I'm most ashamed to say.
When she'd go out shopping she'd buy everything she'd see.
What she couldn't pay for she'd have sent home C.O.D.

One day six big deliveries backed right up to Billy's door.
They asked him to accept the goods while they went after more.
It didn't take Bill long to get his hat and coat.
When Liz came home that night she found a little note.

143
Chinning Music

This song is another masculine satire on women, of which type this volume affords several examples. Like several pieces of this type, this one admits man's weakness for women and only tries to give good advice as to the kind that should be chosen. I have only one text of the song, and have not found it reported in any other collection.

"Chinning Music," sung by Mrs. Guy B. Johnson, Oneonta, Blount County, 1953. She has known it about forty years.

Oh, how do you reck-on he feels when he sits down

to his meals, And his chin-ning, chew-ing mu-sic just be-

gins. He can be out work-ing hard, he can find her in the

Chorus

yard Chin-ning to her neigh-bor o'er the fence. Oh, there's

no use be-gin-ning Try-ing to stop a wo-man's chin-ning,

You might's well try to stop a cir-cle saw. My ad-vice is

to drop it, There's no use to try to stop it. Wo-man's

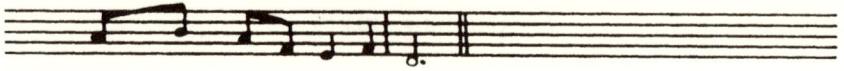

tongue will run for-ev-er-more.

Oh, how do you reckon he feels
When he sits down to his meals,
And his chinning, chewing music just begins?
He can be out working hard,
He can find her in the yard
Chinning to her neighbor o'er the fence.

Chorus:
    Oh, there's no use beginning
    Trying to stop a woman's chining.
    You might's well try to stop a circle saw.
    My advice is to drop it.
    There's no use to try to stop it.
    Woman's tongue will run forevermore.

Oh, I have ofttimes asked
Why a woman talks so fast.
She will come with every bit of news.
She will talk a man to death
While he's trying to get his breath.
Woman's tongue will run to beat the Jews.

It is nice to go out courting
Of those who like the sporting.
So, boys, go to it while you're young.
But if you wish your money to save
And to shun an early grave,
Marry one that's blind and deaf and dumb.

Now I've oft thought it'd be nice
If a woman would just speak twice
And then would let her talker take a rest.
But you can bet your bottom dollar
That she'll keep on with her holler
Until she's in the sweet land of the blest.

Oh, how happy men would be
If the girls could only see
That they don't always have to talk to their love.
But in talk they'll be leader
Even when they see Saint Peter,
And he stops them at the Pearly Gates above.

It is nice to go out courting
Of those who likes the sporting.
So, boys, go to it while you're young.
But take a wise old man's advice,
Though they all may look so nice,
Marry one that's blind and deaf and dumb.

144
Home, Sweet Home To Me

This piece is interesting because it shows that in a land where nearly every home has some kind of religious motto about "Home, Sweet Home" there can still be some detached and humorous treatment of the sentiment. Possibly a comic songster or music-hall creation, this piece smacks more of folk origin. At least it seems to have undergone much alteration in oral tradition. It has not been reported in other collections of folk songs.

"Home, Sweet Home To Me," sung by Miss Drucilla Hall, Millport, Lamar County, 1952.

On the Fourth of July at a country fair, A man went up in a balloon. Had to go up right to the clouds, Make a circle around the moon. When he got up about ten mile high, The gas in his balloon went........ He came down in a parachute and he could only say: "I ain't got no feather bed to land on when I fall. I may land in a river or on top of City Hall. Next time I'll never get on a

house top high-er than a tree. An-y old place that I hang

my hat will be home sweet home to me."

On the Fourth of July at a country fair
A man went up in a balloon.
Had to go up right to the clouds,
Make a big circle around the moon.
When he got up about ten mile high,
The gas in his balloon went . . . . . .
He came down in a parachute
And he could only say:

"I ain't got no feather bed
To land on when I fall.
I may land in a river
Or on top of City Hall.
Next time I'll never get on a house top
Higher than a tree.
Any old place that I hang my hat
Will be home, sweet home to me."

My brother Bill, who lives out West,
It breaks my heart to say,
Cowboys caught him dead to rights
With a neighbor's horse one day.
When I got there my poor brother Bill
Had a rope tied around his head.
Cowboys standing all around,
This is what he said:

"I ain't got no 'ticklar limb
To hang on when I swing.
You may hang me high until I die,
I only ask one thing:
I'd like to be hung on a high 'simmon limb
So all my friends can see,
But any old limb that you hang me on
'Ll be home, sweet home to me."

145
The Old Miller

This attack on the rascality of millers is old and widespread. For English references consult Dixon *(Ancient Poems, Ballads and Songs.* pp. 204-206) and Ebsworth *(Roxburghe Ballads,* VIII, 611-612). More American texts than English have been reported. For references to these texts see Randolph (I, 359) and Brown (II, 440). The L.C. Checklist (pp. 79-80; 258) lists texts from New York City, North Carolina, Ohio, Virginia and Florida.

A

"The Old Miller," sung by Mrs. Ramie Hankins, Vernon, Lamar County, 1952.

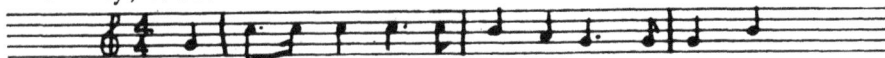

There was an old man who lived a-lone. He had three

sons to full men grown. And when he came to make his will

he could-n't set-tle noth-ing but a lit-tle old mill.

Fod-dy in-ky dink dink, Fod-dy ink dy.

There was an old man who lived alone.
He had three sons to full men grown,
And when he came to make his will,
He couldn't settle nothing but a little old mill.
Foddy inky dink dink, foddy inka day.

First he called in his oldest son.
"Son, my days are almost gone.
You this mill I intend for to will.
Tell me the toll you intend for to take."
Foddy inky dink dink, foddy inda day.

"Father, father, my name is Jack,
And out of every bushel I'll take a peck,

And if by this a fortune I should make
That's the toll I intend for to take."
Foddy inky dink dink, foddy inka day.

"You're a fool," the old man said.
"You've not completely learned my way.
To you this mill I will never will,
By that toll no man can live."
Foddy inky dink dink, foddy inka day.

Next he called in his second son.
"Son, my days are almost run.
You this mill I intend to will.
Tell me the toll you intend to take."
Foddy inky dink dink, foddy inka day.

"Father, father, my name is Jeff,
And out of ever bushel I'll take half,
And if by this a fortune I can make,
That is the toll I intend for to take."
Foddy inky dink dink, foddy inka day.

"You're a fool," the old man said.
"You've not completely learned my way.
To you this mill I will never will,
By that toll no man can live."
Foddy inky dink dink, foddy inka day.

He next called up his youngest son.
"Son, my days are almost run.
You this mill I intend for to will.
Tell me the toll you intend for to take."
Foddy inky dink dink, foddy inka day.

"Father, oh father, my name is Jack.
I'll take the whole turn and swear to the sack,
And if by this a fortune I should make,
That is the toll I intend for to take."
Foddy inky dink dink, foddy inka day.

"You're not a fool," the old man said.
"You've completely learned my way.
And this mill I intend for to will,
For any man can take that and live."
Foddy inky dink dink, foddy inka day.

The old man rolled up his eyes and died.
The old woman shouted hallelujah and cried.
The old man closed his eyes and died.
The old woman shouted hallelujah and cried.
Foddy inky dink dink, foddy inka day.

B

"Little Old Mill," sung by Mrs. Mary Todd, Sulligent, Lamar County, 1952. Seven stanzas, essentially A.

146
Brian O'Lynn

The editors of the Brown Collection (II, 459) report that this bit of satire first on the Scots and later on the Irish goes back to at least the sixteenth century. Brown has one five-stanza version. See references also in Randolph (III, 231), who records that William A. White in his *Autobiography* (p. 26) "remembers that in Kansas, in the 1870's, he sang a song about 'Barney O'Flynn,' who had no breeches to wear and got him a sheepskin to make a pair." The L.C. Checklist (pp. 37; 40) lists it from New York City and Washington, D.C. Apparently the Alabama Irish liked the joke. They had great access to it, for it appeared in at least 30 songsters through the years, in 12-14 stanza versions.

For example, *Banner Songster* (N.Y. p. 54), *Charley O'Malley Irish Songster* (N.Y. 1862, p. 23), *Donnybrook Fair Songster*, (N.Y. 1872), *The "Bryan O'Lynn" Songster* (N.Y. c. 1872, p. 1), *Elton's Illustrated Song Book* ("a highly popular comic song, as sung by the late Tyrone Power," N.Y. p. 158); *Fattie Stewart's Comic Songster* (N.Y. c. 1863, p. 69); *Harp of Erin Songster* (N.Y. c. 1872); *Hart's Plantation Songster* (N.Y. c. 1862, p. 26); *Hooley's Opera House Songster* ("as song by S.S. Purdy," N.Y. c. 1863, p. 66); *Howe's 100 Choice Songs* (Boston, 187-, p. 16); *New Singer's Journal, No. 51* (N.Y. 18--, p. 373); *Oil On The Brain Songster* (Cincinnati, 1865, p. 42); *Old Ireland's Vocal Gems* (Philadelphia, after 1850, p. 78); *The People's Handbook Series, 156 Popular Songs* (N.Y. 1896, p. 25); *Popular Songs* (N.Y. 1861, p. 168); *Stephen's Fenian Songster* (N.Y. 1866, p. 72); *Trifet's Multum Im Parvo* (N.Y. c. 1890, p. 10); *Unsworth Burnt Cork Lyrics* (N.Y. c. 1859, p. 60); *The Wearing of The Green Songster* (N.Y. 1866, p. 57); *Wehman's Irish Songs Book* (N.Y. 1887, p. 70); The tune was used for a parody called "Widow Mulroony's Ball," in *The Donny-Brook Fair Songster* (N.Y. c. 1863, p. 18); and "A new version of 'Bryan O'Lynn' as sung by Fred May" was printed in *The Frisky Irish Songster* (N.Y. c. 1862, p. 61).

"Brian O'Lynn," from the Alabama Archives, collected by Mary A. Poole, with the following note: "The following comic song was sung for many years among the Irish element of Mobile from the beginning of American time."

Brian O'Lynn, his wife and wife's mother,
They all went over the bridge together.
The bridge it broke, they all went in.
"First to the bottom," said Brian O'Lynn.

Brian O'Lynn had no breeches to wear.
He cut up a sheep skin to make him a pair.
The skinny side out, the woolly side in.
"Best for cold weather," said Brian O'Lynn.

147
The Dutchman Song

Comical dialect songs are more of the music-hall, minstrel show and comic songster than of folk tradition. This piece I suspect to be of an origin outside of folk creation. There is, probably, no anti-Dutch sentiment intended in the song, since Alabamans would be largely or wholly ignorant of the Dutch. "Dutch" would probably mean "German." I have not found this piece in the songsters or in any other collection of folk songs. I have only one text.

"Dutchman's Song," sung by Mr. Claude Springfield, Vernon, Lamar County, 1952. He might have learned this piece when he was singing in a quartet thirty or forty years ago.

Oh, shen-tle-mens and la-dies, chust in time,

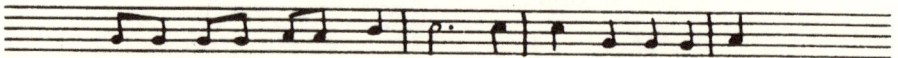

Swid-dy wid-dy win-ky tum fum, Come lis-ten now un-to

my rime, Swid-dy wid-dy win-ky tum fum. My clothes is made

of cash-mere, Swid-dy wid-dy win-ky and I-rish fum. Pike

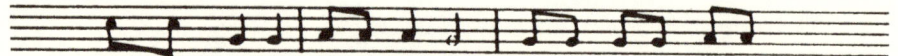

come micke rum mu lov-er ap-pears, Swi-dy wid-dy win-ky

Chorus

tum fum. Sing tur-e ur-e, tur-e ur-e, Swi-dy wid-dy win-ky

tum I-rish fum. Sing tur-e ur-e, tur-e ur-e, Swid-dy

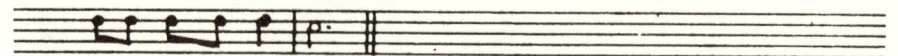

wid-dy win-ky tum fum.

Oh, shentlemens and ladies, chust in time,
Swiddy widdy winky tum fum.
Come listen now unto my rhyme,
Swiddy widdy winky tum fum.
My clothes is made of cashmere,
Swiddy widdy winky and Irish fum.
Pike come mike rum mu lover appears,
Swiddy widdy winky tum fum.

Chorus:
    Sing ture ure, ture ure,
    Swiddy widdy winky tum Irish fum.
    Sing ture ure, ture ure,
    Swiddy widdy winky tum fum.

Oh, they carried the Dootchman home to his bride,
Swiddy widdy winky tum fum.
She called him Tod Tam drunken swide,
Swiddy widdy winky tum fum.
Then he begins to curse and ran'.
Swiddy widdy winky and Irish fum.
She bust him over the head with a big tin pan.
Swiddy widdy winky tum fum.

Oh, they send Jack Parver, an old doctor,
Swiddy widdy winky tum fum.
"Of all the sick mans you're the vurst,"
Swiddy widdy winky tum fum.
"If you drank so much beer, by Tam you'll burst,"
Swiddy widdy winky tum fum.

Oh, they lays this Dootchman on his bed,
Swiddy widdy winky tum fum.
By Tam this Dootchman he gone dead,
Swiddy widdy winky tum fum.
They take him and catch him up in the slats,
Swiddy widdy winky and Irish fum.
He's good for nothing but to poison rats,
Swiddy widdy winky tum fum.

Now, shentlemens and ladies, my song is done,
Swiddy widdy winky tum fum.
And I hope that I've offended none,
Swiddy widdy winky tum fum.
I leaves my lager on the shelf,
Swiddy widdy winky and Irish fum.
If you want any more you can sing it yourself.
Swiddy widdy winky tum fum.

VI
PARODIES OF SONGS

148
Down on the Farm

Nostalgic sentiment about the wonders of farm life apparently were rather common in the 19th century. One song entitled "Down on the Farm" was composed by Gustabus Du Bois and copyrighted by Oliver Ditson in 1889; another by the same name was copyrighted in 1890 by Oliver Ditson & Co. The song given below apparently written by Raymond A. Browne, the music by Harry von Tilzer, and published in 1902, and was a great success (Spaeth, *History of Popular Music,* p. 306). Despite, or because of, the romantic picture of life on the old homeplace, the song became popular with the folk. But the folk likewise rebelled against the false picture, as seen in the fact that parodies, at least two, were written of it. For one parody see below; for another see Brown (III, 241).

A

"Down On The Farm," sung by Mr. Claude Springfield, Vernon, Lamar County, 1952. He used to sing in a quartet. Perhaps this song is from those days. He does not remember.

As a boy I used to dwell in that home I loved so well,
Way down among the clover and the bees.
And the morning glory vine round the cottage used to twine,
And the robin redbreast sang among the trees.

Chorus:
Many weary years have passed since I saw the old folks last,
And the music steals around me like a charm.
Every old familiar face has its kind and loving face
In my childhood's happy home down on the farm.

There were children young and gay; there were old folks old and gray,
And a mother dear to keep us from all harm,
And I spent many happy hours roving wild among the flowers
In my childhood's happy home down on the farm.

And today as I go near that old farm I loved so dear,
A stranger comes to meet me at the door.
In this old familiar place there I see a stranger's face,
Not the old familiar faces as of yore.

B

"Down On The Farm," sung by Mrs. Nettie Coleman, Tucson, Arizona, 1952. She learned it in Greene County, Alabama, some forty years ago. One stanza and chorus.

149
Parody of "Down On The Farm"

For a general headnote see No. 148. This particular parody was published, almost exactly as sung here, in *Harper Bros. European Circus Songster* (N.Y. 189-, p. 5).

"Parody of the same," sung by Mr. Claude Springfield, Vernon, Lamar County, 1952. He probably learned this parody from his quartet days. He does not remember exactly when or how he learned it.

I re-mem-ber when a boy how my heart would

leap with joy, When some-one would speak of

home and farm so dear, Of Moth-er's old red

shawl and mot-toes on the wall, All go far to

Chorus

make me feel sad and drear. Then don't men-tion

the farm to me where I climbed the ap-ple tree.

I'll take an ax and cut off my right arm. For

I'd rath-er go to jail and no one to go my

bail Than to go and spend one hour down on the

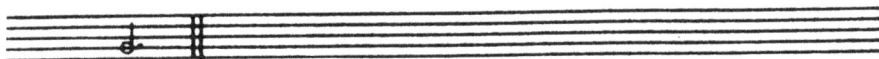

farm.

I remember when a boy how my heart would leap with joy
When someone would speak of home and farms so dear,
Of Mother's old red shawl and mottoes on the wall,
All go far to make me feel sad and drear.

Chorus:
Then don't mention the farm to me where I climbed the apple tree.
I'll take an ax and cut off my right arm.
For I'd rather go to jail and no one to go my bail
Than to go and spend one hour on the farm.

We had brickbats there for soap, wiped our faces on a rope.
E'en my watch and chain, it lost its little charm.
Every hayseed that you'd pass would have whiskers made of grass.
And I liked to starved to death down on the farm.

150
Maggie Jones

Parodies of popular songs are not uncommon in folk tradition, as several songs in this volume attest. Usually the parodies are not so old as other folk songs, and they are therefore likely to come down to us in rather full versions. The present song is a good example. The comic subject and treatment are typical of Alabama funny songs. I have not found this one in other collections, and I have only one text.

"Maggie Jones," sung by Mrs. Lily Turner, Crane Hill, Cullman County, 1952. She does not know how old it is. The tune is, "Shade of The Old Apple Tree."

Miss Maggie Jones she was a homely maiden,
And she owned a homely apple tree.
Miss Maggie's face was freckled, heavily laden.
To tell the truth, she was homelier than me.
One day as I was passing by the garden,
Miss Maggie Jones and I had a chance to spy.
She said, "If you will pick for me some apples,
I will bake for you an apple pie."
So I climbed up the old apple tree,
For a pie was a rare thing to me.
She stood down below with her apron spread so
For to catch all the apples you see.
It looked like a picnic to me.
Just then the limb broke, holy gee.
I broke several bones and half killed Maggie Jones
In the shade of the old apple tree.

My dear old father was an eager fighter,
And mother she was quite a fighter too,
Especially fighting with my dear old father.
She'd beat him till he was black and blue.
Perhaps you'll find some soft spot in the woodshed,
Where he can sleep his little jag away.
There's one thing I can say about my parents,
In the house they'll never fight again, I'll say.
They'll go out under the old apple tree,
For they have lots more room there you see.
Then mother'll start in with a big rolling pin
And tan poor father till he can hardly see.
In the fight they upset a bee hive,
To find that the bees were alive.
They didn't sting pa, but, gee, they stung ma,
In the shade of the old apple tree.

151
You Drove A Buick

Setting words to a popular tune, like parodying, is a common folk practice. "You Wore A Tulip" (words by Jack Mahoney, music by Percy Wenrich; copyrighted by Leo Feist, New York, 1914) was apparently one of the more frequently imitated songs. Hand (*Western Folklore, IX* 1950, 43f.), for instance, gives three miners' parodies and cites another. My Alabama parody of this song was probably more popular than the one text would indicate. Dating the parody is difficult. It probably comes from the later days of the Model T Ford, when the Buick was more conspicuous in "modernity" than was the Ford.

"You Drove A Buick," sung by Miss Drucilla Hall, Millport, Lamar County, 1952. Tune of "You Wore A Tulip."

Bill, do you remember that old Kentucky town,
A girl named Susy Brown, that was all time hanging round?
I took her to a picnic in my little Ford one day,
And then you came along and stole her heart away.

You drove a Buick, a big yellow Buick,
And I drove a little tin Ford.
As you passed by me, you both tried to guy me.
Your ignorance I ignored.
In a mudhole you stuck, Bill, your front wheel you stuck, Bill.
Your engine puffed and roared.
I pulled your Buick, your big yellow Buick
In my little tin Ford.

152
Parody of "Home, Sweet Home"

In the midst of the many "Home, Sweet Home" mottoes and the sometimes rather heavy sentiment of Alabama folk songs, it is pleasant to hear a song about a home that was not so sweet, of conditions not always ideal. This parody illustrates well humor and detachment from the cliches of everyday life.

"Parody of 'Home, Sweet Home'," sung by Mr. Claude Springfield, Vernon, Lamar County, 1952. He has been singing it for nearly fifty years. It is probably a result of his quartet-singing days.

When you're having heaps of fun and getting full of beer,
There's no place like home.
When your feet get tangled up and you walk on your ear,
There's no place like home.

You pull on the door but lose it with a bound.
The bannister will keep you from the ground.
You set on the steps till the milkman comes around.
There's no place like home.

When your wife's relations come to visit you,
There's no place like home.
They bring all their trunks and they stick like glue,
There's no place like home.

'Tis hard to give up the best room that you've got,
And go and sleep on an old hard cot
With a brother-in-law who's just half shot,
There's no place like home.

It's hard to get up in the middle of the night,
There's no place like home,
And look for paregoric without any light,
There's no place like home.

The little baby cries just on one track,
And you step on the point of a rusted carpet tack.
Your wife sticks her cold feet in the middle of your back.
There's no place like home.

153
Just Tell Them That You Saw Me

This sentimental piece was written by Paul Dresser, the brother of Theodore Dreiser. Theodore, in speaking of his brother's songs, refers to "the accuracy with which they (the songs) set forth the moods, the reactions and the aspirations of the exceedingly humble, intellectually and emotionally," and poses: "What other than an innocent-minded and deeply illusioned and unsophisticated democracy could this indicate?" (Spaeth, *History of Popular Music*, p. 277). Spaeth says: "The song had a tremendous sale. There were photographic slides to illustrate the sad story. The phrase: 'Just tell them that you saw me,' became a snappy farewell of a young man about town." He says further that there were many parodies. Stout (*Folklore From Iowa*, p. 63) reports it as a folk song. It apparently was once more popular in Alabama than my two texts indicate. My parody shows its former popularity, and the reaction against the heavy sentiment.

A

"Wayward Girl," sung by Mrs. Nola Browne, Millport, Lamar County, 1951. Tune same as "Oyster Stew."

While strolling down the street one day
Upon a pleasure bent,
I met a girl who shrank from me,
And whom I recognized,
A schoolmate in a village far away.
"Is that you, Madge?" I said to her;
She quickly turned away.
"Don't turn away, Madge, for I'm still your friend.
Next week I'm going back to see the old folks and I thought
Perhaps a message you would like to send."

Chorus:
"Just tell them that you saw me and they will know the rest.
Just tell them that I'm looking well you know.
Just whisper if you get a chance to Mother dear and say,
I love her as I did long, long ago."

"Your face looks pale, your eyes are dim.
Come tell me are you ill?
When last we met your eyes shone bright and clear.

Come, come, Madge, and go with me,
A change will do you good.
Your mother wonders where you are tonight."
"I'd like to see them all again,
But not just yet, you know.
It's pride alone that's keeping me away.
Just tell them not to worry,
For I'm all right, don't you know.
Just tell them that I'm coming home some day."

B

"Just Tell Them That You Saw Me," sung by Mr. Claude Springfield, Vernon, Lamar County, 1952. Essentially the same version as A.

154
Oyster Stew
Parody of "Just Tell Them That You Saw Me"

Spaeth (*History of Popular Music,* p. 277) says there were many parodies of "Just Tell Them That You Saw Me." This one, however, is the only one I have collected. It shows a vigorous reaction against the sentiment of the song.

"Oyster Stew," sung by Mrs. Ruth Clements, Holt, Tuscaloosa County, 1952.

A man hap-pened to an ac-ci-dent up-on a rail-road

train, A-try-ing to ride and would not pay his fee. The

doc-tors they con-sult-ed, ex-am-ined him and said: "We'll

have to saw his leg off at the knee." They tried to give

him chlo-ro-form but he would-n't take the stuff. Said:

"Go a-head while I'm brave and strong. And while you're

saw-ing off the leg, oh, please, sir, let me sing." They

did and then he start-ed up this song: "Just tell them

that you saw me and I was los-ing flesh. To ups and downs

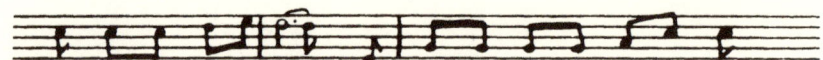

will al-ways be a slave. Just whis-per if you get a chance

to moth-er dear and say, Her dar-ling boy has one foot

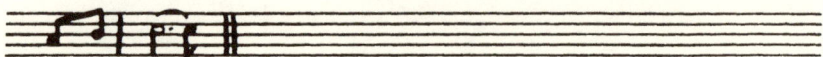

in the grave."

A man happened to an accident upon a railroad train,
A-trying to ride and would not pay his fee.
The doctors they consulted, examined him and said:
"We'll have to saw his leg off at the knee."
They tried to give him chloroform but he wouldn't take the stuff.
Said, "Go ahead while I'm brave and strong.
And while you're sawing off the leg, oh, please, sir, let me sing."
They did, and then he started up this song:

Chorus:
 "Just tell them that you saw me and I was losing flesh,
  To ups and downs will always be a slave.
 Just whisper to mother dear if you get a chance,
  Her darling boy has one foot in the grave."

I went to a church festival about three weeks ago,
Was just because I had nothing else to do.
Of course I stayed for supper, which was fifty cents a chair.
The waiter brought me in some oyster stew.
I dipped my spoon into the stuff and found it was all milk.
I swore I'd never go there any more.
At last one lonely oyster came strolling up the top.
He looked me in the face and bravely said:

"Just tell them that you saw me and I was in the soup.
I've been brought here just sixteen times alone.
Please, Mister, don't you eat me, I'm the only one they have.
Remember, you have children all your own."

155
Sweet Marie

The music of this popular song was written by Raymond Moore, the words by Cy Warman, journalist and versifier, in 1893. It was first sung by Moore in the musical show *Africa,* which opened in the Euclid Opera House in Cleveland. Charles Hopper sang it later in the same show in Pittsburgh. It "was an immediate success and soon the whole country was singing and whistling its dainty measures" (Spaeth, *History of Popular Music,* p. 268). Its wide popularity among the folk is attested to by the fact that it was parodied. It is not widely reported as a folk song. Ford *(Traditional Music in America,* p. 379) gives it.

A

"Sweet Marie," sung by Mrs. O.C. Powell, Titus, Elmore County, 1952, from a manuscript which she wrote down months earlier from memory. She does not remember when or how she learned it.

I've a secret in my heart, Sweet Marie,
A tale I would impart, Love, to thee.
Every daisy in the dell
Knows my secret, knows it well,
And yet I dare not tell Sweet Marie.
When I hold your hand in mine, Sweet Marie,
A feeling most divine comes to me.
Every wave that sweeps the shore
Seems to sing it o'er and o'er,
Seems to say that I adore Sweet Marie.

Chorus:
Sweet Marie, come to me; I love thee, Sweet Marie,
Not because your face is fair, Love, to see.
But your soul so pure and sweet
Makes my happiness complete,
Makes me falter at your feet, Sweet Marie.

Every morn when I awake, Sweet Marie,
Seems to me my heart will break, Love, for thee.
All the world is full of spring,
Full of warbles on the wing,
And I listen while they sing, Sweet Marie.
When the sunset tints the west, Sweet Marie,
And I sit down to rest, Love, with thee,

Every star that studs the sky
Seems to stand and wonder why
They're so dimmer than your eyes, Sweet Marie.

B

"Sweet Marie," contributed by Mrs. M.V. Tarwater, Fayette, Fayette County, 1952, from a manuscript. she does not remember when or how she learned it. Three stanzas and Chorus. Essentially version A.

C

"Sweet Marie," contributed by Miss Drucilla Hall, Millport, Lamar County, 1952, from a newspaper clipping. She did not know the tune. Two stanzas and chorus. Essentially version A.

156
Parody of "Sweet Marie"

See the note above. This parody probably dates from the Spanish-American War, 1898, which was only five years after the song was first published. The tune being simple and rhythmical, it was probably quite popular during this war, both for the original song and for parodies. I have not found this parody reported elsewhere.

"Parody of 'Sweet Marie,' " sung by Mrs. Mary Drake, Huntsville, Madison County, 1953. She claims to have written it.

From the fields of war I come, sweet Ma-rie.

Will you kiss me wel-come home, Love, to thee? I am

on-ly skin and bones, all my sweet-est songs are groans,

And I'm full of ar-my prunes as can be.

From the fields of war I come, sweet Marie.
Will you kiss me welcome home, Love, to thee?
I am only skin and bones, all my sweetest songs are groans,
And I'm full of army prunes as can be.

Oh, I got it in the neck, sweet Marie.
I am but a shattered wreck, don't you see?
In the mud and rain I slept, while the very heavens wept,
And the buzzards vigil kept over me.

When I enlisted I was fat, sweet Marie.
There never was a Thomas cat spry as me.
I could lift a barrel of beer, I could run like a deer.
And there never was a tear in my 'ee.

Now I'm thinner than a ghost, sweet Marie.
You could make a hitching post out of me.
Every joint that's in my frame is with feeble stiffness lame.
Oh, Tahenna (sic) was no name for the spree.

Now I'm with you once again, sweet Marie,
Although you seem not to i-den-ti-fy me.

Now that I am on my feet and will have a chance to eat,
I'll accumulate more meat than you see.

From those bitter quinine pills — ouch! oh, gee.
And from thirty ague chills I am free.
Now I live almighty high, and I soon will be as spry
As the boy you kissed goodby, sweet Marie.

VII
FUNNY SONGS

157
Old Zachariah Fell In The Fire

This nonsense sequence jingle is reported in the Brown Collection (III, 185), from South Carolina (JAFL, xliv, 436), Georgia (Henry, *Songs Sung in the Southern Appalachians,* p. 242; JAFL, xlvii, 339), Mississippi (JAFL, xxvi, 143), Texas (PFLST, xii, 251), Arkansas (*Ozark Folklore,* I, 7). The L.C. Checklist (p. 194) reports a text from Florida. I collected it in Alabama from only one family. The changes in the versions of father and daughter are interesting.

A

"Old Zachariah," contributed by Mr. Gilbert Davis, Montgomery, Montgomery County, 1953. Spoken. He learned it from his father around sixty years ago in Fayette County.

Old Zachariah fell in the fire.
Fire was so hot he jumped in the pot.
Pot was so little he jumped in the kettle.
Kettle was so black he jumped in the crack.
Crack was so high he jumped in the sky.
Sky was so blue he jumped in a canoe.
Canoe was so long he jumped in the pond.
Pond was so deep he jumped in the creek.
Creek was so shallow he jumped in the tallow.
Tallow was so soft he jumped in the loft.
Loft was so rotten he jumped in the cotton.
Cotton was so white he stayed all night.

B

"Old Zachariah,"sung by Mrs. Frances Downing, Vernon, Lamar County, 1952. She learned it from her father, Mr. Gilbert Davis. Her changes are mostly through omission of lines. Since her particular branch of the family likes comic songs, she will probably teach this one to her children.

Old Zach-a-ri-ah he fell in the fire. The fire's

so hot he jumped in the pot.

Old Zachariah he fell in the fire.
The fire's so hot he jumped in the pot.
The pot was so black he jumped in the crack.
The crack was so high he jumped in the sky.
They sky was so blue he jumped in the canoe.
Canoe was so shallow he jumped in the tallow.
The tallow's so soft he jumped in the loft.
The loft was so rotten he jumped in the cotton.
The cotton was so white he stayed all night.

C

"Old Zachariah," a fragment spoken by Mrs. Maggie Lee Hayes, Vernon, Lamar County, 1952. She has largely forgotten the little song. She is the sister of Mr. Gilbert Davis, and like him enjoys these old funny songs, but never did sing them as much as he did. Her children, to whom she repeated these things, are not, apparently, carrying on the tradition.

158
Old Rosin the Beau

This song, either under the above title or as "Old Rosin the Bow," was perhaps the most popular comic song of the mid-nineteenth century. It was apparently first published, in America, in Philadelphia in 1838, as a "favorite comic song dedicated with much respect to the members of the Falcon Barge by the publisher." It was arranged by J.C. Beckell (Dichter and Shapiro, *Early American Sheet Music,* p. 101). The words and music are apparently anonymous, though probably of Scotch origin. The song was used for at least four political parodies between 1840-75. When Henry Clay, who was born in a district of Hanover County, Virginia, called The Slashes, was campaigning against James K. Polk for the Presidency, the Whigs used the tune of "Old Rosin" for two campaign songs, "The Mill-Boy of The Slashes," and "Old Hal of the West." One of Lincoln's campaign songs was "Lincoln and Liberty," written by F.A. Simpkins, to the tune of "Old Rosin." In the General Grant-Horace Greeley Presidential campaign in 1872, a group of independents nominated for their ticket Charles O'Conor and John Q. Adams, and campaigned with the song "Straight-Out Democrat," to the tune of "Old Rosin, the Beau" (Spaeth, *History of Popular Music,* p. 83). The song was also popular in the songsters. It appeared in *The New Negro Forget-Me-Not-Songster* (N.Y. 1848, p. 94); *The Negro Minstrel* (Glasgow, 1850, p. 10), and *Beadle's Dime Song Book, No. 3* (N.Y. 1859, p. 61). Further evidence of the song's wide popularity is the fact that the tune continued to be used for other songs in the songsters — in *Put's Golden Songster* (N.Y. 1858, p. 27) "He's the Man for Me," is sung to the air of "Rosin the Bow"; *Beadle's Dime Union Song Book, No. 3* (N.Y. 1862) has the song "Aloft & Alow" to the same air; and *Camp Song for the Soldier* (N.Y. 1864) has two songs to the tune, "Uncle Sam's Grant" and "The Union Forever." For a bibliography see Randolph (IV, 371). The L.C. Checklist (pp. 299; 342-343) lists it from California, New York City, Ohio and Kentucky. The song apparently is not popular in Alabama. My one text, however, is full.

"Old Rosin," sung by Miss Drucilla Hall, Millport, Lamar County, 1952. She probably learned it from her father, Mr. John Hall.

When I was young and pret-ty, The girls
all called me their beau. But now I'm old and
ug-ly They call me old Ros-in, their beau. Old
Ros-in, old Ros-in, old Ros-in, their beau. They
call me old Ros-in, their beau.

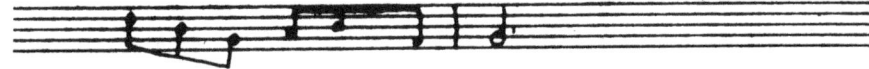

When I was young and pretty,
The girls they all called me their beau.
But now when I'm old and ugly,
They call me old Rosin, their beau.

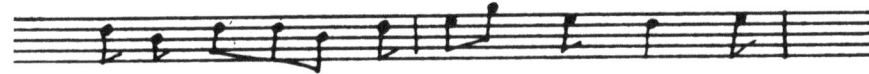

Chorus:
    Old Rosin, old Rosin, old Rosin their beau.
    They call me old Rosin, their beau.

When I am dead I reckon
The ladies will want to, I know,
Just lift up the lid of my coffin
And look at old Rosin, their beau.

Take four or five tall ones, young fellows,
And stand them all around in a row,
And drink a half gallon bottle
To the health of old Rosin, their beau.

Just take a couple of fellows,
And let them all staggering go,
And dig a deep hole in the meadow,
And in it throw Rosin, their beau.

Just get a couple of tombstones;
Place one at my head and my toe.
And on it place an inscription:
Farewell to old Rosin, their beau.

159
George Buck

This nonsense song, like many other folk songs, includes or excludes stanzas at will. These floating stanzas are often about animals, about hunting, working, or against women and marriage. I have not found this particular combination of stanzas anywhere else. George Buck is not a usual ballad name, and might well have been a local name. However, the L.C. Checklist (p. 114) lists this title from New York City. I have only one text.

"George Buck," sung by Mr. Isaac Rollins, Wedowee, Randolph County, 1953. He sings it as a comic song.

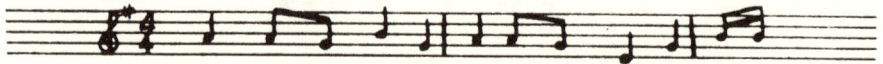

George Buck he said be-fore he was dead To nev-er
let your wo-man have her way. She will cause you to weep,
she will cause you to mourn. She will cause you to lose
your home.

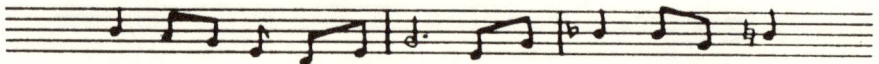

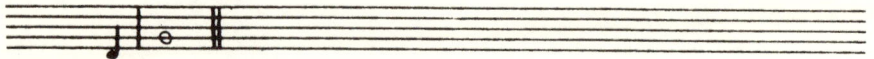

George Buck he said before he was dead
To never let your woman have her way.
She will cause you to weep, she will cause you to mourn.
She will cause you to lose your home.

See a rabbit on a log and I ain't got no rabbit dog,
And I took me a sprout and I flayed that little rabbit out.
And a rabbit on a stump, and I think he's about to jump.
And I hope he will make it some day.

Got them chickens in my sack
And them bloodhounds on my track,
And I'll take them to my cabin fo' long.

160
Sam Simon

This nonsense piece should be compared with the several similar ones in this volume. They are sung for the pure joy of singing and for their comic value. I have not found this one elsewhere.

"Sam Simon," sung by Mrs. Ercelle Hand, Saragossa, Walker County, 1953. She has sung it some forty years.

There was an old Sam Simon, And a young Sam Simon,

And young Sam Simon will be Sam Simon When old Sam

Simon is gone.

There was an old Sam Simon
And a young Sam Simon,
And young Sam Simon will be Sam Simon
When old Sam Simon is gone.

161
The Old Gray Horse

This comic song about a man and his horse has not been widely reported. Randolph (II, 415) gives two texts. Sharp *(English Folk Songs from the Southern Appalachians, II, 220)* gives four stanzas of a related piece. Dobie *(Texas Folk-Lore Society Publications, 6, 1927, pp. 123-124)* gives an "Old Gray" song found in Texas. I have only one Alabama text.

"The Old Gray Horse," sung by Mrs. Eva Hollis, Vernon, Lamar County, 1952.

Last Monday morning being troubled in mind,
I started a long journey, my fancies to find.
None being in company but me and my horse,
And this unto him I began to discourse.

"Long time, Old Gray, we have traveled together,
Through rain and through snow and sometimes in warm weather,
And why should you falter and hang your head down,
For once I'm in a hurry to get to the town."

"You need not abuse me although you're a man,
For you know I will carry you as far as I can.
And as for my courage you need not to doubt,
For the honor of my country I'll never give out.

"You know very well when you give me my due,
You ride me over rocks without any shoe,
Over hills and high mountains and all sich rough ground.
At all those abuses I never do frown."

"At those hard abuses you need not to scorn.
I feed you very well upon fodder and corn.
And every time I warm my feet,
I give you all the oats you are able to eat."

"Yes, yes, Master, all this I do know.
You feed very well and you ride very slow.
But when you get drunk I pay for it all.
You ride very hard and feed not at all."

162
Necktie's Up Behind

This amusing description of some of the hazards of being dressed
up is a take-off of a minstrel/music-hall creation. Presumably the original was composed by Thomas P. Westendorf and copyrighted by
the John Church Co., New York City, in 1891 (*Wehman's Collection
of Songs, No. 32,* N.Y. 1891, p. 2). The differences in the language
of the two versions is interesting. That of the published version is
simpler, less bookish than the folk version. My informant, a school
teacher for nearly fifty years, probably learned the song when he was
in Missouri for a short stay in his youth. The language of his version
affects the stilted phraseology of the stereotypical "professor." In
the published version, there is only a distant similarity in most of
the verses, but I quote one for comparison. I have not found this
song reported in other collections of folksongs.

There's nothing can prevent it, no matter how one tries,
For neckties are in fashion, and they are bound to rise;
They'll do it too, I warn you; at least I think you'll find
That when you don't expect it, your necktie's up behind.

"Necktie's Up Behind," sung by Mr. Andrew Johnson, Vernon,
Lamar County, 1952.

When you at-tend a par-ty and gy-rate with the girls,

The ex-er-cise is hear-ty, your brain with plea-sure

whirls. But oh that pain-ful feel-ing when sud-den-ly

you find the na-ked truth re-veal-ing: your neck-tie's

Chorus.

up be-hind. Your neck-tie, neck-tie, your neck-tie, neck-

tie, your neck-tie's up be-hind. Your neck-tie, neck-tie,

your neck-tie, neck-tie, your neck-tie's up be-hind, it's

up be-hind.

When you attend a party and gyrate with the girls,
The exercise is hearty , your brain with pleasure whirls.
But, oh, that painful feeling when suddenly you find
The naked truth revealing: your necktie's up behind.

Chorus:
    Your necktie, necktie, your necktie, necktie;
    Your necktie's up behind.
    Your necktie, necktie, your necktie, necktie;
    Your necktie's up behind, it's up behind.

On some night when you're calling upon your sweetheart fair,
Oh, is it not appalling as you your love declare;
As the words come hard and harder, quite suddenly to find,
In the midst of love's sweet ardor, your necktie's up behind.

In this queer situation, no matter how one tries,
There is no expiation; the necktie's bound to rise.
'Tis useless to regret it; by fate it is designed,
And when you least expect it, your necktie's up behind.

163
The Beaver Cap

Unaccountably this song, with its very singable words and tune, has not been widely popular with folk singers. Randolph (III, 45) gives a one-stanza fragment and cites a reference to Henry *(Songs Sung in the Southern Appalachians,* p. 32) and to Belden *(Ballads and Songs,* p. 435). Belden's is a full version. The song is not widely sung in Alabama, but it is known by the people who like funny songs. Both my versions are complete.

A

"The Beaver Cap," sung by Mrs. Mona Johnson, Vernon, Lamar County, 1952. She has sung it for at least thirty years.

I'll sing you a song, it won't take long
About my life concerning,
About the beaver cap I wore
Before my locks were turning.

Chorus:
    Sing fact a la, sing toot a low,
    Sing fact a la la day.

I went down town one lovely day
To buy me a hat, sir.
And the very first thing they showed to me
Was a broad brimmed beaver hat, sir.

I bought me one and took it home
And hung it on the bed, sir.
And every time I turned around
I tried it on my head, sir.

I went to work the very next day
A-feeling very fine, sir.
And Mama set her old gray hen
In my new beaver hat, sir.

I took them eggs one by one,
You bet I had some fun, sir.
I threw them at my mama's head,
And banged her as she run, sir.

My daddy came home the very next day.
You bet I steeped around, sir.
He drew those blisters on my back
With that broad brimmed hat, sir.

B

"Beaver Cap," sung by Mr. Joe Pennington, Vernon, Lamar County, 1953.

Went to town the oth-er day to buy me a hat, sir.

The first thing he showed me was broad brim bea-ver cap,

Chorus

sir. Whack ta la too-dle la, whack ta la la day.

Went to town the other day
To buy me a hat, sir.
The first thing the clerk showed me
Was a broadbrim beaver cap, sir.

Chorus:
    Whack ta la, toodle la, whack ta la la day.

I bought that cap. I took it home
And hung it on the bed, sir.
Every time I woke up
I tried it on my head, sir.

I went to work the very next day
Feeling very flat, sir.
When I come home my mommy set a hen
In that old beaver cap, sir.

I took those eggs one by one.
You bet I had some fun, sir.
I banged them at my mommy's head.
I banged them as she run, sir.

My daddy came home the very next day.
You bet he made me hop, sir.
He raised the blisters on my back
With that old beaver cap, sir.

He beat me and he banged me
And he tormented my life out of me, sir.
And the only remedy that I could find
Was marry me a wife, sir.

I hugged those girls; I kissed those girls.
I took them on my lap, sir.
And all the while they was picking fur
From my old beaver cap, sir.

I married my love; she was a dove,
The idol of my life, sir.
If she abused my beaver cap
It kindly raised my Irish, sir.

164
She Don't Wear No

This piece was undoubtedly of comic-songster or minstrel origin. It was sung as a nonsense song. Although more "risque" than the stanza in "Send For The Ladies," these stanzas were sung straight-forward, like the words of any other song. I have only one text. I have not found the song in any other collection.

"She Don't Wear No — Yes She Do," sung by Mrs. Maggie Lee Hayes, Vernon, Lamar County, 1952. It is a "silly song."

She don't wear no--yes she do, She don't wear no--

yes she do, She don't wear no--yes she do. She don't wear

no chim nor shoe.

She don't wear no — yes, she do.
She don't wear no — yes, she do.
She don't wear no — yes, she do.
She don't wear no chem nor shoe.

She don't wear no — yes, she do.
She don't wear no — yes, she do.
She don't wear no — yes, she do.
Yes, she wears them drawers like you.

165
Jennie Jenkins

The editors of the Brown Collection (III, 102) say this song is "presumably a derivative of the very widely known and sung 'Miss Jennia Jones,'" although "Jennie Jenkins" itself has not been widely reported. See Brown for references to New Hampshire, Vermont, Virginia and Missouri. The L.C. Checklist (pp. 194; 289) lists texts from Virginia, North Carolina, California and Mississippi. My four texts indicate rather wide popularity in Alabama.

A

"Jennie Jenkins," sung by Mrs. Martha Jane Snyder, Tucson, Arizona, 1952. She learned it in Greene and Tuscaloosa Counties, Alabama, seventy years ago.

Will you wear white, Jane, oh, Jane? Will you wear
white, Jen-nie Jen-kins? I won't wear white, for the
col-or's too light. I'll buy me a tur-ly wur-ly high.
I'll buy me a tur-ly wur-ly dou-ble ru-tle sil-ky ju-by
per-ly fide brown, Jen-nie Jen-kins.

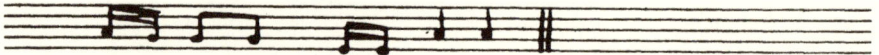

Will you wear white, Jane, oh, Jane?
Will you wear white, Jennie Jenkins?
I won't wear white, for the color's too light.
I'll buy me a turly wurly high.
I'll buy me a turly wurly double ruble
    silky juby perly fide brown, Jennie Jenkins.

B

"Jenny Jenkins," sung by Mr. Mose Pennington, Nauvoo, Walker County, 1953.

Oh, will you wear the red, dear, oh dear,
Will you wear the red, Jenny Jenkins?
I won't wear the red, for the colors they are dead.

Chorus:
 Go buy me a folly dolly dilly dolly
 Double boodle surple juicy binder
 To wear with my rovin' Jenny Jenkins.

Oh, will you wear the yeller, dear, oh dear,
Will you wear the yeller, Jenny Jenkins?
I won't wear the yeller, for the colors they are shaller.

Oh, will you wear the blue, dear, oh dear,
Will you wear the blue, Jenny Jenkins?
I will wear the blue, for the colors they are true.

C

"Dora Della Jenkins," from the Alabama Archives, collected by Mrs. Ila B. Prine from Mrs. Corie Lambert, Mobile, Mobile County, no date.

You wear black, Anna Jenkins.
I wouldn't wear black,
For it's the color of the back.

I'll buy me a tol-o-rol-a rice-en.
I'll buy me a tol-o-rol,
A double role-a-dell-a bum
To wear with my Dora Della Jenkins.

You wear blue, Anna Jenkins.
Well, I would wear blue
For the color's so true.

You wear red, Anna Jenkins.
Well, I wouldn't wear red,
For it's the color of the head.

You wear white, Anna Jenkins.
Well, I wouldn't wear white,
For the color is so bright.

D

"Jenny Jenkins," sung by Mrs. Nola Browne, Millport, Lamar County, 1952. A fragment.

166
Buy Me a Rocking Chair

The only other example of this song that I have found is in Randolph (III, 46). The beginning of his version is practically the same, although a "china doll" is desired instead of the "rocking chair" in my version. Thereafter both songs develop in a similar way though with different articles.

"Sweet Mother, Dear," sung by Miss Drucilla Hall, Millport, Lamar County, 1952.

Buy me a rock-ing chair, rock-ing chair; Buy

me a rock-ing chair, sweet Moth-er, dear.

Buy me a rocking chair, rocking chair,
Buy me a rocking chair, sweet Mother, dear.

What will I buy it with, buy it with,
What will I buy it with, sweet Daughter, dear?

Sell Father's feather bed, feather bed,
Sell Father's feather bed, sweet mother, dear.

Where would your father sleep, father sleep,
Where would your father sleep, sweet Daughter, dear?

Sleep in the boarder's room, boarder's room,
Sleep in the boarder's room, sweet Mother, dear.

Where would the boarder sleep, boarder sleep,
Where would the boarder sleep, sweet Daughter, dear?

Sleep in the washtub, washtub,
Sleep in the washtub, sweet Mother, dear.

Where would I wash at, wash at,
Where would I wash at, sweet Daughter, dear?

Wash in the river, the river,
Wash in the river, sweet Mother, dear.

What if the clothes was to wash away, was away,
What if the clothes was to wash away, sweet Daughter, dear?

Have the dog to watch them, watch them,
Have the dog to watch them, sweet Mother, dear.

What if the dog was to run away, run away,
What if the dog was to run away, sweet Daughter, dear?

Tie his tail to a hickory stub, hickory stub,
Tie his tail to a hickory stub, sweet Mother, dear.

What if his tail was to pull in two, pull in two,
What if his tail was to pull in two, sweet Daughter, dear?

Glue it back with gluing wax, gluing wax,
Glue it back with gluing wax, sweet Mother, dear.

167
When I Was A Little Boy

This funny song, like the fiddle tune, gathers and loses stanzas at the whim of the individual singer. The stanzas in the one Alabama text suit the song less than they do a half dozen others. The song has not been widely reported. The Brown Collection (III, 353) gives one text that is similar to mine only in the first stanza. I have not heard this song called a fiddle tune, but I would not be surprised if it is. If not a fiddle tune, it is what the folk like to call "a crazy song." Shearin (*Syllabus,* p. 38) lists a similar title for Kentucky.

"When I Was A Little Boy," sung by Mr. Andrew Aldrich, Hubberts-ville, Fayette County, 1953.

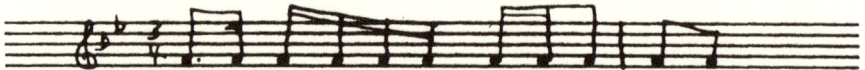

When I was a little boy
About sixteen inches high,
Oh, how I courted them pretty little girls,
And how my mammy cried.

. . . .
Whiskey for to sell.
How can a young man stay at home
When the girls all look so well?

Somebody stole my old coon dog,
And I wish he'd bring him back.
He'd run the big coons over the fence
And the little ones through the crack.

Saturday night I stole a horse,
Sunday I went to meeting.

Monday morning just fore day
Old folks give me a beating.

Saturday night my wife she died,
Sunday she was buried.
Monday was my courting day,
And Tuesday I was married.

168
When Father Was A Little Boy

The language of this piece sounds like a music hall or songster production. It probably dates around the middle of the nineteenth century. Nobody else has reported it as a folk song.

"When Father Was a Little Boy," contributed by Mr. H. T. Burns, Wedowee, Randolph County, 1951. He has known it over sixty years.

When father was a little boy,
The world was not so gay.
I love to hear him tell of how
He passed the time away.

He walked four miles to school each day,
In weather foul or fair,
A coonskin cap upon his head
And goose grease on his hair.

One day a new lad came to school
And sat in front of dad.
Dad liked a little fun,
But he really wasn't bad.

He spied a bright red string
Upon the young lad's neck.
He raveled yarn in great and full;
There must have been a peck.

When dad had reached the end of the string,
The lad was not aware
That dad had stripped him of his
Suit of flannel underwear.

169
Had A Fine Sash

This nonsense piece is undoubtedly of folk origin. The individual stanzas are found in any number of other songs. Such stanzas are added or dropped at the wish of the individual singer. I have not found this fragment elsewhere.

"Had a Fine Sash," contributed by Mrs. C.P. Connor, Millport, Lamar County, 1952.

Had a fine sash,
As fine as silk.
Any man that walks with me
Calls me white as milk.

I had a little dog,
His name was Blue.
Put him on the track;
He fairly flew.

I had a little pig.
I fed him with cheese.
I fed him so much
Till his tail fell off.

It give me a thomp.
Oh give me a nail.
I'll make my pig
A homemade tail.

170
Where Shall I Go?

This piece seems more likely a folk than a music hall, minstrel or songster creation. This is typical folk humor. The situations and treatments are close to the folk. The language is relaxed. This song does not occur in other collections.

"Where Shall I Go?" sung by Miss Drucilla Hall, Millport, Lamar County, 1952. She has sung it forty years.

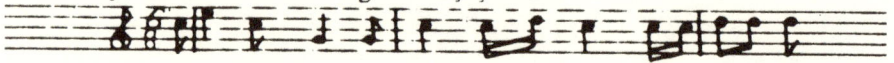

As I walked out one moon shiny night,
As I met a big dog, he offered to bite.
Yan, Yan, big dog; now don't you bite me.
Ah, oh, where shall I go?
Uh, oh, what shall I do?
Oh, I want to go home.

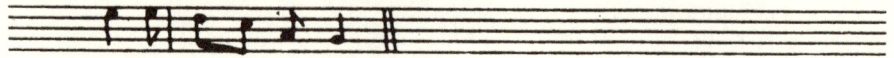

As I was walking round the well,
My foot slipped and in it I fell.
So farewell, world, and howdy do, girl.
Uh, oh, what shall I do?
Uh, oh, where shall I go?
Oh, I want to go home.

When I was lying on my death bed,
They shook the old brandy keg over my head.
I thought to my soul they'd kill me stone dead.
Uh, oh, what shall I do?
Oh, I want to go home so bad.

171
Saint Jonah

This piece of nonsense must have arisen as a take-off on the name
Jonah. Perhaps it is useless to wonder why or how. I have not found
the song anywhere else. I have only one text.

"Saint Jonah," sung by Miss Drucilla Hall, Millport, Lamar County,
1952. She has known it some thirty years.

I sent Saint Jon-ah. I sent him down to the field-ah

To see a-bout his hor-ses-ah. He was gone so long-ah I

had to go af-ter him-ah. And you rec-kon where he was

at-ah. He was set-tin' on a lit-tle log-ah.

I sent Saint Jon-ah.
I sent him down to the field ah
To see about his horses ah.
He was gone so long ah
I had to go after him ah,
And you reckon where he was at ah?
He was setting on a little log ah.
And you reckon what he was doing ah?
He was playing a little corn stalk fiddle ah.
You reckon what he was playing ah?
He was playing my wife's big toe is as long as my finger ah.

172
My Sweetheart's Gone to the Fair

Such nonsense funny songs as this one were more popular, I understand, a generation ago than they are now. I have not seen this song in any other collection.

"My Sweetheart's Gone to the Fair," sung by Mrs. Nancy Ann Bates, Crane Hill, Cullman County, 1953. She has known it for at least fifty years.

My sweetheart's gone to the fair,
Poor little thing she's a way off there.
Whenever she returns there'll be a chance for me,
Slicka day lilacs bloom.

Chorus:
　　Shu li, shu li, shu li floom,
　　Sho lika shi lika shu lika tume,
　　My heart shall lika day he li floom,
　　Shu licka day violets bloom.

I wish I was on yonders hill.
I'd sit down and cry my fill.
Every tear would turn a mill,
Slicka day lilacs bloom.

173
Trouble On Your Mind

In the treatment of an imaginative — or careless — singer a song can undergo many changes. This one seems a case in point. The chorus appears to be a distant-cousin to Brown's "Troubled in Mind" (III, 344). The other parts, however, seem to have drifted in from several songs. The first stanza is a floater, and is sung in many songs, especially comic or nonsense songs. The second stanza must appear in at least a dozen separate songs. The third stanza is a favorite in Negro songs (see Brown, III, 544). Such a composite is subject to constant change.

"Trouble On Your Mind," sung by Mrs. Nancy Ann Bates, Crane Hill, Cullman County, 1953.

Cheeks are like a cher-ry, cher-ry like a rose. Oh,

how I love them pret-ty lit-tle girls There ain't no-bo-dy

Chorus

knows. Hain't that trou-ble on your mind, Sa-rah? Hain't

that trou-ble on your mind? Trou-ble, trou-ble, trou-ble

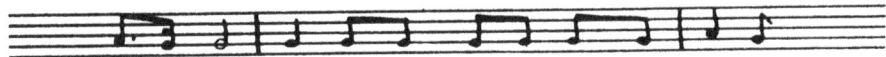

on your mind. Trou-ble don't kill us all, we'll live a

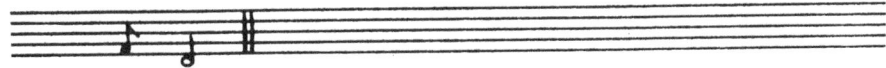

long time.

Cheeks are like a cherry,
Cherry like a rose.
Oh, how I love them pretty little girls
There ain't nobody knows.

Chorus:
   Hain't that trouble on your mind, Sarah?
   Hain't that trouble on your mind?

Trouhle, trouble, trouble on your mind.
If trouble don't kill us all,
We'll live a long time.

Wish I had a big white house,
Sixteen stories high,
And every story in that house
Was filled with chicken pie.

June bug has a glossy wing,
Lightning bug has a flame,
Bed bug got no wing at all
But he hets there just the same.

174
Hop Light, Ladies

This song should perhaps be called "I Don't Mind the Weather so the Wind Don't Blow," for this line seems always to occur, whereas the "Hop Light, Ladies" line does not. The song has not been widely reported. The Brown Collection (III, 119) gives a brief bibliography. Randolph (II, 323) reports it a part of "Jump Jim Crow." The L.C. Checklist (pp. 150; 168) lists texts from Virginia and Mississippi. In all cases the song has not been reported being longer than one fourline stanza. My A version is much longer. The first stanza of the A text seems borrowed from a different song, perhaps a jingle about animals, for which see specimens in Brown (III, 203).

A

"What Does the Red Bird Say to the Crow?" sung by Mrs. Nola Browne, Millport, Lamar County, 1951. She learned it from her father fifty years ago.

What does the red bird say to the crow,

What does the red bird say to the crow, What

does the red bird say to the crow? I don't

mind the wea-ther so the wind don't blow.

What does the red bird say to the crow?
What does the red bird say to the crow?
What does the red bird say to the crow?
I don't mind the weather so the wind don't blow.

Hop light, ladies, your cake's all dough.
Hop light, ladies, your cake's all dough.
Hop light, ladies, your cake's all dough.
You needn't mind the weather so the wind don't blow.

It's raining now and soon gonna snow.
It's raining now and soon gonna snow.
It's raining now and soon gonna snow.
I don't mind the weather so the wind don't blow.

Hop light, ladies, your cake's all dough.
Hop light, ladies, your cake's all dough.
Hop light, ladies, your cake's all dough.
You needn't mind the weather so the wind don't blow.

B

"Hop Light, Ladies," sung by Mrs. Nancy Ann Bates, Crance Hill, Cullman County, 1953. She has sung it for at least sixty years.

Hop light, la-dies, the cake's all dough.

Hop light, la-dies, the cake's all dough. Hop

light, la-dies, the cake's all dough. Nev-er

mind the wea-ther so the wind don't blow.

Hop light, ladies, the cake's all dough.
Hop light, ladies, the cake's all dough.
Hop light, ladies, the cake's all dough.
Never mind the weather so the wind don't blow.

175
Lazy Mary, Will You Get Up?

This song is related to the more common "Whistle, Daughter, Whistle." Randolph (III, 121) has a song called, "She Won't Get Up," which is more the idea of this song. Randolph's version, however, just wants to get the girl out of bed; whereas the Alabama version tries to get her up first for breakfast, then for dinner, and finally for supper. The rewards are different in the two versions. The L.C. Checklist (p. 221) reports a text from Texas.

"Lazy Mary," sung by Miss Drucilla Hall, Millport, Lamar County, 1952.

La-zy Ma-ry, will you get up, will you get up, will you get up? La-zy Ma-ry, will you get up, will you get up this morn-ing?

Lazy Mary, will you get up, will you get up, will you get up,
Lazy Mary, will you get up, will you get up this morning?

What will you give me for my breakfast, for my breakfast, for my breakfast,
What will you give me for my breakfast if I get up this morning?

Ham and eggs. (Spoken)

No, no, Mother, I won't get up, I won't get up, I won't get up,
No, no, Mother, I won't get up, I won't get up this morning.

Lazy Mary, will you get up, will you get up, will you get up,
Lazy Mary, will you get up, will you get up today?

What will you give me for my dinner, for my dinner, for my dinner,
What will you give me for my dinner if I get up today?

Chicken pie. (Spoken)

No, no, Mother, I won't get up, I won't get up, I won't get up,
No, no, Mother, I won't get up, I won't get up today.

Lazy Mary, will you get up, will you get up, will you get up,
Lazy Mary, will you get up, will you get up this evening?

What will you give me for my supper, for my supper, for my supper,
What will you give me for my supper if I get up this evening?

A nice young man with red rosy cheeks. (Spoken)

Yes, Mother, I will get up, I will get up, I will get up,
Yes , Mother, I will get up, I will get up this evening.

176
Hop Along, Sister Mary

This song is one of several in folk tradition about goats. Like so many folk songs, also, it consists of several entities stitched together. The last two stanzas, where married life is discussed, bear no relationship to the beginning. Further the Chorus obviously was lifted verbatim from a song called "Hop Along, Sister Mary" which apparently was composed by M.H. Foley, sung by Foley & Sheffer and widely published in the songsters. For example: *Harrigan & Hart's Gree Leaf Songster* (N.Y. 188-, p. 47); *Olympia Quartette Songster* (N.Y. 18--, p. 41); *Sheffer & Slavin's "Kick Me Again" Songster* (N.Y. 18--, p. 6).

I have not found this song in any other collection.

"Hop Along, Sister Mary," sung by Miss Drucilla Hall, Millport, Lamar County, 1952.

There was a man named Rosenthal,
Who bought a goat some time last fall.
He did not buy it for his kid,
But bought it for himself instead.

Chorus:
　　Hop along, Sister Mary, hop along, hop along,
　　Hop along, Sister Mary, oh hop hop along.
　　You'll get there by and by.

There was a man who craved a kid
For his sweet delightful Miss.
And when that kid he tried to steal,
She hit so hard it made him squeal.

Bill Johnson loved a widow gay,
And he left his wife one winter day.
But then the widow saw his scale (?)
And left him lonesome, sad and pale.

It is not true that married guys
Live longer than a bachelor wise.
But married men live such a while
That life seems longer by a mile.

177
Send For The Ladies

This piece was probably a music-hall production. It probably has
altered into the version a fragment of which I give here. I have not
found the song reported in any other folk song collection. It is a
banjo or fiddle song and probably was fairly popular when square
dances were more widespread. Yet when my informant played it
for me he first made all the women present leave the room.

"Send for the Ladies Come to the Ball," sung and fiddled by Mr.
J.B. Estes, Millport, Lamar County, 1952. He has known it perhaps
forty years.

Send for the la-dies, say come to the ball. Don't

come to-mor-row night, need-n't come at all.

Send for the ladies come to the ball.
Don't come tonight, needn't come at all.

Send for the ladies come to the ball.
Hiked up her left leg and showed it to us all.

Send for the ladies come to the ball.
Hiked up her shimmy tail and show it to us all.

178
Going Up Hippocreek

It seems certain that this song is the remains of the song "Going Up Cripple Creek." In all likelihood this latter song refers to the mining rush in Cripple Creek, Colorado, although there is a Cripple Creek, Virginia, which was a mining district. See Brown (III, 354) for a brief discussion. The L.C. Checklist (pp. 67-68) gives 24 entries. The one Alabama fragment, hardly more than a nonsense stanza, indicates lack of popularity in the state.

"Going Up Hippocreek," sung by Mrs. Crosley, Vernon, Lamar County, 1952.

Going up a hippocreek, going in a run,
Going up a hippocreek, gonna have some fun.
I roll my britches up above my knees.
Wade old hippocreek where I please.

179
A Medley

This item shows folk ingenuity in singing. My informant, who has sung so many songs of other people, here puts together five songs and makes one of her own, interlarding the known songs with transitions of her own. "Sweet Adeline" was written by Richard Gerard and Harry Armstrong (pub. 1903); "The Old Oaken Bucket" is the most famous song of Samuel Woodworth; apparently it was written around 1818, but was not published until 1834, "adapted to a favorite Scotch air," "Jessie, the Flower o' Dumblane"; however, the tune that has become familiar to Americans was written by George Kiallmark, an Englishman, and appeared in print in the 1870's; "In the Evening by the Moonlight" was written by the great Negro minstrel and composer James A. Bland; "Rufus" is a familiar folk song; "Massa's in de Cold, Cold Ground" is, of course, Stephen C. Foster's work, of 1852. (For full discussion of these popular songs see Spaeth, *History of Popular Music.)*

"A Medley," sung by Miss Drucilla Hall, Millport, Lamar County, 1953. She has sung it for many years.

Sweet Ad-e-line, sweet Ad-e-line, with-in my heart
for you I pine. In all my dreams your fair face beams.
You are the flow-er of my heart, sweet Ad--. I'd sell
my socks, I'd sell my shoes for one more drink from the
old oak-en buck-et, the i-ron bound buck-et, the moss
cov-ered buck-et that hangs In the eve-ning by the moon-

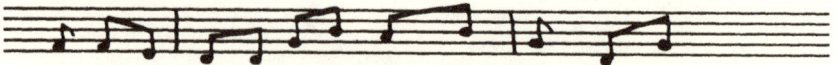

light you could hear those dar-kies sing-ing. In the eve-

ning by the moon-light you could hear those bells now

ring-ing. How the old folks would en-joy it. They would

sit all night and lis-ten as we sang one song for my

Ru-fus Ras-tus John-son Brown, what you gon-na do when

the rent comes round? What you gon-na say, what you

gon-na pay? You won't have a nick-el at Judg-ment Day.

You know I know Mas-sa's gon-na put you out in the snow.

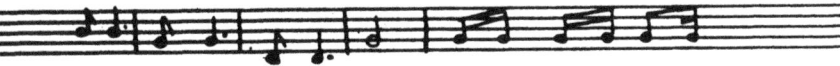

Ru-fus Ras-tus John-son Brown, what you gon-na do when

the rent comes Down in the corn-field hear that mourn-

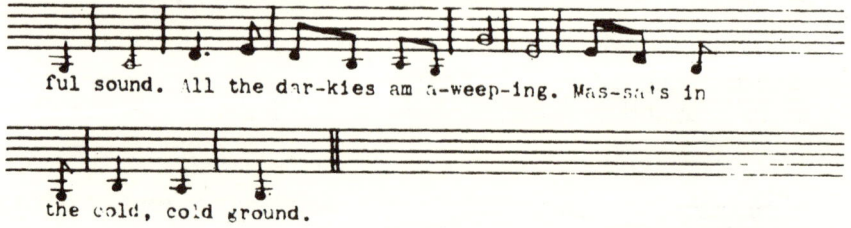

ful sound. All the dar-kies am a-weep-ing. Mas-sa's in

the cold, cold ground.

Sweet Adeline, sweet Adeline, within my heart for you I pine.
In all my dreams your fair face beams.
You are the flower of my heart, sweet Ad- - - - -.
I'd sell my socks, I'd sell my shoes for one more drink from
The old oaken bucket, the iron bound bucket,
The moss covered bucket that hangs
In the evening by the moonlight you could hear those darkies singing,
In the evening by the moonlight you could hear those bells now ringing.
How the old folks would enjoy it.
They would sit all night and listen as we sang one song for my
Rufus Rastus Johnson Brown,
What you gonna do when the rent comes around?
What you gonna say, what you gonna pay?
You won't have a nickel at Judgment Day.
You know I know Massa's gonna put you out in the snow.
Rufus Rastus Johnson Brown,
What you gonna do when the rent comes
Down in the cornfield, hear that mournful sound.
All the darkies am a-weeping.
Massa's in the cold, cold ground.

VIII
ANIMAL SONGS

180
Simon Slick

This song is rather widespread. The headnote to the Brown Collection (III, 567) points out that it is a mixture of two or three pieces — "Liza Jane" and "Whoa, Mule" at least. In fact this piece presents an excellent example of what can happen when a song from the songster or music hall is taken over by the folk. "Simon Slick" is repeated almost without variation from the versions that appeared in various songsters, always without any chorus. The two choruses in my versions are, therefore, attached by the folk because the folk lyric ordinarily has a chorus. Songsters that "Simon Slick" was published in include: *Andy Collum's Latest & Best Banjo Songs* (N.Y. 1881, p. 36); *George S. Knight's Songs & Recitations* (N.Y. 1880, p. 56); *John M. Turney, The Coons Around Our Block Songster* (N.Y. 1879, p. 54); *John Walsh's Gem Of The Emerald Isle Songster* (N.Y. 1881, p. 30); *Murphy & Mack's Jolly Sailor's Songster* (Pittsburgh, 1883, p. 55).

See Brown for a long list of references. The L.C. Checklist (p. 365) reports it from California.

A

"Kicking Mule," sung by Miss Drucilla Hall, Millport, Lamar County, 1952. She has sung it thirty-five years, and does not remember how she learned it, but probably from hearing neighborhood girls singing it.

There was a man in our town whose name was

Si-mon Slick. Owned a mule with a de-mon eye.

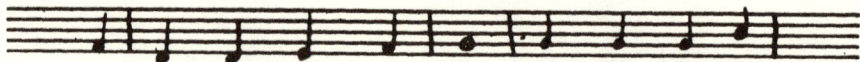

Oh, how that mule could kick. Wink his eye and

swish his tail and greet you with a smile. Gent-

ly tel-e-graph his leg and raise you half a mile.

There was a man in our town
Whose name was Simon Slick.
Owned a mule with a demon eye.
Oh, how that mule could kick.
Wink his eye and swish his tail
And greet you with a smile.
Gently telegraph his leg
And raise you half a mile.

Chorus:
    Hold that mule, Miss Liza Jane,
    Hold that mule I say.
    Hold that mule, Miss Liza Jane,
    Don't let that mule get away.

Kick you quick as lightning,
Had an iron jaw.
The very thing to have around
To tame your mother-in-law.
I tell you, boys,
That mule won't do to trust.
Kicked the . . . . . . .off the track
And never broke the crust.

Kicked the feathers off a goose,
Broke another's back.
Stopped the Texas railroad train
And kicked it off the track.
Stopped the steamboat with his head,
Kicked it out of sight.
Kicked the skating rink in two.
At nine o'clock at night.

Skater standing on his head
Gasping for his breath.
Poked his hind feet down his neck
And kicked himself to death.

B

"Simon Slick," sung by Mrs. Mona Johnson, Vernon, Lamar County, 1953.

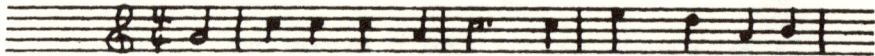

There was a lit-tle man, His name was Si-mon

Slick. He owned a mule with dream-y eyes And

chorus

how that mule could kick. And all that mule

could say was ah-he-haw. And all that mule could

say was ah-he-haw-he-haw-he-haw.

There was a little man,
His name was Simon Slick.
He owned a mule with dreamy eyes
And how that mule could kick.

Chorus:
    And all that mule could say
    Was ah-he-haw.
    And all that mule could say
    Was ah-he-haw, he-haw.

He'd kick you quicker than lightning.
He had an iron jaw.
He was the very thing to have around
To tame your mother-in-law.

He stopped a steamboat with his head.
He kicked it out of sight.
He kicked a boarding house in two
At twelve o'clock at night.

181
Chicken In The Bread Trough

This short nonsense song was probably originally a fiddle or banjo tune. The words are used to relieve the constant repetition of the music. Ford *(Traditional Music of America,* p. 36) gives it as a square-dance tune. My informant played it as a banjo song. It seems to be a greater favorite with Negroes than whites. For a considerable bibliography see Brown (III, 205). It turns up as the final stanza in "Run, Nigger, Run" in Randolph (II, 338). The L.C. Checklist (pp. 54; 127) lists texts from Mississippi, Washington, D.C., and California.

"Chicken In The Bread Trough," sung by Mr. J.B. Estes, Millport, Lamar County, 1952, as a banjo song.

Chick-en in the bread trough scratch-ing out dough. Gran-ny, will your dog bite? No, child, no.

chorus

Gran-ny, will your dog bite, Gran-ny, will your dog bite? No, child, no. Gran-ny, will your dog bite, Gran-ny, will your dog bite? No, child, no.

Chicken in the bread trough
Scratching out dough.
Granny, will your dog bite?
No. child, no.

Chorus:
    Granny, will your dog bite,
    Granny, will your dog bite?
    No, child, no.
    Granny, will your dog bite,
    Granny, will your dog bite?
    No. child, no.

All around the graveyard
And right through the kitchen.
Come on little boys
And let's go fishing.

182
Jaybird Sitting On A Hickory Limb

This is one of three songs in this volume about the jaybird, a kind of song very popular with Negroes. The stanzas and chorus in such a song as this one are floaters and are likely to be found in several songs. See, for instance, "Jaybird died with the Whooping Cough" in this volume. For references and paralled texts see Brown (III, 132, stanza 7, and p. 201, version D).

"Silly song," sung by Miss Malissa Richardson, Kennedy, Lamar County, 1952. She has sung it for at least fifty years and does not remember where she learned it.

A jay-bird sit-ting on a hick-o-ry limb, All a-

cross ov-er to Jor-dan. I upped with a rock And hit

him on the shin, Oh, Je-ru-sa-lem ! Shine on, shine

on, All a-cross ov-er to Jor-dan; Shine on, shine

on, Oh, Je-ru-sa-lem !

A jay bird sitting on a hickory limb,
All across over to Jordan.
I upped with a rock and hit him on the shin,
Oh, Jerusalem!

Shine on, shine on,
All across over to Jordan;
Shine on, shine on,
Oh, Jerusalem!

183
Old Cow Died of Whooping Cough

Folk singers like to make up comic songs about diseases of animals. Apparently one of the most humorous diseases is the whooping cough. See also in this volume the similar song, "Jay Bird Died With The Whooping Cough." Although there are many similar songs to the present one I have not found exactly this one reported anywhere.

"Old Cow Died of Whooping Cough," sung by Miss Anna Allen, Birmingham, 1952.

Old cow died of whoop-ing cough, Ba-by cow died of

meas-les, Fa-ther died with a spoon in his mouth And

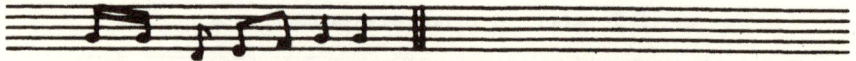

car-ried it off to Je-sus.

Old cow died of whooping cough,
Baby cow died of measles.
Father died with a spoon in his mouth,
And carried it off to Jesus.

184
Sir Piggy

This piece is probably originally English although it has been Americanized. This treatment of animals is not so usual as the songs about jaybirds with whooping cough, and the like, for which see several items in this volume. This particular song I have not found elsewhere.

"Sir Piggy," sung by Mrs. Fannie McCulley, Gordo, Pickens County, 1952. She learned it from her mother.

One morn-ing Sir Pig-gy put on his fine clothes,

Tak-ing his cane, out walk-ing he goes. He went to the

tav-ern and called on the wait-er For to hur-ry and bring

him some wine. He went on to the house where Miss Puss

dwell-ed. Bow-ing po-lite-ly asked if all were well. Miss

Puss got an-gry and thought it was cruel. Pig-gy and Tow-ser

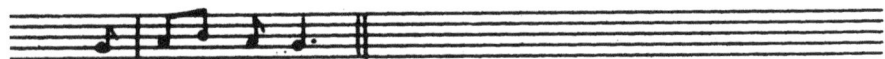

both bent on a duel.

One morning Sir Piggy put on his fine clothes;
Taking his cane, out walking he goes.
He went to the tavern and called on the waiter
For to hurry and bring him some wine.
He went on to the house where Miss Puss did dwell.
Bowing politely, asked if all were well.
Miss Puss got angry and thought it was cruel.
Piggy and Towser both bent on a duel.
Piggy fired a shot off Towser's tail.
The judge said Towser should ride on a rail.

185
Chicken Pecking On A Tambourine

The nonsense stanzas in this comic piece are floaters; that is, they turn up in several songs. I have not found them in this order in any other song. Compare this piece with other nonsense songs in this volume.

"Chicken Pecking On A Tambourine," sung by Mr. Richard Sullivan, Fayette County, 1952. A county comic, he has sung this piece some fifty years. Now self-conscious about it, he will sing only when prodded.

As I went down to a ta-ter patch, tou-rink, dur-ink,

fol-dink a-di-de-o, 'SI went down to the ta-ter patch,

Up jumped an old hen and she did scratch, tum-a-rink, tum-

a-rank, tum-a-roe.

As I went down to a 'tater patch,
Tou-rink, dur-ink, fol-dink a-di-de-o.
I went down to the 'tater patch,
Up jumped an old hen
And she did scratch,
Tum-a-rink, tum-a-rank, tum-a-ro.

Went to the river and couldn't get across,
Tou-rink, dur-ink, fol-dink a-di-de-o.
Went to the river and couldn't get across,
Paid five dollars
For an old blind hoss,
Tum-a-rink, tum-a-rank, tum-a-ro.

Rode him in and he didn't want to go,
Tou-rink, dur-ink, fol-dink a-di-de-o.
Rode him in and he didn't want to go,
And I picked up a tune
On my ole banjo,
Tum-a-rink, tum-a-rank, tum-a-ro.

Bridle and a saddle hanging on the shelf,
Tou-rink, dur-ink, fol-dink a di-de-o.
Bridle and a saddle hanging on the shelf,
If you want any more
You can sing it yourself,
Tum-a-rink, tum-a-rank, tum-a-ro.

Up jumped an old hen and told me of her dream,
Tou-rink, dur-ink, fol-dink a-di-de-o.
Up jumped an old hen and told me of her dream,
All the chickens a-pecking
On a tambourine,
Tum-a-rink, tum-a-rank, tum-a-ro.

186
Jaybirds Gave A Concert Free

The folk like songs about birds and animals. The jaybird seems the favorite subject, as several pieces in this volume show. This nonsense piece, which does not seem to be a fragment, is typical. All the singers desire is some excuse for singing a line or two.

"Jaybirds Gave a Concert Free," sung by Mrs. Herring, Gordo, Pickens County, 1952. She has known it for some sixty years.

Jay birds gave a con-cert free, Up in the boughs of

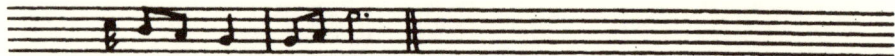

a ma-ple tree, ha ha ha.

Jaybirds gave a concert free,
Up in the boughs of a maple tree.
Ha ha ha.

187
Jaybird Died With the Whooping Cough

The jaybird is the subject for many songs, especially in Negro and pseudo-Negro singing. In several pieces he dies of the whooping cough. For references to the subject see the Brown Collection (III, 201). My one Alabama fragment was sung as a bit of nonsense, by a white man imitating a "Negro song." White *(American Negro Folk-Songs,* p. 243) reported it as a Negro song from Alabama.

"Yonder Come a Rabbit," sung by Mr. W.A. "Lawyer" Davis, Aliceville, Pickens County, 1952. He probably learned it in Pickens County, but he might have got it as a student at the University of Alabama.

Jay-bird died with the whoop-ing cough; seed-
tick died with the col-ic; Yon-der come a frog
with a fid-dle on his back. Gwine a-way to
de fro-lic. Oh, yon-der come a rab-bit ta hun-
uh, Oh, yon-der come a rab-bit ta hun-uh, dere.

Jaybird died with the whooping cough,
Seed tick died with the colic.
Yonder come a frog with a fiddle on his back,
Gwine away to de frolic.
Oh, yonder come a rabbit, ta hunuh,
Oh, yonder come a rabbit, ta hunuh dere.

IX
LITERARY SONGS

188
The Cottage Girl

Wordsworth's poem "We Are Seven" has not been reported before as a folk song. This piece illustrates how a song is usually changed when it goes into folk tradition. Undoubtedly the words for the song were taken from a school book, then altered into a more familiar phraseology. My informant said that she used McGuffey's Reader in school. In this book Wordsworth's poem is somewhat altered from the original. McGuffey and my song both omit the first stanza. For convenience in comparison I footnote the readings in McGuffey and in Wordsworth's text.

"The Cottage Girl," sung by Mrs. Maggie Lee Hayes, Vernon, Lamar County, 1952. She does not remember when or how she learned it, but thinks it was probably from her school book. She used *McGuffey's New Third Electic Reader*. See page 189 of the Henry Ford reprint (1939). The tune is roughly equivalent to the hymn "Must Jesus Bear His Cross Alone?"

I met a lit-tle cot-tage girl; She was eight

years old, she said. Her hair was thick with man-y a

curl That clus-tered round her head.

I met a little cottage girl;
She was eight years old, she said.
Her hair was thick with many a curl
That clustered round her head.

She had a rustic woodland air,
And she was wildly clad;
Her eyes were fair, and very fair;
Her beauty made me glad.

"Sisters, brothers,[1] little maid.
How many may you be?"

"How many? Seven in all," she said,
And wondering looked at me.

"And where are they? I pray you tell."
She answered, "Seven are we.
And two of us at Conway dwell,
And two are gone to sea.

"Two of us in the church-yard lie,
My sister and my brother;
And in the church-yard cottage I
Dwell near them with my mother."

"You say that two at Conway dwell,
And two are gone to sea.
Yet ye are seven. I pray you tell,
Sweet maid, how this may be."

Then did the little girl^2 reply,
"Seven boys and girls are we;
Two of us in the church-yard lie
Beneath the church-yard tree."

"You run about, my little maid.
Your limbs they are alive;
If two are in the church-yard laid,
Then ye are only five."

"Their graves are green, they may be seen,"
The little maid replied.
Twelve steps or more from mother's^3 door,
And they are side by side.

"My stockings there I often knit,
My kerchiefs^4 there I hem;
And there upon the ground I sit,
And sing a song^5 to them.

"And often after sunset, sir,
When it is light and fair
I take my little porrige^6
And eat my supper there.

"The first that died was sister^7 Jane;
In bed she moaning lay
Till God released her from^8 her pain,
And then she went away.

"So in the church-yard she was laid;
And when the grass was dry^9
Together round her grave we played,
My brother John and I.

"And when the ground was white with snow,
My brother John was forced to go,
And he lies by her side."

"How many are you then?" said I,
"If they two are in heaven?"
Which was the little maid's reply:[11]
"O, master, we are seven."

"But they are dead, those two are dead;
Their spirits are in heaven."
'Twas throwing words away, for still
The little maid would have her will
And said, "Nay, we are seven."

Alternate readings. W means Wordsworth, M, McGuffey:

1. W and M: Sisters and brothers
2. W and M: maid
3. W: my mother's; M: mother's
4. W: kerchief; M: kerchief
5. W: And sing a song; M: I sit and sing
6. W and M: porringer
7. W: sister; M: little
8. W: of; M: from
9. W: And when the grass was dry; M: And all the summer dry

189
Maid of Athens

Byron's famous poem has been included in numerous collections of popular songs, including many minstrel songsters, though I have not seen it reported anywhere as a folk song. It appeared in *Souvenir Minstrel* (N.Y. 1836, p. 163) with the notation "Words by Byron, Music by Kiallmark," with the Greek translated. It was included in the *Universal Songster, or Museum of Mirth* (London, 1846, I, 98), with the refrain translated. It was published also in *The English Minstrel: Containing A Selection of The Most Popular Songs Of England, No. 11* (Glasgow, 1850, p. 39), three stanzas with the following chorus:

Oh, hear my vow before I go,
Oh, hear my vow before I go.
My dearest life, I love you!

It was published in numerous other songsters in America. For example: *The Berry's Song & Dance Book* (N.Y. 1873, p. 16); *Forget-Me-Not Songster* (N.Y. 1847, p. 1); "Sung by J.L. Carncross of Carncross & Dixie's Minstrels," *The Greenback's Songster* (N.Y. 18--, p. 18); "Music by Henry R. Allen," *Illustrated Popular Songster* (N.P. 18--, p. 1); "Words by Byron, Music by Kiallmark," *Love's Songster* (N.Y. 18--, p. 185); *Pastor's Song Of Flags Songster* (N.Y. 18--, p. 112); *Singer's Journal No. 1* (N.Y. 18--, p. 7); *Singer's Journal No. 4* (N.Y. 18--, p. 45); *Sam Hogue's Minstrels Songs* (Liverpool, 1873, p. 9); *Tilt Skirt Songster* (N.Y. 18--, p. 44, 2 6-line stanzas, with Greek included and translated in a footnote); *Up In A Balloon Songster* (N.Y. 18--, p. 52, Greek translated); *Wehman's Good Old Songs No. 1* (N.Y. 18--, p. 62). The song was popular enough to be parodied at least once. I give the Byron part of a medley *(Kiss Behind The Door Songster,* N.Y. 1872, p. 13):

Maid of Athens ere we part
Give oh give me back my heart,
And it's if you want to hire me
Step into Mickey Magher.

The story behind my one Alabama text indicates a certain popularity in the state. My informant told me that she learned the song from a book of instructions on how to play the organ. In 1890 her father bought an organ. Included in the back of the instruction book were the words and music for"Maid of Athens.'' She said that several persons in the neighborhood bought organs, and always this particular piece of music was included in the book of instructions. My informant remembers distinctly that soon after they had bought their organ, a neighbor came over from Wetumpka and spent the Sunday with her. This lady sang and played "Maid of Athens." She had recently bought an organ, and this poem had been included in her book of instructions.

I have asked the oldest dealers of pianos and organs in Montgomery and Birmingham if they know anything about this practice of including songs, especially such a song as this, with sales of their instruments. All say that they know nothing about it. Probably the practice has long since been discontinued.

My text differs from Byron's original and from all the other versions of the song that I have seen. Probably the poem was once more popular as a song than it now appears.

"Maid of Athens," sung by Mrs. O.C. Powell, Titus, Elmore County, 1953.

Maid of Athens, ere we part
Give oh! give me back my heart
Or, since that has left my breast
Keep it now and take the rest.
Then hear my vows before I go.
Oh! hear my vows before I go.
My life, my soul, I love you.
My dearest maid, I love you.
Then hear my vows before I go.
My life, my soul, I love you.

Maid of Athens, I am gone.
Think of me, Sweet, when alone.
Though I fly to Istanbul,
Athens holds my heart and soul
Then hear my vows before I go.
Oh! hear my vows before I go.
My life, my soul, I love you.
My dearest maid, I love you.
Then hear my vows before I go.
My life, my soul, I love you.

190

The Bridge

Longfellow's poem "The Bridge" was set to music by Miss M. Lindsay in 1861 (published by Oliver Ditson & Co; see Dichter and Shapiro, *Early American Sheet Music*, p. 159). This setting abridges Longfellow's poem rather sharply (see Carl Carmer, *Song of the Rivers of America*, p. 7). Pound *(Syllabus,* p. 67) reported this piece as a folk song, saying it is a "Fragment giving three stanzas and part of a fourth of Longfellow's poem." Very likely this fragment derives from the Lindsay setting. Probably my one Alabama text comes from the Lindsay setting, but it is greatly changed in places. At times it is closer to Longfellow's original than to Lindsay's setting. Undoubtedly the poem appeared in school books in Alabama. This text might be a setting from these books. Of the original poem, my song includes stanzas one, six, seven, eight, nine, ten, twelve, fourteen and fifteen. In footnotes I give the Longfellow readings for particular words and phrases.

"The Bridge," sung by Mrs. O.C. Powell, Titus, Elmore County, 1953. She does not remember when or how she learned it.

I stood on the bridge at mid-night As the clocks

were strik-ing the hour, And the moon rose o-ver the ci-ty

Be-hind the dark church tower. And like those wa-ters

rush-ing A-mong the wood-en piers A flood of thoughts

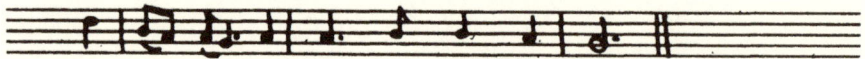

came o'er me That filled mine eyes with tears.

I stood on the bridge at midnight
As the clocks were striking the hour,
And the moon rose over[1] the city
Behind the dark church tower.

And like those waters rushing[2]
Among the wooden piers
A flood of thoughts come o'er me
That filled mine[3] eyes with tears.

How often, oh! how often![4]
In the days that had gone by,
I had stood[5] on that bridge at midnight
And gazed on the[6] wave and sky.
How often, oh! how often
I had wished the[7] ebbing tide
Would bear me away on its bosom
O'er the ocean wild and wide.

For my heart was hot and restless
And my life was full of care,
And the burden laid upon me
Seemed greater than I could bear.
But now it has fallen from me,
Lies buried[8] in the sea,
And only the sorrow of others
Throws its shadow over me.

I[9] think how many thousand[10]
Of care-emcumbered men
Each bearing his burden of sorrow
Have crossed that[11] bridge since then.
Forever[12] and forever[13]
As long as the river flows,
As long as the heart has passions,
As long as life has woes,

The moon and its broken reflections[14]
And its shadows shall appear
As a[15] symbol of love in Heaven
And its weavering image here.[16]

The following are the Longfellow readings:

1. o'er
2. Stanza six
3. my
4. Stanza seven
5. I stood
6. that
7. that the
8. It is buried

9. And I
10. Stanza twelve
11. the
12. And forever
13. Stanza fourteen
14. reflection
15. the

191
Little Yellow Bird

Robert Louis Stevenson's poem "Time To Rise" (more popularly known as "Birdie With a Yellow Bill") turns up almost unaltered as a folk song. My informant said that the piece has been sung in her family as long as she can remember. She believed that nobody else sang it. She did not know that it was Stevenson's poem. I have not found it reported in other selections.

"Little Yellow Bird," sung by Mrs. Sophie Lou Chambliss, Assistant Warden of the Alabama State Prison for Women, Wetumpka, 1953. The only difference between her version and Stevenson's poem is the substitution of "my" for "the" in the second line.

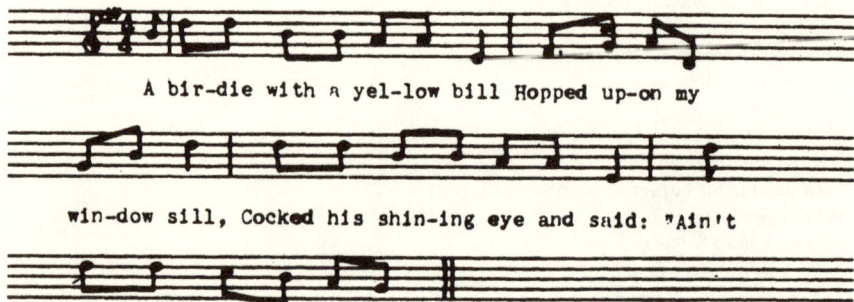

A bir-die with a yel-low bill Hopped up-on my

win-dow sill, Cocked his shin-ing eye and said: "Ain't

you shamed you sleep-y head?"

A birdie with a yellow bill
Hopped upon my window sill,
Cocked his shining eye and said,
"Ain't you shamed you sleepy head?"

192
Little Boy Blue

This piece illustrates the folk treatment of a literary work. Eugene Field's poem "Little Boy Blue" was undoubtedly published in school books used in Alabama. As a favorite literary piece, it was apparently taken out of the books and sung. This song is not far removed from the poem. Probably it has not undergone much oral transmission. Yet the poem has undergone certain changes in phraseology, and, more important, has had added to it a completely new stanza, the second. For comparative purposes, I have footnoted all variations from the original poem.

"Little Boy Blue," sung by Miss Drucilla Hall, Millport, Lamar County, 1952. She does not remember when or how she learned it. She believes that she probably did not get it out of a school book.

The lit-tle toy dog was cov-ered with dust, But

stur-dy and stanch he stands. And the lit-tle toy

sol-dier is red with rust, And his mus-ket molds in

his hand.

The little toy dog was[1] covered with dust,
But sturdy and stanch he stands.
And the little toy soldier is red with rust,
And his musket molds in his hand.[2]
Time was when the little toy dog was new,
And the soldier was passing fair.
And that was the time when our Little Boy Blue
Had[3] kissed them and put them there.

When the Little Boy Blue closed his eyes and went to sleep,[4]
He prayed the Lord his soul to keep.
"God bless my daddy too; he has been so kind and true,"
Said our Little Boy Blue as he went to sleep.

"Now, don't you go till I come," he said,
"And don't you make any noise!"
So, toddling off to his trundle-bed,
He dreamed[5] of the pretty toys.
And as he was dreaming, an angel band[6]
Awakened our Little Boy Blue.
Oh! the years are many, the years are long,
But the little toy friends are true!

Ay, faithful to Little Boy Blue they stand,
Each toy[7] in the same old place,
Awaiting the touch of a little boy's hand,[8]
The smile on the dear little face.[9]
And the wonder, as waiting the long years through
In the dust of a[10] little chair,
What has become of our Little Boy Blue,
Since he kissed them and placed[11] them there.

Below are the readings in Field's poem:

1. is
2. hands
3. Kissed them
4. This stanza is not in the original poem. The echo of the children's prayer, "Now I Lay Me Down to Sleep," is interesting.
5. dreamt
6. song
7. Each in
8. of a little hand

9. of a little face
10. that
11. put

INDEX

This index is to titles, first lines, refrains and choruses, and variants of all these; to first lines of "floater" stanzas; and occasionally to a line, not the first, that the song may be known by. If the same title, first line, refrain or chorus occurs in variants of a song, the number is given only for the first time it appears. Numbers are to songs, not pages. Titles are given without quotation marks. All lines are in quotes. Letters in parentheses indicate what kind of line each is: (1) refers to "line," (r) to "refrain," (c) to "chorus," (f) to "floater."